Lost Cove, North Carolina

Contributions to Southern Appalachian Studies

1. *Memoirs of Grassy Creek: Growing Up in the Mountains on the Virginia–North Carolina Line.* Zetta Barker Hamby. 1998

2. *The Pond Mountain Chronicle: Self-Portrait of a Southern Appalachian Community.* Edited by Leland R. Cooper and Mary Lee Cooper. 1998

3. *Traditional Musicians of the Central Blue Ridge: Old Time, Early Country, Folk and Bluegrass Label Recording Artists, with Discographies.* Marty McGee. 2000

4. *W.R. Trivett, Appalachian Pictureman: Photographs of a Bygone Time.* Ralph E. Lentz II. 2001

5. *The People of the New River: Oral Histories from the Ashe, Alleghany and Watauga Counties of North Carolina.* Edited by Leland R. Cooper and Mary Lee Cooper. 2001

6. *John Fox, Jr., Appalachian Author.* Bill York. 2003

7. *The Thistle and the Brier: Historical Links and Cultural Parallels Between Scotland and Appalachia.* Richard Blaustein. 2003

8. *Tales from Sacred Wind: Coming of Age in Appalachia. The Cratis Williams Chronicles.* Cratis D. Williams. Edited by David Cratis Williams and Patricia D. Beaver. 2003

9. *Willard Gayheart, Appalachian Artist.* Willard Gayheart and Donia S. Eley. 2003

10. *The Forest City Lynching of 1900: Populism, Racism, and White Supremacy in Rutherford County, North Carolina.* J. Timothy Cole. 2003

11. *The Brevard Rosenwald School: Black Education and Community Building in a Southern Appalachian Town, 1920–1966.* Betty J. Reed. 2004

12. *The Bristol Sessions: Writings About the Big Bang of Country Music.* Edited by Charles K. Wolfe and Ted Olson. 2005

13. *Community and Change in the North Carolina Mountains: Oral Histories and Profiles of People from Western Watauga County.* Compiled by Nannie Greene and Catherine Stokes Sheppard. 2006

14. *Ashe County: A History; A New Edition.* Arthur Lloyd Fletcher. 2009 [2006]

15. *The New River Controversy; A New Edition.* Thomas J. Schoenbaum. Epilogue by R. Seth Woodard. 2007

16. *The Blue Ridge Parkway by Foot: A Park Ranger's Memoir.* Tim Pegram. 2007

17. *James Still: Critical Essays on the Dean of Appalachian Literature.* Edited by Ted Olson and Kathy H. Olson. 2008

18. *Owsley County, Kentucky, and the Perpetuation of Poverty.* John R. Burch, Jr. 2008

19. *Asheville: A History.* Nan K. Chase. 2007

20. *Southern Appalachian Poetry: An Anthology of Works by 37 Poets.* Edited by Marita Garin. 2008

21. *Ball, Bat and Bitumen: A History of Coalfield Baseball in the Appalachian South.* L.M. Sutter. 2009

22. *The Frontier Nursing Service: America's First Rural Nurse-Midwife Service and School.* Marie Bartlett. 2009

23. *James Still in Interviews, Oral Histories and Memoirs.* Edited by Ted Olson. 2009

24. *The Millstone Quarries of Powell County, Kentucky.* Charles D. Hockensmith. 2009

25. *The Bibliography of Appalachia: More Than 4,700 Books, Articles, Monographs and Dissertations, Topically Arranged and Indexed.* Compiled by John R. Burch, Jr. 2009

26. *Appalachian Children's Literature: An Annotated Bibliography.* Compiled by Roberta Teague Herrin and Sheila Quinn Oliver. 2010

27. *Southern Appalachian Storytellers: Interviews with Sixteen Keepers of the Oral Tradition.* Edited by Saundra Gerrell Kelley. 2010

28. *Southern West Virginia and the Struggle for Modernity.* Christopher Dorsey. 2011

29. *George Scarbrough, Appalachian Poet: A Biographical and Literary Study with Unpublished Writings.* Randy Mackin. 2011

30. *The Water-Powered Mills of Floyd County, Virginia: Illustrated Histories, 1770–2010.* Franklin F. Webb and Ricky L. Cox. 2012

31. *School Segregation in Western North Carolina: A History, 1860s–1970s.* Betty Jamerson Reed. 2011

32. *The Ravenscroft School in Asheville: A History of the Institution and Its People and Buildings.* Dale Wayne Slusser. 2014

33. *The Ore Knob Mine Murders: The Crimes, the Investigation and the Trials.* Rose M. Haynes. 2013

34. *New Art of Willard Gayheart.* Willard Gayheart and Donia S. Eley. 2014

35. *Public Health in Appalachia: Essays from the Clinic and the Field.* Edited by Wendy Welch. 2014

36. *The Rhetoric of Appalachian Identity.* Todd Snyder. 2014

37. *African American and Cherokee Nurses in Appalachia: A History, 1900–1965.* Phoebe Ann Pollitt. 2016

38. *A Hospital for Ashe County: Four Generations of Appalachian Community Health Care.* Janet C. Pittard. 2016

39. *Dwight Diller: West Virginia Mountain Musician.* Lewis M. Stern. 2016

40. *The Brown Mountain Lights: History, Science and Human Nature Explain an Appalachian Mystery.* Wade Edward Speer. 2017

41. *Richard L. Davis and the Color Line in Ohio Coal: A Hocking Valley Mine Labor Organizer, 1862–1900.* Frans H. Doppen. 2016

42. *The Silent Appalachian: Wordless Mountaineers in Fiction, Film and Television.* Vicki Sigmon Collins. 2017

43. *The Trees of Ashe County, North Carolina.* Doug Munroe. 2017

44. *Melungeon Portraits: Exploring Kinship and Identity.* Tamara L. Stachowicz. 2018

45. *Always Been a Rambler: G.B. Grayson and Henry Whitter, Country Music Pioneers of Southern Appalachia.* Josh Beckworth. 2018

46. *Tommy Thompson: New-Timey String Band Musician.* Lewis M. Stern. 2019

47. *Appalachian Fiddler Albert Hash: The Last Leaf on the Tree.* Malcolm L. Smith with Edwin Lacy. 2020

48. *Junaluska: Oral Histories of a Black Appalachian Community.* Edited by Susan E. Keefe with the Junaluska Heritage Association. 2020

49. *Boone Before Boone: The Archaeological Record of Northwestern North Carolina Through 1769.* Tom Whyte. 2020

50. *From the Front Lines of the Appalachian Addiction Crisis: Healthcare Providers Discuss Opioids, Meth and Recovery.* Edited by Wendy Welch. 2020

51. *Writers by the River: Reflections on 40+ Years of the Highland Summer Conference.* Edited by Donia S. Eley and Grace Toney Edwards. 2021

52. *Wayne Howard: Old Time Music, the Hammons Family and Mountain Lore.* Lewis M. Stern. 2021

53. *Lost Cove, North Carolina: Portrait of a Vanished Appalachian Community, 1864–1957* Christy A. Smith. 2022

Lost Cove, North Carolina

Portrait of a Vanished Appalachian Community, 1864–1957

Christy A. Smith

Contributions to
Southern Appalachian Studies, 53

McFarland & Company, Inc., Publishers
Jefferson, North Carolina

LIBRARY OF CONGRESS CATALOGUING-IN-PUBLICATION DATA

Names: Smith, Christy A., 1972– author.
Title: Lost Cove, North Carolina : portrait of a vanished
Appalachian community, 1864–1957 / Christy A. Smith.
Other titles: Portrait of a vanished Appalachian community, 1864–1957
Description: Jefferson, North Carolina :
McFarland & Company, Inc., Publishers, 2022 |
Series: Contributions to Southern Appalachian studies 53 |
Includes bibliographical references and index.
Identifiers: LCCN 2021045792 | ISBN 9781476686080 (paperback : acid free paper) ∞
ISBN 9781476644226 (ebook)
Subjects: LCSH: Lost Cove (N.C.)—History. | Mountain life—
North Carolina—Lost Cove. | Yancey County (N.C.)—Rural conditions. |
Lost Cove (N.C.)—Genealogy. | BISAC: HISTORY / United States /
State & Local / South (AL, AR, FL, GA, KY, LA, MS, NC, SC, TN, VA, WV)
Classification: LCC F264.L67 S65 2022 | DDC 929.3756873—dc23
LC record available at https://lccn.loc.gov/2021045792

BRITISH LIBRARY CATALOGUING DATA ARE AVAILABLE

ISBN (print) 978-1-4766-8608-0
ISBN (ebook) 978-1-4766-4422-6

© 2022 Christy A. Smith. All rights reserved

*No part of this book may be reproduced or transmitted in any form
or by any means, electronic or mechanical, including photocopying
or recording, or by any information storage and retrieval system,
without permission in writing from the publisher.*

Front cover image: Velmer Bailey family walking back from
church; Hosea, Velmer, Priscilla, Servilla, Isaiah, and Eugene
(1952) (photograph provided by Chad Fred Bailey)

Printed in the United States of America

McFarland & Company, Inc., Publishers
Box 611, Jefferson, North Carolina 28640
www.mcfarlandpub.com

*To the Lost Cove families and their descendants
and in loving memory of my mother,
Emma Johnson Smith*

Table of Contents

Preface   1
Introduction: Boundaries, Routes, and Debates   5

One. Lost Cove's Beginning   13
Two. Lifeways of the Families   23
Three. The Prosperous Years: Railroads and Timber   41
Four. Moonshine in the Mountains   57
Five. Mountain View Free Will Baptist Church and Lost Cove School   66
Six. Families   99
Seven. The End of a Community   146

Appendix: Sketches of Lost Cove Interviewees   161
Lost Cove Speaks   165
Chapter Notes   167
Bibliography   175
Index   181

Preface

It is inconceivable to me that an ethical relation to land can exist without love, respect, and admiration for land, and a high regard for its value. By value, I of course mean something far broader than mere economic value; I mean value in the philosophical sense.[1]
—Aldo Leopold

I am 10 years old when I step onto the railroad tracks with anticipation. My heart races and I can't wait to see this ghost town, hidden in the Nolichucky Gorge. My head swirls with vivid thoughts as I dream of a life in these mountains. A life filled with adventure and determination, a life full of love for family and land.

As a child, the outdoors was my playground. My parents, Walter and Emma, always hiked and took trips close to our house. I grew up in Erwin, Tennessee, a small railroad town bordering Madison and Yancey counties in western North Carolina. From Cherokee, North Carolina, to the Shenandoah Valley in Virginia, the Blue Ridge Parkway offered an outlet for our adventures. The Cherokee and Blue Ridge Mountain ranges became my refuge, and I was eager to explore what nature had to offer and listen to the stories along the way.

Growing up, stories about Lost Cove and the railroad echoed through my grandparents' house, told mainly by my great-grandfather, Harley "Hank" Sherman Johnson, and grandfather, Robert Franklin Johnson. Both men worked for the Carolina, Clinchfield, and Ohio (CC&O) Railroad and the CSX Railroad in Erwin, Tennessee. Hank or "Old Pop" as we called him, told his grandchildren and great grandchildren stories of men killed while building the railroad, trains derailing, floods ravaging the railroad tracks along the Nolichucky and stories of moonshine.

Once built by immigrant hands, the Carolina, Clinchfield, and Ohio Railroad became one of the costliest railroads to build. Immigrant men were buried along the Nolichucky and Toe rivers as well as along Alta Pass, North Carolina. The 18 tunnels and 13 miles of track were blasted and laid by hard-working men from Northern Europe to Africa. My great-grandfather spoke of many trains derailing back in the days of steam engines, of nameless bodies buried alongside the tracks around Cane Bottom past Lost Cove, a stretch of flat land that housed railroad gangs in shanty houses or railroad cars along the sidetracks and where several houses stood. Stories of floods ravaging the rails along the gorge were fascinating to hear. His stories often recounted his years on the railroad, experiences that he or my grandfather, Robert, not only saw but lived.

As I walk the railroad tracks I imagine bodies buried under or next to the tracks. In the Nolichucky Gorge, there isn't much room to maneuver on either side of the railroad tracks. On one side is the raging river; on the other side are mountains or rock cliffs. I questioned my great-grandfather many times about these accidents. Why were the bodies never sent to the families? Did their families even know the men had died? He told me that most immigrant men didn't even have family in the United States, that most came alone to make enough money to send for their family later. He told me that building the railroad meant prospering, that sending the dead bodies back to the families or hauling them out of the mountains would cost the railroad company too much, so they buried them right there, under or beside the tracks.

As we hike on the tracks, we listen carefully for trains. It is easy to hear the trains heading south because the vibrations are felt and echoes of the engine bounce off the mountainsides. But when trains head north, the train is gliding because of the steep grade, and the engine can barely be heard. My great-grandfather and grandfather told me stories about their days on the railroad. Old Pop spoke of his runaway train with no brakes screaming down the Nolichucky Gorge and into the Erwin yard. The steam engine brakes started fading in the upper part of the gorge. Of course, steam engines were less reliable than the modern-day diesel. With the gorge grade at 1.38 percent, the steepest part of the rail line sent him screaming down into the Erwin railyard. Unlike Old Pop, who retired from the railroad early, his son, an engineer, didn't retire until 1985.

My grandfather "Bob" drove the trains to Spartanburg, South Carolina, pulling coal cars through the gorge and down the steep tunneled tracks of Alta Pass, North Carolina. Once, his train lost its brakes heading down the mountain into Marion, North Carolina. His buddy, Phillip Mashburn, said the train was bobbing left to right, swerving like a rooster tail through the tunnels. The men in the caboose held on for dear life, counting their holy blessings. Thank goodness, no train sat at the bottom of Alta Pass because a wreck could have happened. My grandfather told many stories about the railroad and his adventures. His grandchildren rode the train several times in the Erwin yard, sitting on his lap, or checking out the passenger cars that sometimes came through. As a child, each of his grandchildren would always sit on his lap and listen to his stories.

Stories from my great-grandfather sometimes included moonshine. Old Pop made moonshine on Upper Higgins Creek in Flag Pond, Tennessee. When he drove the steam engines through the Nolichucky Gorge, he would stop at Lost Cove, so he could buy some of the best moonshine around. One can understand why Lost Cove, with lively springs running off the mountains along the tracks, had the best moonshine.

While the stories of the railroad lingered through my imagination, my thoughts remained focused on Lost Cove, the landscape and the people who lived there. My family always walked the railroad tracks from Unaka Springs into the Nolichucky Gorge. Many residents walked the same tracks every day just to make it to Erwin. The hike to Lost Cove is about three miles from Unaka Springs, Tennessee. In the early 1900s, the Unaka Springs Hotel was a booming locale. People from New York to Florida would travel by train to sit in the mineral springs. It is said that Al Capone stayed there often when he travelled to Johnson City, Tennessee. Unaka Springs had a luxury hotel that sat next to the railroad tracks. The CC&O made frequent stops at the hotel to pick up passengers heading to Erwin or Asheville, North Carolina.

The landscape along the Nolichucky River is rugged, and chiseled rock outlines the mountainside. The fast-rolling Nolichucky roars in the gorge. Its vibrant waters crash against the landscape, creating an echo that bounces off the mountains. Up in the gorge, you make sure you have good ears. The trains run like clockwork: one chugs south, and then, thirty minutes or so later, one glides north. You definitely don't want to get caught on the railroad tracks when the trains are hauling through the gorge. The lack of space between the trains, the mountains, and the river can scare you. I got caught on the tracks between the rock walls and the rail several times. The distance between the train and rock walls is less than five feet in some spots; the train cars make your body quiver as they pass by.

Along the railroad tracks is Devil's Washing Bowls. This is sometimes where rafters stop along the ride down the Nolichucky. The beautiful mountain stream has three washing bowls. A trail runs next to the stream, which rushes down the mountain during early spring and summer. Most people walk up to the very top of the stream to zip down into a bowl. The highest bowl is the best because the natural stream creates a flume, which shoots an eager rafter out into the bowl.

Past the bend from the North Carolina state line and trestle bridge, the trail to Lost Cove starts from the edge of the tracks. The hike up the long, steep and rocky truck path is easy for a kid like me. I take pictures of the sunlight catching the ferns and fresh moss on the rocks and play in the natural springs that crossed the truck trail. The beautiful landscape makes me feel as if I am lost in time, reflecting on the people and their life in this community. I can picture their life … simple yet free from the woes of the outside world.

As we reach the top of the trail, a huge boulder welcomes visitors to Lost Cove. I always know once I see that rock that the old wooden houses are just around the corner. Even through the 1990s there were numerous houses, crop buildings, and barns in the cove. The houses sit deteriorating, and the wallpaper peels back the hands of time. Fresh springs gurgle from beneath the forest floor. Despite the occasional hiker, the beautiful upland settlement remains hidden in time.

Over the years, I compiled newspaper clippings, articles, and excerpts written on Lost Cove. The information that I found on Lost Cove through research only represents a small percentage compared to the informative, in-depth interviews from residents along the way. To me, this book best exemplifies Lost Cove's history and people. The interviews I gathered provide the historical stories and information needed to write this book. My informants guided me in every step, allowing me to catch up to *their* spoken words.

I am grateful for the many stories of the history, lifeways, and people of Lost Cove told to me by former residents J.C. Bryant, Geneva Tipton McNabb, Homer Tipton, and Isaiah Bailey. Interviews with Lost Cove preacher Verno Davis, Betty Peterson, Norman Canoy, Roy Guthrie, Joseph Bailey, Camille McNabb Flett, Teresa Miller Bowman, Jim Johnson, and Richard Bailey provide a glimpse of events and family memories. Photos from Joseph Bailey provide a glimpse of the Tipton, Miller, and Bailey families. Photos by Teresa Miller Bowman show school pictures and the Miller families. Photos from Chad Fred Bailey, Hosea's son and Isaiah's nephew, provide an in-depth look at lifeways within the community. Camille McNabb Flett's pictures show her grandfather Dock Landon Tipton's family and her mother. Photos from Regina Cornett, J.C. Bryant's granddaughter, and Jeff Bryant, his son, provide a look at Lost Cove structures and pictures of the Miller and Bryant families. All informants were especially warm and have become a part of my family. Their stories are embedded in my mind and I will never forget their patience, kindness, love, and friendship. Their life in Lost Cove was one of complacency, fulfillment, hardship, and strife. I appreciate Samuel Byrd from Burnsville, North Carolina. His kind leadership and determination enabled me to attain more interviews from informants in Yancey and Unicoi counties. I also commend the ladies at the Yancey County Library, Mrs. Frankie Murphy and Melanie Stallings. I appreciate their kindness and direction for allowing me to find more materials needed to write this book. I am proud of this book. I believe that Lost Cove history will live on, without being erased from the memories of the residents and descendants.

I appreciate Dr. Roberta Herrin for guiding me into Appalachian Studies during my undergraduate years. To the wonderful, wise mentor, Dr. Tess Lloyd, appreciation is due for encouraging my interest in Appalachian culture and history, as well as guiding me to capture the best stories residing among Appalachian people. Dr. Kevin O'Donnell, my friend and former professor, deserves praise for his patience and direction. Dr. Marie Tedesco merits commendation for her guidance and counsel in helping me pursue my master's degree, and allowing me to strengthen my roots.

Eventually, the large compilation of materials collected will be placed in the Archives of Appalachia at East Tennessee State University. I commend Jeremy Smith and Ryan Bernard and previous staff from the Archives. Time after time, I asked for documents, manuscripts, photographs, and files. Their generous help enabled me to collect the best-documented materials pertaining to Lost Cove. To all my family and friends I thank you for your patience and persistence in pushing me to complete this work. Without you, I would still be idling.

I hope that Lost Cove residents and their descendants will enjoy this book. I tried my best to capture the truth through interviews. I appreciate their kind words and help in guiding me to find more information, as well as finding other residents and descendants. My intention is to preserve the history, lifeways, and people of Lost Cove. I believe it is important to document Appalachian culture, and tell the stories of Lost Cove people; stories that stood silent until now.

Introduction

Boundaries, Routes, and Debates

> *Deep in the remote back country of the Unaka and Bald Mountains of western North Carolina where that state borders with eastern Tennessee, nature reclaims the fields and pastures, the cabin and church yards of "Lost Cove."*[1]
> —Everett M. Kivette

For more than 60 years, Lost Cove has remained desolate. Formerly a self-sustaining, thriving community, Lost Cove is now, according to historian Pat Alderman, "one of eastern America's most legendary Ghost Towns."[2] The settlement is prime hunting territory, with springs, rolling fields, and flat lands that cater to the avid hunter. Its rich soil and forest enabled families to live without the chaos of everyday society's woes and helped them form a sustainable community. Lost Cove boundaries, routes, and debates have filtered through newspaper articles from North Carolina to California for more than 50 years, painting a legendary settlement that wooed the outsider's love of Appalachia.

The history of this settlement, situated high above the Nolichucky and South Toe rivers, demonstrates how families in remote communities throughout the Appalachians survived from the Civil War era until the mid–twentieth century. Here, families and land unite in order to survive. Interactions with the outside world are limited. There are no crossroads or highways, only boundary lines and paths that stretch along Narrow Branch from Poplar, North Carolina; Flat Top Mountain (Joe Lewis Fields) by way of Spivey Mountain or White Oak Flats in Yancey County; and the Clinchfield railroad, now called the CSX.

Lost Cove has always been physically isolated. The cove lies at the edge of Mitchell, and Yancey counties in North Carolina, and in Unicoi County, Tennessee.[3] The topography of Yancey County is rough, and the elevation of the ridges close to the North Carolina–Tennessee border rises above 5,000 feet. The nearest town is Poplar, North Carolina. White Oak Flats is the second closest community, as well as the Sioux community of Yancey County. While Unicoi County hugs the border of North Carolina, Lost Cove sits peacefully below the Pisgah Mountain Range.

The cove's elevation is around 2,500 feet, but the boundary lines rise to 3,000 feet. Lost Cove is situated about 1.5 miles above the gorge of the Nolichucky River (known as the Toe River in North Carolina), and the gorge is great for the avid kayaker and rafter. Rafting companies often tell Lost Cove stories to their clients as they guide rafters down the Nolichucky Gorge. Lost Cove's boundary lines collide with the Pisgah National Forest. Flat Top Mountain overlooks the settlement, rising at 4,716 feet. On the opposite side of Lost Cove sits the Unaka mountain range. The range climbs from 3,000 to 5,500 feet. The Appalachian Trail runs across the Spivey mountain range and into the Unaka Mountains, slightly touching the edge of Lost Cove. When people hike the Flat Top Mountain trail into the cove, the Appalachian Trail markers guide the hiker in the right direction to Unaka Mountain. Many AT hikers have walked into Lost Cove just to catch a glimpse of the community.

Several passages enabled families to haul goods to and from the markets, and allowed interactions with the outside world. The path beyond the Poplar Bridge in North Carolina winds around the southern edge of the community. The narrow, rocky path runs some two miles before reaching the first house. Most residents trekked into Poplar hauling crops or goods to trade at the local store. The Poplar train depot, located three miles or more above the Lost Cove community, contained a general store, where neighbors bartered and traded goods. Families interacted, bartered,

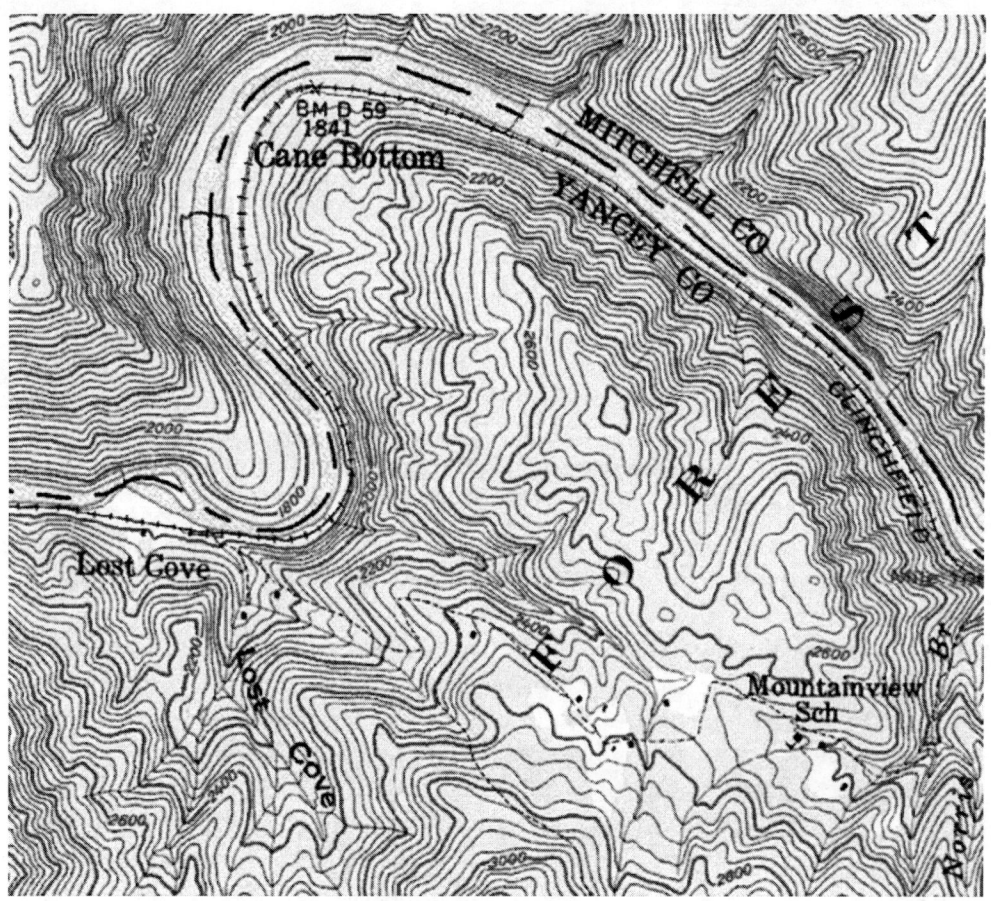

Lost Cove USGS map

and hauled crops from the Ramsey Township, Green Mountain, Huntdale, and Sioux communities as well.

The path along Flat Top Mountain overlooks the community, some five miles from the edge of Joe Lewis Fields. The old trail is reachable by heading on 19W over Spivey Mountain and into White Oak Flats. The trail is windy, steep, and rough. At one point, the trail became a sled trail, allowing White Oak Flats families to haul goods into Lost Cove. Many horse riders used this path to reach the cove, but now, from years of hard winds and storms, uprooted trees, rock gardens, and steep terrain, ATVs and horses attempting to reach the community encounter resistance.

There have never been real roads into the cove, only a rutted sled trail that curves around the mountains into White Oak Flats. Betty Peterson, cousin to J.C. Bryant, lived in White Oak Flats as a child. Her brothers and sisters often went into Lost Cove to see their cousins. The old ragged road begins at the edge of Lost Cove near John Miller's homestead and ends near the Bryant's homestead in White Oak Flats. For many years, families sometimes used this sled trail to carry crops and herbs to the country store in Poplar. In the later years, Betty's two brothers tried to build a road into Lost Cove from the border of their property. Both trails are tilted now. Years of springs overflowing and gulley-washers have damaged both trails. New trees have grown in and around the trails, creating a new forest fresh with new life.

The last route into the cove is by way of Unaka Springs. Hikers usually park their cars past the old Unaka Springs Hotel and up the mountain toward the cemetery. A rutted trail, opposite the cemetery, winds down to the railroad tracks. In the 1980s, our family could drive the cars down the rutted trail. The trail was smooth until years of decay and rain washed it back to its natural state. Hikers trek nearly three miles on the railroad tracks then up a steep, rocky old logging road. The trail lies past the North Carolina state line via the CSX rail line. The ascent is windy and long. One can hear northbound trains chug up the Nolichucky Gorge, resonating across the mountains. The old road carried many lives and products from the railroad to the community. Hard labor and construction kept this road manageable for decades.

Mr. Samuel Byrd, great-great-grandson to Stephen "Morgan" Bailey, explained to me that Lost Cove may be an upland settlement.[4] The land sits at a relatively high elevation and could be considered a plateau. Lost Cove's terrain is a wide and long sloping ledge with flat areas that serve as a close backdrop on the east, south, and southwest corners of the boundary lines. The cove's water supply came from streams like Norris Branch, Lost Cove Branch, and Big Branch. The branches provided the water necessary for crops, animals, and moonshine, while springs provided fresh water to every house. The mountain settlement had plenty of pristine land. Lost Cove nestles on nearly 350 acres of land, and amid its fertile landscape, a small but thriving community found plenty of land to grow crops, maintain orchards, and raise animals.

From the community's inception around the Civil War era until the early twentieth century, Lost Cove was self-sufficient, but as the twentieth-century timber industry began dwindling, and railroad transportation routes grew, the cove dwellers began relying on the outside world for further needs. The post-industrialization era and the trigger of World War II forced families throughout the Appalachians to leave their homelands. The Appalachian people poured into neighboring cities for jobs and advancements in education. Men in Lost Cove began entering military services and marrying women from neighboring towns. J.C. Bryant left to serve in Japan, and Okie Bailey entered the Navy. Others, like Isaiah Bailey and his sister Priscilla Bailey Knode, wanted to further their education. Ironically, as we shall see in subsequent chapters of this book, the dependence on the outside world contributed to the death of the community.

Many people question how families could live in the rugged terrain along the Nolichucky Gorge for almost a century. Questions about its topography, boundaries, and families often conflict with or contradict stories told by outside newspaper articles, which often distort views in order to catch public attention and elicit emotional responses, especially when it pertains to Appalachia.

There is little written documentation about Lost Cove, and what exists is sometimes contradictory. The information drawn from newspaper clippings paints a rugged community with no communication with the outside world, a community isolated with only a beaten down shack that rests next to the railroad tracks, where mail or goods are dropped off and trains stop for passengers. Some accounts and interviews were published in local newspapers of Sullivan, Unicoi, and Washington counties in Tennessee and in Yancey, Buncombe, Durham, and Alamance counties in North Carolina from 1950 to 2015. In the 1950s, most of the newspaper clippings from North Carolina were written by Doris Dumond. The articles became distorted as more newspapers across the country reprinted Ms. Dumond's articles. News about the cove reached beyond the mountain region. Lost Cove, North Carolina, intrigued readers from many states. Newspaper articles from California, New Mexico, Mississippi, Iowa, Florida, Wisconsin, Texas, and Ohio spin tales of the deserted community.

Lost Cove appeared in newspapers across the United States because of its isolation. Headlines read: "North Carolina Community Is Isolated from Rest of World," "Lost Cove Is Really Lost Town," and "Lost Cove, North Carolina, Asks Outside World to Say Hello." These reprinted articles are a just a small number of newspaper headlines that made a fuss about Lost Cove. The headlines were changed in several states, but most newspapers reprinted the same stories, even if they distorted the truth.

The underlying problem is that the articles never addressed major details about Lost Cove. Lost Cove did have contact with the outside world. Families and passengers rode trains to and from Asheville, North Carolina, and Erwin, Tennessee, and beyond to see family members, and to shop for goods not made in the community. Several Lost Cove residents worked for the railroad. Interaction with fellow workers kept them informed about railroad news. Timber was a major commodity for Lost Cove families and trains would stop on the sidetrack to load and unload it for the community. Residents would trade their goods at general stores in Poplar, North Carolina, and Erwin, Tennessee. Mail was delivered by train and dropped off at the post office, called Caro-Tenn, which enabled families to receive news about the neighboring towns and their families. When the post office closed, one community leader, Swin Miller, handled the mail for the residents, sometimes traveling to Poplar to take the outgoing mail to the store for delivering.

The earliest newspaper accounts of Lost Cove were related to moonshine. The reluctance to publish how content and self-reliant Lost Cove residents were is another story yet to be told through the early newspaper accounts. Most accounts of Lost Cove didn't make headlines until the later years, when the community began to decline. There are small accounts of the early years of Lost Cove, when the first chapel was built, or when moonshine, timber, and trading goods were how families survived. There are some small reports on church services and cleansings, on education and teachers, or on doctors reaching the community to help pregnant women. But no major research has ever been conducted on Lost Cove.

No, the outside world's fascination with Appalachia and the people who live here has always drawn outside commentary and articles. The mere thought of Appalachia draws images of mountain people who are rugged, illiterate, and desperate, but yet that doesn't stop the Northerner, Midwesterner, and Westerner from writing articles about the land or people. Lost Cove captivated the outside world and placed it in the center of news across the country.

Numerous newspaper articles on Lost Cove can't compare to the historical documents found in this research. Several Appalachian vertical files in the Archives of Appalachia contain railroad accounts and maps, books, and photos relevant to Lost Cove. These accounts hold valuable information in order to construct the railroad chapter in this book. There are several historical books that reveal information on the cove.

One print source that discusses the cove is John Preston Arthur's *Western North Carolina: A History from 1730 to 1913*, an informative historical account of the settlements, railroads, manners, customs, and boundaries of western North Carolina. Arthur's information provides one of the first glimpses into Lost Cove's history. The accounts of Lost Cove are minimal, but Arthur's book contains information about the dispute over boundary lines between North Carolina and Tennessee especially when it came to the territory along the Nolichucky and Toe rivers.

The dispute over the Lost Cove boundary lines began in 1887. North Carolina Governor A.M. Scales appointed James M. Gudger to meet with the Tennessee commissioner and North Carolina surveyor J.R. Neal to determine where along the Nolichucky River the state line crossed into North Carolina. The commissioners agreed where the state lines crossed the Unaka and Iron Mountains but not the Lost Cove boundaries. A disagreement followed when the Tennessee commissioner advised that the line run south from a peak north of the Nolichucky that sat at the mouth of Lost Cove Creek, almost three quarters of a mile east from the line that Neal surveyed to the same stream. The difference made J.R. Neal's line run closer to Devil's Creek instead of Lost Cove Branch.

Mr. Gudger adamantly disagreed with the Tennessee commissioner. He had the original surveying documents from 1799, which he used to determine the previous lines. In the end neither side would come to an agreement, but Gudger finally conceded the small line dispute. In a letter sent to Governor Scales, Commissioner Gudger explained that he felt North Carolina could afford to concede the small territory. While there is no new evidence to determine where the original line ran, the boundaries of Lost Cove still remain in North Carolina.

A North Carolina historian, Lloyd R. Bailey, Sr., mentions the cove in his in-depth account of the Toe River Valley in *The Heritage of the Toe River Valley: Avery, Mitchell, and Yancey Counties, North Carolina*. The articles on Lost Cove are informative and descriptive. Accounts of Lost Cove families, churches, and history are found throughout the seven volumes. Bailey's books blend historical information with church documents, genealogy, articles on towns, and testimonies from families who lived in the western counties of Avery, Mitchell, and Yancey. Lloyd Bailey, Sr., is a descendant of the Baileys from Yancey County.

From Unicoi County historian Pat Alderman, the books *All Aboard*, *In the Shadow of the Bald*, and *The Wonders of the Unakas in Unicoi County* present some information about the cove, although Alderman is focused mostly on East Tennessee and western North Carolina history. Also, Alderman once interviewed Chester and Carrie Bailey, a married couple from Lost Cove. The interview appears on a videotape by local station WSJK-TV and can be found in the media center at East Tennessee State University. The last known information on Lost Cove is from Donald McCourry. McCourry provides photographs in *The Appalachian Eagle* along with newspaper articles about Lost Cove. The short book allows readers to catch a glimpse of the community through photos.

Beyond the writers mentioned, most secondary sources deal with Appalachia more generally, not Lost Cove specifically. These books and articles provide insight into the social, cultural, and economic aspects of the Appalachian people, and these insights are applicable to the experience of Lost Cove residents. Books by Deborah McCauley, Howard Dorgan, and Bill J. Leonard trace religious doctrines and practices throughout the Appalachians. Railroad books by William Way, James A. Goforth, and Mary Hattan Bogart provide historical facts about the Carolina, Clinchfield, and Ohio (CC&O) Railroad. Books by Ina and John Van Noppen, John C. Inscoe, and Paul Paludan describe Civil War conflicts in western North Carolina. Articles by Patricia Beaver and Deborah McCauley reveal community traditions in Appalachia. Other secondary sources by Loyal Durand, Gordon McKinney, Wilbur R. Miller, and Jess Carr demonstrate how families in western North Carolina dealt with moonshine making, revenue enforcements and wartime conflicts.

The most important accounts of Lost Cove used are the oral history interviews I conducted in 2007, 2009, 2012, and 2017 residents. During the time that I interviewed most residents, descendents, and owners of Lost Cove lands, they lived in Unicoi County, Tennessee. Homer Tipton lives in Ohio. Roy Guthrie lives in Barnardsville, North Carolina. Joseph Bailey lives in Hampton, Tennessee. Norman lives outside Greenville, South Carolina. I conducted interviews in several settings. Interviews with Samuel Byrd and Trina Fox were conducted by telephone and at the Yancey County Library. I recorded most of the interviews on a digital voice recorder. There are no known manuscripts or diaries from Lost Cove residents available.

The recordings will be deposited in the Lost Cove Collection in the Archives of Appalachia at East Tennessee State University. The Lost Cove Collection includes photographs released to the author, interviews by the author, railroad file citations, a list of books on file, articles from magazines and newspapers, and photographs from collections already included in the Archives of Appalachia.

Since these informants and their families lived in Lost Cove during different time periods, the data about the settlement occurs during its early, middle, and later periods. Responses by the informants contain genealogy data and lifeways of the families. Sometimes my informants' accounts contradicted the written accounts in newspapers and local history books. Determining which source is correct is sometimes difficult. However, the written sources and the interviews agree on at least one thing: the love that residents of the cove had for their isolated homeland, even though the pressures of modern life lured them away from it.

ONE

Lost Cove's Beginning

The cove's beginning was primitive and rough. Its only contact with the outside world was by mountain footpaths, long, steep, and tedious.[1]
—Pat Alderman

Born out of the chaos of the Civil War and persevering through the Great Depression, Lost Cove was a remote mountain community made possible by the determination and strength of the people who resided on the slopes of the boundary between North Carolina and Tennessee. The life of this once-thriving community during the nineteenth and twentieth centuries reveals how the cove developed, lifeways in the cove, how the community survived, and why the community became deserted.

Lost Cove is said to have been a sanctuary from the tax collector and Indian, and a "moonshiners' haven."[2] There has long been controversy about when the first settler arrived in Lost Cove and how the community received its name. One theory suggests that members of Daniel Boone's group were the first to settle in the cove, while another theory claims that Stephen "Morgan" Bailey first settled there before the Civil War era. A theory about the naming of Lost Cove addresses the boundary dispute between North Carolina and Tennessee, while another theory states that the railroad named the community.

Frank Elliott and J.L. Lonon proclaim from accounts that members of Daniel Boone's group may have formed the community. In an article in *Blue Ridge Country* magazine, Frank Elliott notes that other "accounts hold that the community was settled by members of Daniel Boone's expeditions."[3] Elliott's account tells about a young girl growing sick and dying during the Boone expedition. Elliott speaks about the young girl's family burying her along the mountainside while they "built two log cabins" to start the community.[4] In J.L. Lonon's book, *Tall Tales of the Rails*, Lonon states that when he visited the cove while it still remained inhabited by the descendants of the first settlers, an unknown woman told him about the settlement's origins:

> During Daniel Boone's trek through the twelve mile Toe-Nolichucky River Gorge, a young girl from one of the families in the Boone group took seriously ill, and as a result her family could not continue with the band. Another family of friends remained behind with them, and during the girl's extended illness, while the men were hunting for game, they found the level plateau near the top of the mountain. There they decided to construct a lean-to shelter for the ill girl, as well as for other family members. Several days after the move, the girl died, and was buried near the hut. Reluctant to leave the grave in the wilderness, the two families decided to

build two log homes, which were soon completed. This, apparently, was the beginning of the settlement.[5]

Lonon also states that "the older lady recalled to me that in her girlhood days (during the Civil War) the Daniel Boone group was joined by other families who were dodging involvement in the war."[6] Daniel Boone did trek through the mountains of western North Carolina, and early settlers did build cabins along the Watauga and Nolichucky rivers. Lonon indicates that "a cemetery located near the school-church has grave markers dating back to the late 1700s."[7] However, though these accounts may hold truth, there are no known written records stating that members of Daniel Boone's group formed the Lost Cove community. Also, Lost Cove residents never talked about the headstones during the interviews. No one ever addressed Daniel Boone's trek or the headstones that are near the school-church. I have never seen any graves as long as I have been hiking into the cove. The only structures that were close to the one-room school-church house were Bob and John Miller's houses. No known grave markers have been found so far.

Since no records indicate whether Lost Cove was formed before the Civil War, the only known written records show that Lost Cove became a settlement during the Civil War and was founded by a Union soldier. Lloyd Bailey, Sr., editor of *The Heritage of the Toe River: Avery, Mitchell, and Yancey Counties, North Carolina*, notes that the first known settler was a Union soldier by the name of Stephen "Morgan" Bailey.[8] Born in 1825, Morgan was the son of John "YellowJacket" Bailey and Lovada "Lovie" Ray. "Yellow Jacket" Bailey got his name because he was hotheaded. Morgan was one of 20 children born to John and Lovada Ray in Relief, North Carolina. Some records show that Morgan had a twin named Hiram. Both married Deyton girls from Mitchell County.

Morgan's maternal grandparents previously owned the land where the town of Burnsville is now located. The land, once called Ray Flats, was owned by Hiram Ray, Lovada's father. Hiram Ray gave John Bailey nearly 160 acres on July 9, 1820.[9] John later deeded more than 100 acres of land to start the town of Burnsville, North Carolina. In 1930, Bailey notes, the city commissioners designated the site as "Bailey Square." A plaque in John Bailey's honor sits in the Burnsville town square underneath Otway Burns' statue.[10] Even today, the statue still stands at the center of the square.

Most of the Bailey family lived either in Yancey or Mitchell County in North Carolina during the middle 1800s. Most census records indicate that many residents who would later reside in Lost Cove lived in the Ramsey Township of North Carolina. Many articles about Morgan Bailey's Union army ties questioned whether he was a Union soldier.

The Fold3 website indicates that Morgan Bailey enlisted in the Union army on June 11, 1864, and was discharged on August 8, 1865, before the Civil War ended. Morgan enlisted in Knoxville, Tennessee, as a volunteer. He enlisted at the age of 39, and his occupation is listed as farmer. His height is listed at five feet 10 inches with dark complexion, dark hair and dark eyes. Morgan swore that he would serve the Union army for three years. The document signed by Sergeant Robert Cummings stated that Morgan would serve against his enemies and obey the president and officers appointed to him. The papers were witnessed by a Mr. Ed Brown.[11]

Morgan served in the Union army (Co. F, 3rd NC Mounted Infantry) under Col. George W. Kirk. Lloyd Bailey contends that Morgan "claimed disability in his pension application, saying that he had fallen off a cliff during a night raid and was seriously injured."[12] There are no records that support this claim. Research shows that he had money due to him when he was discharged. Morgan received an amount of $71.67 for his clothing account, and $300.00 due for pay. On the company muster rolls, the remarks listed show that Morgan was discharged on August 8, 1965.

According to the National Archives in Washington, D.C., Morgan Bailey filed for his pension papers on October 17, 1878.[13] There are no extant records stating if Morgan filed for a pension earlier than the date indicated. Morgan may have entered Lost Cove before 1864 and re-entered the cove again in 1865 after his discharge from the North Carolina Third Mounted Infantry. Morgan Bailey's parents lived in nearby Relief, North Carolina. Lost Cove is close to Relief, just past Poplar along the South Toe River. Alderman does suggest that Morgan came into the cove shortly before the Civil War "with simple tools, family, and work animals."[14] Other members of Lost Cove also state that Morgan came into the cove before the Civil War.

Since Morgan hunted, some say he saw the territory as perfect land to live on, to raise livestock, and have a family. In an article published in the *Daily News*, Velmer Bailey, great-grandson of Morgan Bailey, recounts how his great-grandfather was the first man to build a cabin in the cove. Since deeds were informal back then, most settlements were not established until the government cleared the land for timber.[15] Isaiah Bailey, Velmer's son, recollects that his great-great-grandfather Morgan Bailey bought land in Lost Cove by trading his shotgun and paying $10 for the land.[16]

Stephen Morgan Bailey pension papers (1878). www.Fold3.com

There is no doubt that Morgan Bailey settled into the cove between 1860 to 1865. Why he moved there is another question. His pension records state that he filed for the pension on October 17, 1878, almost 14 years after he was in the infantry. The land is good hunting terrain and Bailey often hunted in Lost Cove, according to interviews. Possibly he was trying to escape the ravages of the Civil War, which brought chaos to the mountains of western North Carolina. Some say that Lost Cove afforded a refuge during the Civil War years to families fleeing its turmoil—and service.[17] This area was a constant (if non-formal) battleground: brothers fighting brothers, fathers against sons, and neighbors against neighbors. As a Union soldier, Bailey understood the chaos of war, especially in the mountains. His family lived not far from Lost Cove, and since he hunted there often, Lost Cove seemed the ideal place to live and prosper.

Gordon McKinney's article "The Civil War in Appalachia" depicts a time of destruction and fear among families in the southern Appalachian Mountains. McKinney states that "communities were destroyed by confrontations as large armies marched across the mountains throughout the war, leaving behind desolated farms and towns and thousands of dead and wounded soldiers and civilians."[18] Around 150,000 men volunteered for the Confederate army and 100,000 for the Union forces.[19] McKinney also notes that many mountaineers opposed forming a southern nation.

Even in nearby Shelton Laurel, close to the Tennessee and North Carolina state lines, war interrupted the mountain people's lives. David Shelton, a young Union sympathizer, often directed and led Union soldiers wanting to escape the war through the mountains of East Tennessee. Trails that ran from Hot Springs, North Carolina, into Shelton Laurel and Devil's Fork, along the Appalachian Trail, allowed soldiers to escape. David Shelton knew this territory well, helping soldiers who wanted to reach Camp Nelson in Kentucky.

In the areas of eastern Tennessee and northwestern Virginia (now West Virginia), most people "supported the national government, while in areas of western North Carolina and northern Georgia, the people were reluctant to leave the Union. The latter people had to accept the reality of the Confederacy in their states and support the Southern war effort."[20] As a Union soldier, Bailey saw many of his comrades fall to the Confederates. With many men in the mountains fighting their neighbors and brothers, his sense of isolation took him far from the front lines of war.

In their book *Western North Carolina Since the Civil War*, Ina and John Van Noppen also note that "the Civil War brought disunion and discord to Western North Carolina."[21] With many young men hiding out in the mountains, the mountains became a refuge from both armies. Phillip Paludan's book, *Victims: A True Story of the Civil War*, stresses how desertion flourished in the mountains due to conscription. Men wanted to dodge the draft, because the draft meant leaving their farms, livelihoods, and families, and might force men to kill, to be in armies that the mountaineer did not want to be in. According to Paludan, western North Carolina and eastern Tennessee housed most deserters. Within the Confederacy alone, North Carolina led the rankings for deserters, with an estimate of 24,000 men and officers. Tennessee ranked second with an estimate of 12,000 volunteers fleeing their rebel ranks.[22]

Thus, if Morgan Bailey was motivated by a desire to avoid the divided loyalties and incessant conflict of the Civil War, Lost Cove's rocky but fertile mountainside may have seemed like a safe haven to him and his first wife, Rebecca Deyton. In an article by Don Haines, "Gone, But Not Forgotten," however, Ulis Miller, who lived in Lost Cove from the age of two to sixteen, states that it is "pure fiction" that Morgan Bailey settled into the cove because of his Civil War leanings.[23] Miller does not dispute that Morgan Bailey was the first person in, "but it had nothing to do with the Civil War."[24] Mr. Miller's statement seems to be true, since Morgan Bailey's family resided in Mitchell County before the Civil War, and since Morgan Bailey resided in Yancey County during the Civil War.

My informants confirm that Morgan Bailey was the originator of the Lost Cove settlement. Mr. Bryant remembers that Lost Cove's first settler was a man named "Bailey."[25] Of course, there were other families who moved into Lost Cove during the early days. In my interview with Geneva Tipton McNabb, who lived in Lost Cove from 1918 to 1926, Mrs. McNabb said that there were around seven families in Lost Cove when she lived there. Her family lived in Lost Cove in the 1880s through the 1930s.

According to Mrs. McNabb, her grandfather, John D. Tipton, was an early settler who owned 230 acres in Lost Cove. Documents found also state that John D. Tipton enlisted into the North Carolina Third Mounted Infantry on the same day that Stephen "Morgan" Bailey enlisted in Knoxville, Tennessee. The Civil War archives show that John D. Tipton enlisted at the age of 30. Tipton was a tall man at six feet two inches. He had a light complexion with hazel eyes and brown hair. Tipton is listed as a farmer from Yancey County. My theory indicates that Morgan Bailey and Tipton were friends before their enlistment. Both men probably traveled together on their way to volunteer for the Union army in Knoxville. Tipton's documents were also signed by Sergeant Cummings and witnessed by Mr. Ed Brown. As soon as Bailey and Tipton signed their documents, the battle for freedom began.

Both men volunteered because they opposed secession from the Union as well as slavery. Slavery didn't exist as much in the higher mountains as it did in Asheville, North Carolina, or Greeneville, Tennessee. Mountain men didn't own as much land and didn't need slaves as those who had many acres to work did, and the economic and social conditions were very different as compared to the plantation farming. In the mountains the Civil War pitted brother against brother, neighbor against neighbor. Men were being conscripted and women were left tending houses, farms, and livestock.

Ora Blackmun writes that the Confederate tax placed on families meant less flour, oats, and corn. The tax meant everyone who had farm products above a specified exemption had to send all products to Confederate warehouses in Greenville, South Carolina.[26] Raids and skirmishes occurred in the mountains during the Civil War because of the tax. Women were even forced to raid Confederate stocks on April 9, 1864. Wives of Union sympathizers stormed the Burnsville, North Carolina Confederate storehouse and carried off bushels of wheat and other foods meant for Confederate families and soldiers. The very next day in Burnsville, some 75 Union sympathizers broke into the ammunition storage and took as much ammunition and as many guns as they could, then destroyed the remaining weapons.[27]

During the Civil War, loyalty divided many men in the regions of Tennessee and North Carolina. Because of the divide, Union army regiments began forming in North Carolina from 1862 to 1863. The Third Mounted Infantry was formed on February 13, 1864, by General John Schofield from Ohio. Schofield granted "Major G.W. Kirk, of the Second North Carolina Mounted Infantry, to raise a regiment of troops in the eastern front of Tennessee and western part of North Carolina. The regiment will be organized as infantry and will be mustered into the service of the United States to serve for three years, unless sooner discharged."[28]

According to "A History of the North Carolina Third Mounted Infantry Volunteers," Major G.W. Kirk, a well-known Union volunteer, began his career with the First Tennessee Regiment as a private in 1862. His determination and dedication as a volunteer soon led him to attain the rank of lieutenant in the Fourth Tennessee. He kept this rank until June 1863 and by late 1863 became captain of Company A, Fifth East Tennessee Cavalry Volunteers. Kirk would be discharged soon after, but was called once again by Schofield to lead as colonel of the Third Mounted Infantry in early 1864.[29]

The Third Mounted Infantry enlisted more than 850 soldiers. Kirk's infantry consisted of Companies A-K. Most men enlisted were from eastern Tennessee and western North Carolina; many were Native Americans. The companies consisted of men from 16 to 48 years of age with a total of 70 or more men to each company. Both Bailey and Tipton enlisted in Company F of the infantry. Most men in Company F enlisted in June, but the enrollment lasted until December 1864. When Bailey and Tipton joined the infantry in Knoxville in June of 1864, Kirk and Companies A-D were in full military operation and ready for war. The first movement from most companies began in Morristown, Tennessee, on June 13, 1864, and ended in Burke County, North Carolina, on July 15, 1864.

There are many inconsistencies with how many men actually participated in the first raid under Kirk. While some companies were not fully formed, the raids were the first military operation of the infantry and consisted of a force between 130 and 300 men. Bailey and Tipton's Company F had not fully formed, so only 23 of the 79 men enlisted in the company, along with a captain and several staff, were eligible to fight in the early raids.[30]

The regiment traveled through Bulls Gap and entered Carter County on June 25, when Kirk enlisted the services of John V. Franklin as a guide. Franklin led the regiment across the Toe River and Cranberry through Mitchell County, North Carolina, and down the mountain to Morganton. Camp Vance sat six miles from the center of Morganton. The camp, named after the governor of North Carolina, served as a conscription camp for the Confederates. Vance's men neared the camp on the evening of June 27, just two days after leaving Carter County. The camp contained close to 250 young conscripts.[31]

Kirk's main objectives after seizing Camp Vance were to press on to Salisbury, North Carolina, to free federal prisoners at the prisoner encampment and to destroy the Yadkin River bridge. On the early morning of June 28, Kirk and his regiment captured 132 prisoners and 48 horses and mules. The infantry had little resistance during the raid, yet 10 conscripts and one officer were killed. On their way back to

Knoxville, Kirk and his infantry, known as Tories and Bushwhackers, battled with a small force of Home Guards, destroyed the Morganton Railroad Depot, scavenged food and recruited 40 men for his command.[32] The Home Guards were units of young and old men from several western North Carolina counties who rounded up deserters and renegades fleeing the war. They protected their towns and citizens yet were sometimes lawless. The group couldn't stop Kirk and his forces.

The Third Mounted Infantry would participate in action at Morristown and Russellville, Tennessee, from October 28 to December 7 of 1864. John Tipton participated in this action. Records indicate that Morgan Bailey, sick, left for North Carolina on September 29, 1864. By November he returned to the infantry. Nearly 400 men from the infantry would fight against Tennessee rebel forces where men often fought their brothers or neighbors. The infantry soon assisted the Fourth Tennessee along Paint Rock, North Carolina, in Madison County. Their forces were to hold and control the passes into North Carolina until rebels evacuated East Tennessee. Once accomplished, the infantry scoured the mountains for any hiding rebels.[33]

During late December 1864, John D. Tipton left on leave to see his family. Along with a friend, Tipton trekked back to Lost Cove during a harsh winter. His visit lasted over five months and the infantry was furious. AWOL notices were issued without knowing the events that occurred in the mountains. Tipton became very sick and could not resume his duties with the regiment. The cold winter trek back to the mountains left him with the flu. His worn out shoes were demolished on the trek. The Union would find him not guilty of going AWOL. Records indicate on the company muster roll in March–April of 1865 that on December 29, 1864, John D. Tipton, listed as a deserter, left with one rifle. This account through government records indicates that Geneva McNabb's account of her grandfather is true. Mrs. McNabb told me that Tipton walked into Lost Cove with a friend around 1864 during the wintertime. Tipton's shoes were worn out and he became sick due to walking with only leaves wrapped around his feet. The families brought in a doctor to nurse Tipton back to health. The government initially claimed that Tipton had gone AWOL, but this charge was later overturned.[34]

Civil War records also indicate who may have left with John D. Tipton that day. According to records, Archibald (Arch) Bennett, a resident of Lost Cove, is reported absent from the regiment on December 29, 1964. He enrolled into the Union army on the same day as Morgan and John D. The day he left with John D., he took with him a spring rifle.[35] The records indicate that Arch was 30 years old and a farmer when he enlisted. According to the documents, Arch deserted to Greasy Cove, which is now in the vicinity of Jackson Love Highway in Erwin. Arch rejoined his regiment in Asheville on May 1, 1865, and his pay was restored. Arch stayed with the regiment until August 1865. While both men were reported deserted, Morgan Bailey stayed with his company.

In February 1865, Colonel Kirk and the regiment were sent to raid Waynesville, North Carolina. With 600 men on the move, the small town of Waynesville endured pillaging of articles and jewelry, and some citizens were beaten. Colonel Robert Love's house burned and the jailhouse prisoners were let loose. There are no documents that state which companies participated in the raids. They continued through

Balsam Gap and escaped Colonel Stringfield's Confederates, of which many were Cherokees. Kirk withdrew and escaped back to Tennessee through Indian Gap, along the Swain County, North Carolina, and Sevier County, Tennessee, line.[36]

The second biggest event for the Third Mounted Infantry came at Stoneman's Raid in April 1865. This raid, designed to end the war, had Kirk and his men in Boone, North Carolina. They were to barricade Meat Camp Road that led through Sampson Gap in Ashe County. After barricading the roads, Kirk transformed the Watauga courthouse into a fort. The Confederates wanted to raid, yet none were available to hit Kirk's camp at Blowing Rock.[37]

Kirk and his regiment would soon travel to Asheville in May 1865. John D. Tipton did not desert the Union army. Another Muster Roll document says he rejoined the army from desertion on May 1, 1865, in Asheville, North Carolina, the same day Arch Bennett rejoined. The documents show that Tipton did not lose his pay due to the fact that he had "erroneously" been reported as a deserter. Tipton finished out his duties and was honorably discharged. Tipton's granddaughter, Geneva McNabb, carries his discharge papers. John Tipton rejoined his company in Asheville after the infantry returned on May 17, 1865. The capture and occupation events in Asheville led to federal control and effectively ended the Civil War in the mountains, as far as Kirk's infantry was concerned. In August 1865, Bailey left the Third Mounted Infantry and Tipton remained in Asheville. An account indicates that Morgan Bailey fell off a cliff at some point during these raids and that is why he was discharged from the infantry due to injury.

Ron V. Killian's book states that the infantry recorded 39 deaths due to disease and battle injury. There were 78 desertion charges among the men, and the regiment experienced five enemy captures. Company D of the infantry had the most Native Americans, while Company F, Bailey, Tipton, and Bennett's company, had the most desertions. The regiment had the most men with surnames in common, and most enlisted in the same month and year from the same small towns. Colonel George W. Kirk officially resigned from his post in May 1865. He left the United States Army on August 8, 1865.[38]

The National Archives records indicate that John D. Tipton filed for his pension on August 2, 1890, and then again on February 18, 1907. John may have been discharged at an earlier date, but there are no known records indicating that he filed for his pension prior to 1890.[39]

Of course, there are no known records indicating when John D. Tipton first bought property in Lost Cove. Mrs. McNabb's documents indicate that John D. Tipton paid $500 to Isaac R. Love and his wife, Mary, for 230 acres of land on September 24, 1902. The land in Lost Cove

> adjoined the lands of said Isaac R. Love and others beginning at a stake in the Dripping Rock Branch below where Wiley Tipton (John's father) now lives at a point where the last line of the 230 acres crosses the said branch then to back line of said 130 acres crosses branch then with old line east to poplar lynn and dogwood there along a steep mountain to 2 lynns and a spruce pine crossing Manors Branch to a sourwood, spruce pine to near bank of a branch then with crossing line to beginning 100 acres.[40]

John D. Tipton became the owner of over one-third of the land in Lost Cove. John and Caroline stayed in Lost Cove until their death. As the years passed and the

John D. Tipton pension papers (1890). www.Fold3.com

children got older, John told two of his sons to split the farm in half. Both brothers built houses in Lost Cove and they and their families took up residence. These brothers were Mrs. McNabb's father, Doctor (Dock) Landon Tipton, and her uncle, Wiley Tipton.[41] The population in Lost Cove grew as more families entered. The Baileys and Tiptons have found their peace of heaven, rested in the mountains of the Pisgah Forest. The solitude and fertile landscape provided independence, identity, and self-endurance.

As with the debate about Lost Cove's first settlers, there are debates over how Lost Cove received its name. Perhaps the name came as a result of Lost Cove's geographic isolation, accessible only by foot (or later, by train). An article in the *Asheville Daily Gazette* on February 22, 1898, titled "Lost Cove Moonshiners," presents a different idea about the name. The article explained that revenue agent A.E. Aiken could not visit the area of Lost Cove due to the boundary dispute between the states of North Carolina and Tennessee. Neither state could claim the area; hence it was a "Lost Cove."[42]

The boundary documents can be found in the N.C. Executive and Legislative Documents. John Preston Arthur claims that Captain James M. Gudger from North Carolina and J.R. Neal, a surveyor, were appointed by Governor Scales to determine at what point the Nolichucky (or Toe) River crosses the state line. Neither the North Carolina nor Tennessee commissioners would yield.[43] Since neither state could claim the jurisdiction of land or determine the state boundary lines, the commissioners named the border territory "Lost Cove."[44]

Others who have written about Lost Cove have passed down their stories from other accounts. In his railroad book, J.L. Lonon states that the "name 'Lost Cove' was given to the settlement by the railroad."[45] However, the name "Lost Cove" was used before the Carolina, Clinchfield, and Ohio (CC&O) was built through the Toe and Nolichucky rivers.

Whatever the origin of the name, it served the settlement well. No matter why or when Lost Cove was settled, Lost Cove was populated by the spirited mountain folk who thrived as families for nearly 100 years. Through pure determination, these families built their homes in the rough, forested wilderness of the Appalachians. Their kinship ties connected each individual to other people, to land, to community, to history, and to identity.[46]

Two

Lifeways of the Families

Families were in frequent contact with their neighbors during an average work day, and informal chains of communication were excellent.[1]
—Durwood Dunn

The Civil War turned Lost Cove into a thriving community. After Morgan Bailey's family moved into the cove, other families followed. By the late 1880s, families such as the Tiptons and Millers nestled into this secluded community.[2] The people of Lost Cove were determined to battle the harsh elements and live a quiet life, away from the chaos of war. Since Lost Cove sits high above the Nolichucky Gorge, the terrain was ideal for an alternate life. Stories that I received when I interviewed the descendants of the original Lost Cove settlers show a glimpse of the inhabitants of Lost Cove and the folkways and customs of these inhabitants.

J.C. Bryant, one of my interviewees, notes that his grandfather and grandmother, Arch and Sindy Miller, moved into Lost Cove around 1926. His grandparents came to help out his relatives Swin and Martha Miller.[3] Since all of the families in Lost Cove were related, the settlement housed generations and generations of Baileys, Tiptons, Millers, and Bryants. Mr. Bryant lived in Lost Cove from the age of two to twenty (that is, between 1934 and 1952). He discusses the physical arrangement of the houses in the cove from 1930s to the 1950s:

> From Lost Cove Station, Mac English's house sat next to Big Branch. After English's house came Aunt Hester and Uncle Wiley's house, then the Millers' house, Frank Bryant's house, Swin Miller's house, Velmer Bailey's house, Clifford Miller's house, Chester Bailey's house, Bob Miller's house, the school and church building, then John Miller's house, and the sawmill.[4]

All in all, there were around 13 houses while Mr. Bryant resided in Lost Cove, not including three houses above Mac English's house in Big Cove. Mr. Bryant did not know who lived in all of them. In addition to the inhabitants who lived in the cove, Mr. Bryant notes that as early as 1915, the railroad section gang lived in the railroad houses in Cane Bottom, down along the river's edge. There were eight to nine houses in Cane Bottom.[5] Cane Bottom is a small stretch of land next to the Nolichucky River, about two miles above Lost Cove, near Poplar, North Carolina. The flat land next to the railroad tracks enabled a second line to be built along the gorge. Some men who maintained the railroad rails, kept them clean of debris or loose rivets, lived here, as well as relatives of Lost Cove residents. Many families lived at Cane Bottom even though it is a small section of land. Most residents relied on the railroad just as Lost Cove residents did.

Families in Lost Cove always relied on one another. For those living in the western mountains of North Carolina, frontier life was marked with poverty. From the 1870s to early 1890s, the only contact the settlement had with the outside world was a rugged and tedious trail that crept two and one-half miles around the mountain to Poplar, North Carolina. The families used a sled to haul their herbs and crops to the trading post in Poplar. In Poplar, the families bartered their goods. Although Lost Cove's settlement changed due to the building of the railroad and the first sawmill in the 1900s, families continued to need one another for survival.

Lost Cove families worked together to provide enough food and shelter for all in the settlement. Mr. Bryant states that "if we lacked an item, we would borrow it from another family, and next year we would return the item. In other words, we borrowed."[6] Pat Alderman's book discusses similar patterns. According to Alderman, because places such as the cove had fertile grounds and lush forest, the families who lived in such locations could produce crops, fruits, and ginseng in order to sustain them. They swapped some of these items for goods such as housewares, kerosene oil, coffee, pepper, and molasses. Items like sugar cane and honey were desirable, for these items were needed for taming the sweet tooth.[7]

Geneva McNabb says they traded food if they needed a hand building an outbuilding or harvesting crops or tending to the animals when a family member was sick or traveling to see family. Others swapped food for linens, wallpaper, or wood. All the families living in the cove helped others. Their self-reliance and sustainability kept them nourished and thriving.

Velmer Bailey's house (1957). Courtesy of Chad Fred Bailey.

Two. Lifeways of the Families 25

Since Lost Cove families made little money, they could not always depend on having ready cash. Fortunately, the mountains provided much that they needed to survive. In Don Haines's article, Trina Presnell Fox, who lived in Lost Cove in the 1920s, remembers how abundant the supply of mulberries, apples, and peaches was, for these fruits provided the basis for jellies and preserves for the families.[8] Fruit trees thrived in the cove. Families had many apple and peach trees so they were able to make apple butter, pies, and cobblers. The beautiful apple orchards were still producing tasty apples in the 1990s. The land where the orchards lay was wide and sloped near Velmer Bailey's barn. Rows of apple trees landscaped the hill. Apples crowded every tree.

John Miller's smokehouse (1985). Courtesy of Jeff Bryant.

Hosea Bailey sitting in Velmer's barn loft (1952). Courtesy of Chad Fred Bailey.

Hosea and Isaiah Bailey walking through Velmer Bailey's cornfield. Velmer's corncrib is at the bottom of the field (1952). Courtesy of Chad Fred Bailey.

    Cove dwellers also had chickens, hogs, and cows for meat. Raising hogs was a dirty job even for a young man. Chickens were kept by the women. Most chickens had plenty of room to roam since there was plenty of land. The cows were kept in the fields along with the horses. The fields yielded hay for the animals. Mr. Bryant states that the abundance of corn, potatoes, cucumbers, tomatoes, and green beans allowed each family to prosper.[9] The fields in the community were filled with crops

Two. Lifeways of the Families 27

Hosea and Priscilla Bailey Knode sitting in Velmer Bailey's chicken coop (1952). Courtesy of Chad Fred Bailey.

during the spring and summer months. The abundant crops raised helped sustain their family and kinfolk through the harsh winters. The families skinned hogs often in the fall. The men would kill several hogs to feed all of the families in the cove.

Kinship was a constant force in the settlement, and its effect could be seen in food processing and storage. Bryant said that at nighttime, after the family picked beans, his aunt Martha would come down to the house. The family would string the beans and lay them on sheets to let them dry. Most of the women in Lost Cove gathered together

Ulis Miller and his calf. Courtesy of Teresa Miller Bowman, Ulis's daughter.

Hazel Miller canning in her home (1948). Courtesy of Teresa Miller Bowman.

to help cook the beans on a boiler and can them. Canning, like drying, was important to the families because it offered food in the wintertime. The women prepared the jars for canning while the men and young boys gathered the crops. The families also shucked corn together.[10]

According to Bryant, each family had a garden. Since almost every house had plenty of spring water when irrigation was needed, the gardens flourished. Bryant says that some of the gardens were flat and some were sloped. The fertile land provided enough crops not just for his family but other families in Lost Cove.[11] Horses were used to till the gardens. The families used the old disc tillers, drawn by the horses, when preparing the soil for planting. One man would guide the horses while another would scatter and plant the seeds after. The women would also help seed the gardens. Once the land was tilled and the seeds planted, the men would help others in the community till their gardens.

Planting tobacco every other year was a constant, and every year the family planted cane. Mr. Bryant states that tobacco did not grow as well as cane or other

Martha Miller sitting on the porch with Unaka Mountain in the background (1952). Courtesy of Chad Fred Bailey.

crops. Bryant and his friend Homer Tipton, who lived with Bryant's family in Lost Cove, used hoes to dig lines for planting the potatoes. Farming and gardening sometimes was done according to the signs. When I interviewed Homer Tipton, he discussed when potatoes were dug: "When the full moon starts going down," Tipton explained, "that's when you want to dig your potatoes."[12]

Many families in the cove relied upon the *Farmer's Almanac* to plant their crops. They knew when the best time was to plant each seed in order to gather plenty of the products. Every family planted their crops by the signs of the moon. Even today, my father plants according to the moon signs and his garden has always produced plenty of crops.

When Lost Cove residents had more than enough crops to fill their root cellars, they sold to the trading post in Poplar, North Carolina. Crops were not the only item produced or sold from Lost Cove. Many families sold herbs. Since the rich forest produced plenty of ginseng, goldenseal, and mushrooms, the families in the cove had other sources of income.

From the early 1930s through the 1940s, Bryant's family sold herbs. Bryant discusses how his family hunted ginseng to sell in Poplar. With ginseng being a predominant herb throughout the southern Appalachians, the rich herb provided a great source of income for the families in Lost Cove. The rich mountainsides below Flat

Swin Miller, Sinclair Conley, and Clifford and John Miller skinning a hog (1952). Courtesy of Teresa Miller Bowman.

Top Mountain were a perfect place for ginseng to grow. The damp forest with thick moss, laurels and rhododendron, and cooler climate allows ginseng to grow abundantly. The ginseng would dry on makeshift pallets and screens while some ginseng would be sold wet. The more ginseng dries the better the yield. Bryant would sell his ginseng and cash good money. Sometimes the family traded the ginseng for other items needed in the household.

While herbs yielded good money, there were other sources of income for the Bryant family. Mr. Bryant states that he, his mother, and his sisters made hook-rugs to sell from the late 1930s to the late 1940s. He notes that his family lived by selling ginseng and hook-rugs. He also states that the rounded and oblong hook-rugs were made from old socks, burlap sacks, lamp oil, soot, and a needle with which Mr. Bryant would weave flowers, such as roses, into patterns. The old socks came from factories around the area. The factories supplied misshaped socks for families to use as materials.[13] The factories giving away the materials were mostly factories in Erwin, Tennessee.

Other families in Lost Cove relied upon the same resources in order to survive. Families such as the Tiptons had horses to till the land and gardens to grow. In Mrs. McNabb's interview, she discussed how her family's garden and livestock provided abundant food for the family:

Poplar, North Carolina. Lost Cove families picked up mail, bought groceries, and traded herbs at Briscoe Peterson's store (1952). Courtesy of Chad Fred Bailey.

> There was always a garden in Lost Cove. My family had plenty of everything to eat: beef, pork, store-canned food, and sausage. A lot of times they had to eat cornbread for breakfast, but it didn't stump me. They also roasted corn and potatoes in the fireplace ashes. The family loved parched corn. Horses and cattle were abundant, as well as apple orchards, wild strawberries, and blackberries.[14]

She commented that there was always plenty of food to eat, and her family never wanted for anything.[15] McNabb spoke about storing cabbage and potatoes in the wintertime by digging holes and covering the cabbage and potatoes with straw. Storing these crops in the ground enabled the family to eat cabbage and potatoes if they did not have enough canned foods to eat. As for storing milk, butter, and fruits, the family deposited the goods along the spring branch, where they dug a hole. The depth of the hole and coolness of the water allowed the milk, butter, and fruits to remain fresh.[16] Everyone in Lost Cove had a cool branch that held their cow milk and butter. A dug-out hole that was sometimes lined with rocks held in the cool waters of the springs.

The children in Lost Cove often helped their families and neighbors with the gardens, orchards, and animals. Of course, chores were assigned every day to the children. Mr. Bryant had to collect wood to cook food and heat the house. His chores also included carrying water from the spring, plowing the fields, and hoeing corn.[17] Mrs. McNabb acknowledges that she and her siblings always had chores. Mostly, she had to find the younger children and send them to the house, or she had to carry water from the spring. Geneva insists that when her parents told her and her siblings to do a chore, they did the chore without saying they did not want to do so.[18]

Hosea, Isaiah, and Miller boy with horse (1952). Courtesy of Chad Fred Bailey.

Geneva knew that her parents relied upon her and her siblings to help. If she didn't, she knew she would be in trouble, the kind of trouble that involved switches. After chores and evening supper, children were made to take a bath. Every family in Lost Cove had a bath inside the home. Families boiled water on the wood stove and the tub would be placed near the stove for families to keep warm. The children bathed one by one.

Geneva remembers that her bathtub sat next to the fire. Her mother kept the fire roaring so she and her siblings would not get cold during bath time, especially during winter. J.C. Bryant also bathed next to the chimney. His mother boiled hot water and made soapy water on the stove. No baths were taken outside even in summer time. In the later years, bathtime pictures would be published in the *Parade* magazine from California. These photos exposed children taking baths outside not inside.

In an article from the *Oakland Tribune*'s *Parade* magazine dated March 8, 1953, Sid Ross and Ernest LaFrance showcased everyday life of families in the cove. While the photos capture church activities, family life, and children at play, there are photos of bath time that depict boys bathing outside in a galvanized tub. According to Chad Bailey, son of Hosea, grandson to Velmer Bailey, these photos are fake and staged. Hosea Bailey is pictured in two pictures, one with his brother and the second with a schoolmate. Both pictures provide a fake illustration of family life in the cove. No families bathed outside.

The photographers wanted the outside world to believe that families in poverty-stricken Appalachia were still bathing outside in the 1950s. Outsiders have exploited the Appalachian region for decades, trying to evoke a bygone culture. The Bailey and Miller families had to be disappointed in the photographers and editor of *Parade* when the pictures appeared in the magazine. While no families made comments about the images, people from across the country viewed the photos as truth. Outsiders always seem to misunderstand Appalachia and the people.

Life in the cove seemed the same as any other place on Earth. Though isolation was the key difference between Lost Cove and a small town, the residents loved their land and people and wanted to live in Lost Cove forever. Residents in Lost Cove lived in quaint houses. Their hands built them, their fingers drew blood, their ropes and tools brought down trees, and their love kept their houses filled with simplistic furnishings.

Most people ask me how they built their houses. What did the interiors look like? How did the families shop for furniture? Did they have dirt floors? Undoubtedly, before the arrival of sawn lumber, houses and barns were built of logs, and one of the remaining structures in the cove at the time of this writing is built of logs covered with weatherboards. Mrs. McNabb states that since around 1910, residents built the houses with wood from the Mac English sawmill. The English sawmill produced boards from walnut, chestnut, oak, and poplar, and the houses built from these materials endured decades of weather. Geneva also describes the chimney of her house, which was built with creek rock. Inside, the fireplace held an iron rod and kettle for cooking beans, meats, and stews.[19] The fireplace was at the center of cooking in most early Lost Cove residences. The fireplace was big with openings on two sides, one side for the cooking and the other side for warming the living area or bedrooms. All of the

Isaiah giving Hosea a fake bath for the newspapers (1952). Courtesy of Chad Fred Bailey.

fireplaces were built with creek rock. The round rocks were then plastered with clay to keep the cool air from seeping into the houses.

The houses had plenty of furnishings and even some frills that offered warmth and security. Featherbeds and quilts kept the residents warm. Mrs. McNabb states that the walls had paper from Sears Roebuck catalogs glued to them. She says, "The family used to laugh at the wallpaper and stand on their heads to read the catalogs." Some homes had clocks. The kitchen had an old-time cook stove with an oven above it for cooking cornbread. The house had a pie cupboard. The kitchen table, made out of hardwood, had two long benches on each side for children's seating.[20]

Velmer Bailey's home had a beautiful detailed clock that sat in his house. Not every house had a clock, so the pendulum clock became sort of a luxury for families since the cove did not have electricity. The family clock sits in Hosea Bailey's home now. Mr. Bryant notes that the family house "was built out of big logs, a log house." Mr. Bryant goes on to say that the family used clay between the logs so the house would remain airtight. Creek rock became the foundation of the house. The logs lay on top of the rock to remain level. The men would cut long poles to make rafters, and then they would make board shingles and cover them. The windowpanes were bought in Johnson City, Tennessee, and the families made their doors out of the lumber from the sawmill.[21] Mr. Bryant adds that weatherboard was also used for siding. He states that from "the 1920s to early 1940s, the sawmills in there, gave each family

Hosea Bailey pours water into a tub with a Miller boy (1952). Courtesy of Chad Fred Bailey.

a pattern for a house…. The lumber was hemlock pine. The pine was the best a person could get at the time."[22] Mac English created house patterns for the people in the cove. The patterned houses, with the fireplaces in the middle, allowed all the families to keep warm during the winter months.

Inside the Bryant house, the walls were plastered in newspaper and pasteboard.

John Miller's house (1976). Courtesy of Chad Fred Bailey.

Stove in Velmer Bailey's house (1980). Courtesy of Chad Fred Bailey.

Velmer Bailey's clock (1980). Courtesy of Chad Fred Bailey.

Even Sears and Roebuck advertisements were sometimes hung on the walls. A big cook stove heated the house. In the kitchen, though, one could feed the chickens through the cracks in the floor. A rug lay on the floor, and in the wintertime when the wind blew, the rug would rise up off the floor. The house had four rooms. The kitchen and dining room were one big room with a separate sitting room and bedrooms. The family used straw beds with feathers on them most of the time. Mr. Bryant's mother made quilts as well. The materials for the quilts came from cotton and scraps from clothes.[23]

The Reverend Bob Miller's house (1980). Courtesy of Chad Fred Bailey.

Structures such as barns, corncribs, and outbuildings enabled the families to store their crops. According to Isaiah Bailey, the Velmer Bailey family owned two big barns, a corncrib, an apple shed, and a wood shed to store the kindling and firewood. The family raised about 40 to 50 bushels of apples a year.[24] The family would

Velmer Bailey's house with barn and chicken coop (1957). Courtesy of Chad Fred Bailey.

Swin Miller's house (1980). Courtesy of Jeff Bryant.

make apple butter or pies, often taking the apples to neighbors to eat or selling them at the trading post in Poplar. Swin Miller's family had a big barn and corncrib too. Since wild animals roamed the mountainsides of Lost Cove, the barns and corncribs helped the families store crops so that the crops could remain fresh and animals could not reach the produce.[25] Bears often tried to reach the apple produce, but because the family sealed the corncribs and kept the barn fastened shut, the bears had no luck.

Mr. Bryant has many stories that involve these barns and sheds. Mr. Bryant notes that Velmer Bailey (Bryant's second cousin), John Miller (Bryant's uncle), and Swin Miller (Bryant's uncle) had apple orchards that supplied a large quantity of apples. John Miller used a smokehouse as an apple house for storing these apples. Velmer also stored his apples in the loft of his barn. Mr. Bryant acknowledges that Velmer's sons and he would get apples to eat at nighttime, though Velmer never said a word to them.

When Velmer came outside to lock up the barn and heard the boys talking, he would turn around and go back to the house until they left the loft. Mr. Bryant notes that Velmer never locked them in the barn.[26] Apples were clearly an important crop. Mrs. McNabb states that her father, Dokter, also owned a huge apple orchard, nearly 115 acres up past the cemetery and along the mountainside. Of course, Mrs. McNabb's family lived in Lost Cove in the earlier years; Bryant lived there later.[27] Hence, we can see the maintenance of traditional subsistence patterns through the years.

Since fresh spring water ran next to every house, the families relied on the water for gardening, cooking, and drinking. According to Mr. Bryant, Lost Cove spring water ran nonstop. Velmer Bailey's house had the best spring water; the water came straight out of the mountain.[28] In a *Johnson City Press Chronicle* article, dated April 3, 1958, Velmer Bailey states that "the water is the best in the world, and contagious diseases seldom reach us."[29] Mrs. McNabb notes that the spring water next to her house overflowed every springtime.[30] Water flowed consistently throughout Lost Cove. The springs came straight from the mountainside. Some springs were lined with pipe so the water would flow away from the ground. Even outsiders talked about the cold spring water that ran through the cove.

Anne Damtoft Campbell and her husband, Robert Fishburne Campbell, an editor with the *Asheville Citizen-Times*, hiked into the cove in 1952. Their visit was short, but Anne recalls how the residents greeted them. Someone offered her a cool drink that was pulled out of a "wire cage set in a frigid mountain spring."[31] Water meant life, and with water so pure it helped bring life into the cove.

Other important aspects of the lifeways of a community are health care and childbirth. If any family member in Lost Cove became ill, the families sent for the doctor by hiking out of the cove to Poplar (or later, by train). According to Mrs. McNabb, Dr. Jeff Cooper, a local Poplar doctor, delivered her in 1918 at her family's house in Lost Cove. Doc Cooper named her "Geneva" after the Swiss city."[32]

Mrs. McNabb also states that her brothers and sisters were born in the family home. In Haines's article, Hazel Miller, Clifford Miller's wife, also states that Dr. Jeff Cooper was the doctor who would come into the cove. Doc Cooper delivered almost all of the babies in Lost Cove during the early 1900s. However, Hazel Miller goes on to say that "most babies in the 1930s and 1940s were delivered by a midwife named Lizzie Howell."[33] According to Mr. Miller, Lizzie also doctored people and stayed in Lost Cove if more than one baby was due about the same time.[34] An account from Roy Guthrie also attests to Lizzie Howell delivering babies.

In an interview with Roy Guthrie, son of Ira Lee and Trula Bryant Guthrie, Roy states that there were two midwives in Lost Cove: Lizzie Howell and Cora Belle Hensley. Roy was delivered by Lizzie on July 2, 1941. Cora Hensley was mainly the midwife for Ramsey Township, but would often help Lizzie Howell when needed in the cove. Mr. Guthrie also spoke about Dr. Cooper, who was a popular doctor for people in the cove. Though Dr. Cooper helped deliver in the early 1900s, he did not deliver babies in the cove during 1930s or 1940s.[35]

The outside world reached Lost Cove not only when doctors and midwives arrived for births and sickness but also by the mail. According to Haines's article, Clifford Miller states that "we picked up our mail at a place called Caro-Tenn, because it was on the North Carolina–Tennessee border. Outgoing mail was placed on a metal arm by the postmaster, and a train would come by and snatch it."[36] Sources say that Wiley Tipton, John D. Tipton's son, ran the post office. Alderman states that Lost Cove's post office was named "Caro-Tenn in honor of the two states that practically bordered their settlement. This post office officially closed in 1920."[37] The post office may have remained open when Isaac MacCall English built a sawmill in Lost Cove. English built a store next to the railroad tracks. English's store would serve as the post office and general store.

After the post office closed, Swin Miller often collected the mail for the families. He walked to Briscoe Peterson's store to drop the mail off and return with goods that he and other families needed. Though Mr. Bailey does not remember a post office in Lost Cove, he does recall his family and others receiving their mail from the Poplar store. Bailey notes that "there was a big box of mail for Lost Cove residents, everyone's mail was put in it, and whoever went up to Poplar would return with the mail." One could walk up to Poplar to get the mail, even though by Mr. Bailey's youth most cove dwellers rode the train to make it easier to bring home whatever groceries they bought.[38]

In many ways, then, the families of Lost Cove were self-sufficient. But there seems to have always been trade with the outside world, even when trade involved hauling products on a sled. Additionally, medical care was provided by doctors and midwifes who lived outside of the settlement. Even mail allowed families to keep in touch with the world outside of the small settlement. While the outside world beyond the settlement brought needed income, care, and mail to the families, two outside influences changed Lost Cove forever: the coming of the railroad and logging. The changes brought in extra money, but they also contributed to the end of passenger trains, and the devastation of the landscape and livelihood of the community.

Three

The Prosperous Years
Railroads and Timber

The railroad allowed Lost Cove and other small settlements such as Green Mountain, Huntdale, Poplar, and Relief to thrive. As the CC&O railway linked the small towns to the outside world, and the way of life in Lost Cove blossomed since the railroad also made it possible to sell timber. With trains stopping at Lost Cove and Poplar stations, families like the Coopers moved into Lost Cove because of work being offered. Thus, passenger and freight trains enabled the families to prosper through trading and timber. But before more families moved into Lost Cove, controversy brewed in the mountains along the Tennessee and North Carolina state lines. Who would build the railroad and when would the railroad be finished? Other controversies involved the Mac English sawmill and the railroad.

The South & Western (S&W) Railway and the Southern Railway debated who had the right of way through the rough terrain of the Nolichucky Gorge. The Southern was backed by J.P. Morgan, a railroad magnate. The Southern Railway would later be controlled by the Norfolk Southern. The S&W was absorbed by George Carter's Clinchfield Company. These companies argued for years in the court systems on the construction and operation of the road and rail lines. The companies and court system took nearly five years to decide who would build the rail lines.

In 1904 in North Carolina, the road northward from Spruce Pine, North Carolina, to the Tennessee state line was sold to the South & Western Railway.[1] The railroad between Spruce Pine and the Tennessee state line was open territory for two major railways wanting to build through the rough Nolichucky Gorge, the Southern Railway and the South & Western Railway. From the late 1890s, the construction of the South & Western Railway (now called the Carolina, Clinchfield, and Ohio Railway or the CC&O) through the rocky Nolichucky Gorge provided a new way of life for Lost Cove residents.

The Clinchfield Railroad was the costliest construction in railroad history as well as the finest example of railway engineering and construction anywhere.[2] According to William Way's book *The Clinchfield Railroad*, there was a bitter altercation between the Southern Railway and the South & Western Railway (now the CC&O). This altercation focused on the construction of the railway from Poplar, North Carolina, to Unaka Springs, Tennessee. When Way gathered his information from the Clinchfield offices in Erwin, he heard this story from the workers:

> In about 1905, the Southern Railway, "considering the C.C. & O. a menace to the integrity of its property," began surveys for a competitive line, presumably to forestall the construction of the Clinchfield, then the South & Western. The Southern was planning to extend its line from Embreeville through the Gorge, and on across the mountains. The two lines crossed and re-crossed, and practically coincided at numerous places. At one point near Poplar, the rights of way of the two companies crossed at grade in a tunnel. Litigation followed, and the Clinchfield, in order to hold its rights, placed a force of men at work on the tunnel approach. It seems that the case was postponed from time to time, and the Clinchfield's construction gang had been reduced to one aged negro with a wheelbarrow and a spade. The Negro remained on his job for about three years, and finally the Southern decided not to construct the line. The point in litigation was not utilized by the Clinchfield, for today it passes along the opposite side of the river.[3]

Thus, a lone African American man whose name is unknown was the only man left to work the railway. Soon after, the Southern Railway opted out of building the line. With the battle over, George Carter's railway could now focus on building one of the costliest railroads of its time.

The treacherous building of the railroad through the Nolichucky Gorge challenged George L. Carter. The landscape, steep and rocky, had to be flattened and the rock chiseled in order for the railroad to be built. The eight-mile stretch of line from Poplar, North Carolina, to Erwin, Tennessee, demanded the hands of men and machine to build and maintain, as well as plans to keep the river from flooding again.

On March 13, 1907, the South & Western Railway, known now as the Carolina, Clinchfield, and Ohio, petitioned a proposed track revision at Lost Cove. The railroad plans mention that the train track should be placed above the high water of 1906. The flood of 1906 overtook the tracks through the Nolichucky Gorge. The tracks needed to be constructed higher so that further flooding would not ravage the tracks.[4]

When the railroad gangs (section men) labored to construct the rails through the Nolichucky Gorge, houses were built for them. Later, section men helped the railroad maintain the lines through the gorge. Whether trains turned over or flooding occurred, the section men fixed or hauled out broken rails and trains. According to Bryant, the camp houses stood about one mile above the Lost Cove train stop in Cane Bottom, between Poplar and Lost Cove proper. There were at least eight or nine houses in Cane Bottom. The section gangs consisted of not only whites but also African Americans. However, the African American workers stayed mostly in abodes called "shanty houses." Mr. Bryant describes the shanty houses as railroad cars that sat on the sidetrack rails. Thus, at Cane Bottom, the sidetracks were used for not only gathering and hauling timber, but also housing people. Though the African American workers were separated from the white workers, Bryant does not remember racism in the work situation.[5]

According to Mary Hattan Bogart, the railroad construction also involved Italians, Germans, and Russians. Even men who came directly off boats from Europe were sent to construct the Clinchfield. Since language barriers were indicated, the contractors hired interpreters for the men. Bogart explains that the men lived in "tar paper shacks, and gambling and drinking were their main pastimes. Consequently, there were many fights and killings in the camps." When explosions or accidents occurred while working on the tracks, many of the immigrants were buried in graves

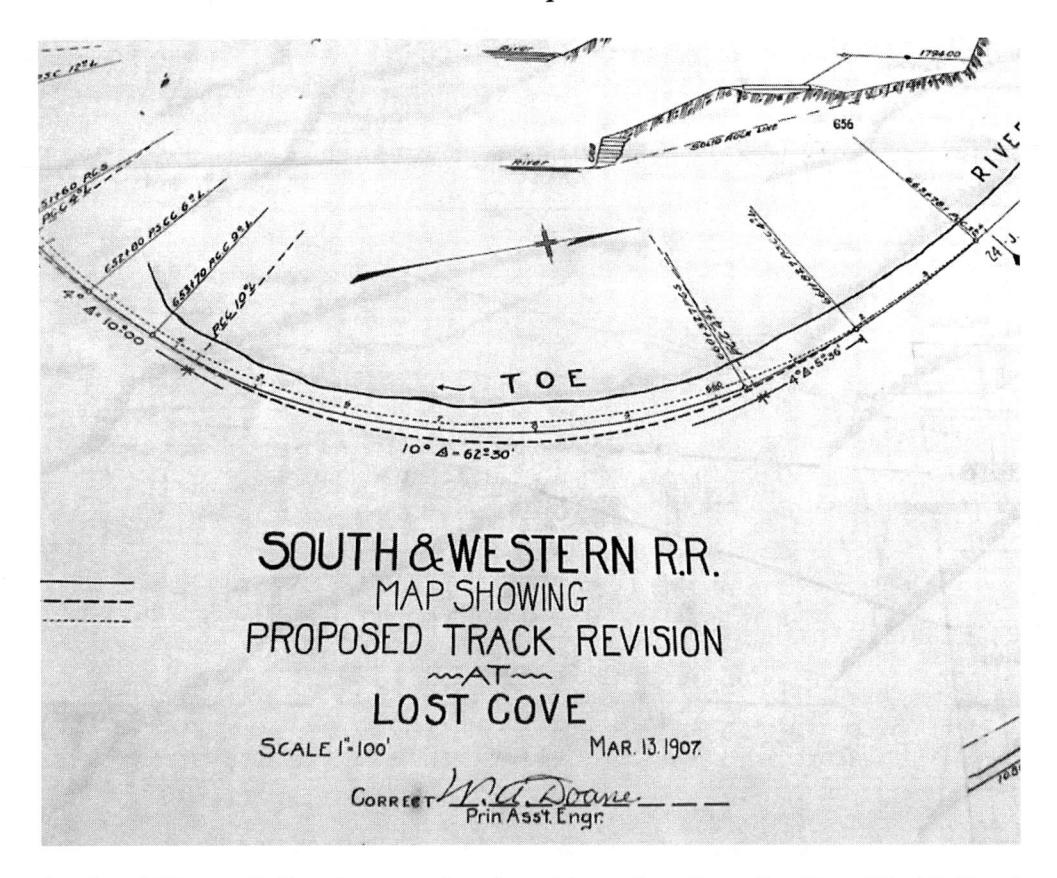

South and Western Railroad proposed track revision at Lost Cove. Carolina, Clinchfield and Ohio Series of Engineer Maps and Drawings. Archives of Appalachia, East Tennessee State University.

alongside the tracks, since they had no families in the United States.[6] Bryant remembers that many African Americans and other section men were buried along Cane Bottom. No headstones or graves are marked. The bodies have never been found or field studies conducted.[7]

Since the section men worked on the rails throughout the day, the trains heading north and south needed to signal the men in order for the trains to not kill or hurt any railroad workers.[8] The earliest account of trains stopping at Lost Cove Station is 1903. The South & Western Railway Company Passenger Train Schedule for No.3 Engine shows an effective schedule starting Wednesday, July 1, 1903. The trains heading south were numbers 5, 3, and 1. Northbound trains were numbers 2, 4, and 6. There were 11 stations between Johnson City and Poplar. Passengers boarded the train at Lost Cove only when flagged, which means that passengers had to request train services or be at the station when the train came through.

In 1903, the southbound trains stopped at Lost Cove around 8:30 a.m. and again at 3:36 p.m. The northbound trains stopped at 1:58 p.m., 9:10 a.m., and again at 2:58 p.m. As the years rolled on, the schedule changed for the settlement.

In Way's book, readers learn that the "enginemen [would] sound whistle at abrupt curves between Unaka Springs and Poplar between 7:00 a.m. and 4:30 p.m., as a warning to section men."[9] In James Goforth's book, *Building the Clinchfield: A Construction History of America's Most Unusual Railroad*, Goforth presents a detailed railroad schedule for the trains. In the September 7, 1908, schedule, the CC & O lists Lost Cove as having a water station.[10] Water stations were necessary for running the steam engines while providing water for the workers. Many small railroad stations had water tanks to keep the steam engines running. The railroad section gang men or the conductor pumped the water into the steam engine boiler during stops. The steam engine could use close to 13,000 pounds of water depending on the coal load. The tanks sat next to the railway, and a valve stretched from the tank to the boiler. The tank became an iconic image along the railroad system. Lost Cove passengers used the rails frequently.

The Lost Cove station stop is number 23 along the line. Stops for Lost Cove were at 9:28 a.m. and 5:50 p.m. There were of course freight trains leaving Lost Cove as well. Freight trains in the morning would leave at 9:17 a.m. on Monday, Wednesday, and Friday. Trains for the afternoon hours, heading north, left at 1:13 p.m. on Tuesday, Thursday, and Saturday.[11]

The railroad provided the perfect opportunity for linking the small settlement to the outside world. In general, railroads throughout Appalachia allowed communities to prosper, even if it meant destroying their sense of place. The railroad not only allowed Lost Cove families to reach the outside world, but also brought the outside world to Lost Cove, as Ronald L. Lewis explains in his article "Appalachian Myths and the Legacy of Coal":

> Railroads returned with manufactured products, such as dry goods, household furnishings, farm supplies, and other items people purchased from mail-order catalogs. The railroad connected local communities to the national markets and, as elsewhere in rural America, exerted a profound influence on the standard of living. They were the lines of communication [in that leading issue Appalachians into the national culture and identity.[12]

Thus, although telephones and paved roads never reached Lost Cove, North Carolina, Lost Cove still had a modern connection with the outside world. When the South & Western Railway (CC&O) was completed from Poplar, North Carolina, to Unaka Springs, Tennessee, Lost Cove became a prominent stop for the trains. While families carried produce to the trading post to sell, they also traveled to the grocery store and doctor by train. Now, the families did not have to walk the treacherous sled trail anymore, even though some still did.

According to the CC&O vertical files located in the Archives of Appalachia at East Tennessee State University, the number of Lost Cove passengers riding the rails southbound in 1917 amounted to no more than 12 per day, while no more than four passengers rode northbound.[13] Way's railroad information does not show the train times for rail stations in 1931, but he does state that "Nos. 37 and 38 will stop at Unaka Springs and Lost Cove on signal."[14] According to Mrs. McNabb, the passenger trains ran south toward Poplar in the morning and north toward Erwin in the afternoon.[15]

Mr. Bryant states that he and his family rode the passenger trains many times. Bryant liked to ride the train to Poplar to get groceries around 12 p.m. Since the trains

Water tank. James Goforth Collection Box 1; CCR Image 3, Accession #80. Archives of Appalachia, East Tennessee State University.

South and Western Railway Company

Passenger Train Schedule No. 3

IN EFFECT WEDNESDAY, JULY 1, 1903

CENTRAL STANDARD TIME

SOUTHBOUND			MILES	STATIONS	MILES	NORTHBOUND		
NO. 5	NO. 3	NO. 1				NO. 2	NO. 4	NO. 6
A. M.	P. M.	A. M.		leave Arrive				
§7 20	†2 00	†7 20		T...JOHNSON CITY...	64	†3 15	†10 47	§4 15
7 23	2 04	7 23	1	. Market Street Crossing.	63	2 10	10 44	4 10
7 35	2 20	7 35	4 9	......OKOLONA......F	59.1	2 58	10 29	3 58
7 42	2 29	7 42	7.3	......MARBLETON...F	56.7	2 51	10 19	3 51
7 46	2 34	7 46	8 4	......TAYLOR'S....F	55.6	2 47	10 14	3 47
7 53	2 40	7 53	10 6	T......UNICOI......	53.4	2 40	10 05	3 40
8 01	2 52	8 01	13 7	......FISHERY......F	50.3	2 30	9 51	3 30
8 08	3 02	8 08	16 2	T......ERWIN......	47 8	2 23	9 41	3 23
8 14	3 10	8 14	18.2	T......LOVE'S......	45.8	2 17	9 33	3 17
8 18	3 16	8 18	19.5	......CHESTOA......F	44.5	2 12	9 28	3 12
8 20	3 20	8 20	20	T..UNAKA SPRINGS...	44	2 10	9 26	3 10
8 32	3 36	8 32	24	......LOSTCOVE......F	40	1 58	9 10	2 58
8 47	3 52	8 47	29	T......POPLAR......	35	1 43	8 47	2 43
8 56	4 09	8 56	32	......PETERSON....F	32	1 34	8 18	2 34
9 02	4 15	9 02	34	T.....HUNTDALE......	30	1 28	7 58	2 28
9 11	4 27	9 11	37	......RELIEF......F	27	1 19	7 46	2 19
9 23	4 43	9 23	41	T..GREEN MOUNTAIN	23	1 07	7 30	2 07
9 33	4 57	9 33	44.4	......FORBES......F	19.6	12 56	7 17	1 56
9 42	5 10	9 42	47 4	T......TOECANE......	16 6	12 47	7 05	1 47
9 57	5 30	9 57	52 4	......SINKOLE....F	11 6	12 37	6 46	1 37
10 10	5 45	10 10	56 3	T......BOONFORD...	7.7	12 25	6 30	1 25
10 17	5 54	10 17	58 6	......PHILLIPS....F	5.4	12 17	6 21	1 17
10 24	6 03	10 24	6 8	......BAILEY'S......F	3 2	12 10	6 12	1 10
10 35	6 45	10 35	64	T...SPRUCEPINE.....		12 00	6 00	1 00
				Arrive leave		NOON	A. M.	P. M.

†—Daily except Sunday.   §—Sunday only.   T—Telephone.   F—Train stops when flagged only.

GEO. L. CARTER,
President.

MEL. H. WEILER,
Trainmaster.

South and Western RR 1903 train schedule. Document provided by Martha Erwin.

turned around in Huntdale, North Carolina, the passengers had one hour to shop. Mr. Bryant's family also rode the trains to Johnson City and Erwin, Tennessee. Even though the trains cost 10 cents to ride, all of Bryant's family traveled with free passes, since Bryant's father, Frank, was a section gang worker on the CC&O.[16]

Getting on the train was something of a ritual. Since Lost Cove Station lay along a 1.38 percent grade, the trains glided down the river past it. In order to stop, the trains had to squeeze their brakes about three-fourths of a mile above the station. The brakeman would jump off the train and place the stool down on the ground for passengers to step up into the train.[17]

CC&O wreck near Poplar, North Carolina (1910s). James T. Dowdy, Sr., Collection, #827, Box 1, Folder 1. Archives of Appalachia, East Tennessee State University.

Sometimes the trains heading into Erwin didn't even stop for Mr. Bryant. Mr. Bryant laughs about his adventures on the train. The engineers knew when J.C. would be riding the train. According to Mr. Bryant, "the trains would blow the whistle twice up above Lost Cove Station. The whistle blowing would signal the brakeman to slow the train down just enough for Bryant to jump on the train."[18] The passenger trains slowed down without stopping for Mr. Bryant, especially when he was the only person riding the train.

Mrs. McNabb also recollects impromptu train rides. She and her friends would "swing the trains" after swimming in the Nolichucky so they could ride up to Cane Bottom where her Uncle Tom Tipton and Aunt June lived. Tom Tipton's house sat next to the Nolichucky River on level ground, in Cane Bottom. The trains would slow down just enough for the kids to jump on and off.[19]

Isaiah Bailey notes that he always rode the train to Huntdale and Erwin. While Mr. Bailey lived in Lost Cove, the cost of riding the passenger trains varied. Mr. Bailey notes that "to ride from Lost Cove to Erwin was 26 cents a person. A kid under 12 was free, and a kid over 12 was 10 cents or 15."[20] Though the passenger trains provided opportunities for the families, Mr. Bryant often walked the railroad tracks to Lost Cove from Poplar, North Carolina, or Erwin, Tennessee. Mrs. McNabb said that even after the family left Lost Cove in 1926, the family often walked to visit family and pick apples in her father's orchard.[21] Even the trains never deterred families from walking the railroad tracks or trail that they had walked for decades. Since the section gang maintained the rails for nearly eight miles in the gorge, many lived in Cane Bottom. The railroad hired several men to cook for the men along the tracks.

Camille Flett, Geneva's daughter, tells a story of a black man that fed her uncles sometimes while they worked on the railroad at Cane Bottom. The black man cooked for the railroad men. He also cooked Italian pasta for her uncles while they worked.[22] Another story comes from Jim Johnson, Dolly Miller's son. Chester Bailey also cooked for the railroad during the early years. He cooked for all of the men working the rails along the Nolichucky Gorge. Chester cooked all day and then returned home every night.[23]

Chester Bailey cooks for the railroad section gang (1940). Courtesy of Jim Johnson.

Three. The Prosperous Years

While the railroad provided an outlet for families to make money, the pine and oak trees along with sawmills also helped Lost Cove thrive by selling lumber and acid wood to companies throughout the region and beyond. Lost Cove families needed timber to survive. When the blight years killed off the American chestnut trees, the once fertile forest became a wasteland. The chestnut tree provided income to many families in western North Carolina. The plush forest provided plenty of timber to make houses, outbuildings, and fences and provided firewood for many families in Lost Cove and throughout the southeast region.

In *Revenuers and Moonshiners: Enforcing Federal Liquor Law in the Mountain South, 1865–1900*, Wilbur R. Miller describes the effects of logging:

> After 1890, as railroads came closer to the great timber stands, lumber companies bought up huge tracts and began a wholesale stripping of the forest, leaving bare slopes subject to erosion. Logging became a full-time occupation as young men migrated to lumber camps in the woods and families settled in company towns surrounding sawmills.[24]

In Lloyd Bailey's 1997 book *The Heritage of the Toe River Valley: Avery, Mitchell, and Yancey Counties, North Carolina*, volume two, Lloyd Bailey, Sr., notes that the first lumber company into Lost Cove was the Caldwell Lumber Company around 1880.[25] No information on the Caldwell Lumber Company is available from the early years, nor are there any records of the company in archives researched.

Since timber was a profitable commodity in the hills of Appalachia, railroads worked side by side with sawmills in order for the product to reach the outside world. As the railroads exported the timber, the sawmills made ties for the railroads. Hemlock, pine, chestnut, poplar, oak, and hickory trees lined the landscape in the Nolichucky Gorge, and the 1907 South & Western Railway (later CC&O) files state specifications for cross ties and switch ties made by sawmills along the railway: "[H]ardwood ties shall be of white oak, chestnut oak, post oak, chestnut, or locust; softwood ties of long leaf yellow pine, cypress, cedar, or catalpa."[26] Along with these specifications, the railroad also instructed what class of wood was desired, how the ties were made, where to lay the ties at the railroad tracks, and what rules to follow for tagging the ties.[27]

No data confirms who brought the Caldwell Lumber Company into Lost Cove. In Pat Alderman's book *In the Shadow of the Big Bald: About the Appalachians and Their People*, Alderman notes that the first sawmill was hauled into Lost Cove "by freight and drug, piece by piece, to its site around 1905."[28] Around 1909, the Unaka Springs Lumber Company, organized by J.J. Hager and J.W. Broce, acquired approximately 6,000 acres of land in the vicinity of Unaka Springs, Tennessee, which is two and one-half miles down the river from the Lost Cove stop.

In a CC&O memorandum dated September 28, 1909, Hager and Broce asked the railway to "put in two or more small mills in the timber, drawing the product to the CC & O railway at stations, Love, Chestoa, Unaka Springs, Lost Cove, and Cane Bottom."[29] No matter who brought in the first sawmill, we do know that after 1910, Isaac McCall English built a sawmill along Devil's Creek just below the Lost Cove area.[30] Mr. English brought his wife, Annie Minerva French English, into Lost Cove. While he set up the sawmill operation, he also built one of the biggest houses in Lost Cove. According to Mrs. McNabb, Mac English's sawmill may have been on her uncle Wiley

Tipton's land.[31] Mr. Bailey observes that Mac English owned around 5,000 acres of land along the Nolichucky River, from Poplar, North Carolina, to Devil's Creek.[32]

Isaac McCall English grew up in the Upper Laurel Township in Madison County, North Carolina. He is the son of James and Mary McCall English. By 1910, Isaac along with his wife, Annie French, lived in Asheville, and his mother lived with the couple. Isaac registered for the World War I draft in 1918 in Bakersville, North Carolina, but there are no records indicating that he actually served. Mr. English and his brothers had always worked in the manufacturing of lumber. There are stories of the brothers travelling often to Johnson City on the Carolina, Clinchfield, and Ohio railway. With lumber on their minds, they saw the plush forest along the Nolichucky River as perfect for a sawmill operation. The 1923 edition of *American Lumberman* includes the following about I. Mac English, brother to J.L English of English and Sons in Asheville:

> [He] owns three saw mills along the Tennessee border and is building a large planing mill. He has quite an extensive plant ... at Caro-Tenn and has another mill under construction at Mac, Tennessee; the town being named after him. The capacity of the operations will be tripled by the improvements and is estimated that there is eight years cut of timber in the holdings at the regular output rate of 60,000 feet a day. Mac English is also postmaster at Caro-Tenn and the leading spirit of that town.[33]

English was designated as the postmaster at a new office established in Yancey County known as Caro-Tenn in 1919.[34] English hired Lost Cove residents to work the timber and load the trucks. Residents such as Dokter Tipton, Wiley Tipton, Velmer Bailey, and Clifford Miller all worked the sawmill. Mrs. McNabb says that her uncle, Wiley, ran the sawmill. Mrs. McNabb states that Mac English owned a commissary in Lost Cove, too, where tobacco, snuff, sugar, and other commodities were purchased.[35] While the men worked the mill, some women cooked for the workers. J.C. Bryant's wife, Dixie Lee Tipton Bryant, had family living in Lost Cove, and Mr. Bryant acknowledges that Dixie's mother worked as a cook for Mac English, while her father worked the sawmill.[36] Almost everyone in Lost Cove worked at the Mac English sawmill.

The sidetrack built along Devil's Creek became a major stop for the CC&O. Because the sawmill sat about a mile above the sidetrack, trucks loaded with timber drove alongside Devil's Creek to bring the lumber or acid wood to the railroad. Alderman notes that English and his brother had "brought in a truck to move the sawed timber to the loading zone."[37]

Because the sawmill produced a large amount of cross ties and acid wood in the Nolichucky Gorge, the railroad needed to make changes to the rails at Lost Cove to keep up with hauling all those wood products. In the CC&O files, a petition was admitted by F.B. Vines of Johnson City concerning the extension of a sidetrack. The letter is addressed to Mr. Vines from the CC&O's general manager, L.H. Phetteplace. The letter states:

> Mr. Brewer has brought to my attention the matter of extending the sidetrack at Lost Cove for business which you expect to offer at that point. He states that you have somewhere in the neighborhood of 8000 cords of acid wood, 11000 cords of pulp wood and 500–600 carloads of logs. This being the case we will be willing to extend the siding under the usual agreement; that is, you to do the grading and furnish the switch timber and ties....[38]

Three. The Prosperous Years 51

In a remitted correspondence from the railroad's industrial agent, Mr. Vines did comply with the railroad rules and regulations. After Mr. Vines graded the roads to "get the Lost Cove sidetrack extended North with sufficient clearance," the sidetrack handled four to five cars for hauling timber, pulp wood, and acid wood to the markets. The railroad began shipping no less than "two cars daily for the next two years and ... may [have] run two cars daily for four years."[39]

For nearly 15 years, Mac English's sawmill shipped acid wood, pulpwood, and railroad ties throughout the eastern United States. Bryant notes that most of the "wood [was] shipped to Kingsport, Tennessee, or Canton, North Carolina."[40] In Haines's article, Clifford Miller recalls making "a living cutting railroad ties and by chopping up dead chestnuts." The chestnuts were shipped to Canton.[41] The large number of cross ties that railroads always needed enabled the sawmill to survive. Since the railroad corporation bought fresh ties needed for laying down the steel tracks, the small sawmills along the Appalachians thrived for many years.

One of the biggest pulp mills that processed timber in Lost Cove is the Champion Fibre Company, a pulp and paper mill. Formed in 1908, the company became the first to make white pulp from chestnut wood. The company also processed southern pines and in 1934 became the first mill to manufacture bleached hardwood pulp.[42] The Clinchfield hauled hundreds of tons of timber to Canton from Lost Cove's mill.

Mac English's sawmill produced some of the best acid wood, pulpwood, and cross ties from the region. Though the chestnut blight of the early 1920s hit western North Carolina, wiping out almost all of the chestnuts, the massive amount of timber along the Nolichucky enabled the families to make good money. Production and money allowed Lost Cove families to thrive. But in 1925, production and money ceased in one day.

According to J.C. Bryant, the land near Devil's Creek caught on fire, and the blaze swept across the mountainside, burning Mac English's sawmill and everything in its sight. Everyone working for English fought the fire wholeheartedly. The fire burned nearly everything in its path, approximately 5,000 acres of land. The Lost Cove settlement was spared.[43] Both Bryant and Bailey tell how the families fought the fire that swept through Lost Cove. Both men stated that their families must have back-drafted the flames or dug ditches surrounding their properties and buildings. Not a single house in the cove was lost. However, Mac English's sawmill burned down. An *Asheville Citizen-Times* article, dated September 10, 1925, addresses the fire that broke out along No Business Ridge area. The fire, which spanned toward Devil's Creek where Mac English's sawmill resided, also reached the historic Unaka Springs Summer Resort.[44] The timber jobs in which Lost Cove residents had worked so hard had dwindled to ashes in one day. Homer Tipton observes that "the fire was the worst in Yancey and Unicoi County history."[45]

Other newspapers such as the *Bristol Herald Courier* and the *Knoxville Journal* provide further details on the 1925 fire. The *Bristol Herald Courier* states that men battled the fire for over 10 days and that many lives were endangered. The "fire covered 5,000 acres and the loss is $500,000. The loss to individuals is $10,000. General Manager Phetteplace of the Clinchfield Railway ordered all of his men to fight the fire as long as necessary."[46] The *Knoxville Journal* provides information on Mac English's sawmill. The fire on No Business Mountain, near Unaka Springs, destroyed the sawmill plant of Mac English. An army of men were bent on saving the Unaka Springs Hotel. The fire smoldered for days after and sentries were left working to prevent sparks from firing up again.[47]

Almost all of the timber near Lost Cove was depleted by the fire. Though most of the timber was gone, English still needed to use the siding track near the state line bridge after the fire. In a letter to Mr. L.L. McIntyre, English wanted to keep using Mack Siding in the spring of 1926 but the railroad decided to remove the frog and switch in January. English advised the railroad that he had machinery coming in and wanted the connection to be on before April 1. The railroad wanted more explanation from English if more shipments were due at the sidetrack.[48]

His request for the switch was granted in July 1926. English was set on keeping the sawmill sidetrack open so he could ship the remaining machinery and the rest of the tradable timber to market. His inquiry about the fire to the railroad set off an investigation. He petitioned the CC&O, now the Clinchfield Railroad Company, to look into the matter. In a memorandum by J.M. Ferguson, created on May 26, 1927, English and the management of the railroad agreed to arbitrate as to question "whether or not they (the Clinchfield Railroad) set out the fire which burned over the tract adjoining that of the Carolina Lumber Company, and whether they set out the fire which destroyed the saw mill and lumber of I. Mac English spoken of in all our reports as the skidder fire."[49] The railroad selected the arbitrators and a hearing proceeded in Burnsville, North Carolina, on June 10, 1927. The eight witnesses arrived in Burnsville on June 9 and reported to Mr. McLaughlin and J.W. Pless, representatives of the railroad. All eight men agreed to testify, board a train in Spruce Pine, and travel to the burned area near Lost Cove on Saturday, June 11. No information details their findings to what or who may have set the fire, or what conclusion was made.

Mac English moved with his family to Asheville in late 1927. He left his two-story house, built with the finest hardwoods, and stepped onto the train bound for Asheville. Though he moved away, Mac English and his adopted son still had correspondences and dealings with the Clinchfield Railroad Company until 1938. English made numerous arguments with the railroad over switches, docks, the shanty house, siding and rails. These arguments would last for nearly 11 years.

According to railroad memorandums from November 1927 to 1928, the company wanted to remove the switch and frog from the main line at English's siding near Devil's Creek, as well as the old timber dock that sits at the sidetrack of Lost Cove. With English no longer producing and milling timber, the railroad's agenda was to clean up the old sheds and construction that resided along the Lost Cove and sawmill tracks. The documents, written mostly by W.C. Hattan and Mr. L.L. McIntyre, the superintendent of the railroad, request action from Mr. English.

English would have to agree to remove the old timber dock from the sidetrack at Lost Cove due to the railroad having no claim but 100 feet on each side of the lines of main track. The railroad wanted to clean the mess up, and if they decided to without approval then a claim could be made by English. The documents show the frustration of the railroad growing because English didn't respond to any inquiries by the railroad. On March 17, 1928, English made contact with Mr. McIntyre. English asked the railroad to keep the siding at the Devil's Creek Mack site. English wanted to load lumber from the site as soon as he "is physically able to get there and do the work."[50] Superintendent McIntyre understands that English wanted an interested party to buy his tract of land along Devil's Creek. The railroad agreed to keep the siding in place for 30 days. In June, English sold his property along the Tennessee–North Carolina line at Devil's Creek. English told the railroad that the people who bought his property would start operating timber production right away.

The tract of land named Mack Siding would be timbered once again by interested parties. Along the Devil's Creek property, an old shanty house sat above the state line bridge, and the railroad asked that the shanty be torn down due to safety concerns. The shanty served as a supply house for equipment and tools. The railroad didn't want to deal with English, but they didn't want him to make a claim against them either. On February 11, 1929, the railroad composed a notice for I. Mac English, sent to Asheville, North Carolina, in regard to the shanty being torn down. The railroad stated that the shanty was causing safety concerns because it could slide right off the mountain and hit the state line bridge.[51]

In April 1929, the railroad received a letter from the Sterling Lumber Company of Hendersonville, North Carolina. The company was in the process of buying English's land and timber and advised the railroad that they would be operating at the property as early as May. The company stated that they had at least six million feet to be shipped and "expect shipments to begin at rate of one car per day."[52] For one year, no shipments moved at Devil's Creek and the railroad remained frustrated. There were no documents in the Archives of Appalachia on the Sterling Lumber Company's operations at Devil's Creek from May 1929 to May 1930.

In May 1930, the railroad made a public announcement that they would remove the siding at Devil's Creek since no activity from the site had been reported. In June, the railroad received a letter from the Sterling Lumber Company. Mr. E.M. Lyda, Sterling's field auditor, advised that the company was in litigation with English and did not want to move the lumber yet due to the involvement. Mr. Lyda believed that all obstacles would be settled between the two parties. The company expected the shipments to move soon and the siding to be cleaned up. Once again, the railroad deferred the removal of the siding at Devil's Creek.

Since English's contract with Sterling was in litigation, it would be up to English to pay costs for removal of the shanty house. In late January 1931, a fire once again spread out onto English's property. The railroad acknowledged that the steam engines, which chugged north and south on the Clinchfield, had scattered fire along the gorge days prior, and the fire could be seen along English's property. A steam engine, No. 95, had extinguished fire at different places along the gorge and was being assisted by Eng. 412 when more fire was scattered.[53] Mr. H.A. Brown of the Clinchfield advised that Mr. Elliott designate four men to tend to the ground fire. The men from Mitchell County were hired to also watch over the property in case a fire arose again. The railroad wanted to make sure that all inquiries with English over his property were settled between the two. Another battle over English's property ensued over the price of his rails.

In July of 1931, Mr. V.E. Elliott addressed the amount of rails English owned:

Mr. English owns 9.06 tons of 85 pound rail that was removed from the Lost Cove Siding. There is also 1,392 lbs. of 65 lb. angle bars with this rail. Using fit prices for this material it will amount to $199.32 for the rail and $27.84 for the angle bars, or a total of $227.16.[54]

The railroad paid Mac English and settled the debt of the rails. Months later, the railroad spoke with English again about removing siding at Devil's Creek. The railroad gave English nine months from September 1931 to ship the rest of the timber out. English wasn't budging just yet. English still needed to use the siding to remove timber, and it wasn't until December 1932 that the railroad pressured Mr. English further. The railroad construction engineer sent a letter to English on January 3, 1933.

Dear Sir:

The cross ties in gauntlet lead to your siding at Devil's Creek will have to be replaced this month, and unless you desire to furnish these ties and resume shipment soon we will have to remove this siding. The agreement covering the construction and operation of this siding provides that the Shipper shall bear the cost of the maintenance of this side track. Our Road master advises that it will take about 180 ten foot cross ties for this gauntlet lead to make it safe for operation.

Please advise at once if you will furnish these ties and pay for their installation or shall we remove this siding.

Yours very truly,

Mr. V.E. Elliott[55]

More letters to English were to follow in regard to removing the switch at Mack Siding. The railroad again gave English until November 1933 to remove any materials, machinery, and siding from Devil's Creek. English kept deferring the removal by telling the railroad that he had lumber sold but shipments were held up. For two years Mac English kept the railroad from removing the siding. He claimed that he still had to ship lumber out or that machinery needed to be shipped. In May 1936, Mac English entered the Clinchfield office of V.B. Elliott. He claimed that part of his materials was removed from the property at Devil's Creek. The railroad provided a list of materials that were owned by Mac English. The list was made into a contract on June 12, 1936. The bill of sale acknowledged the amount of $84 due to I. Mac English. The railroad purchased the remaining materials of rail, angle bars, bolts, and spikes from him. The long-awaited removal of the siding began.

In August 1938, a letter from J.M. English & Son's Company in Asheville, North Carolina, requested that the railroad keep the siding open for the timber to be shipped out and asked if the company could get land there for a lumber yard. In the letter, Mr. C.E. English stated that I. Mac English had died six weeks earlier. He assumed that the English & Son's Company was trying to salvage all they could of the property.[56] No records after 1938 indicate that J.M. English secured the siding along the state line bridge. The railroad eventually removed the siding, shanty, and materials related to Mac English.

In 1930, according to census records, Mac and Annie lived in Washington County, Tennessee. Guy, their adopted son, was nine years old. Mac's occupation was manager at the Johnson City U.S. Bobbin and Shuttle Company. The company made bobbins for the textile industry. Records show that Isaac McCall English died on July 7, 1938, at the age of sixty-two. His cause of death shows that he died from a cerebral embolism with a contributory cause from arterial sclerosis. He passed away in

Maryville, Tennessee.[57] His wife, Annie Minerva French English, died on February 16, 1957, at the age of seventy-four. They both are buried in the New Salem United Methodist Church in Knoxville, Tennessee. Records indicate that when Annie died, her death certificate informant was Guy Piercy.[58] Research conducted shows no legitimate death or birth information on Guy English (Piercy). The only information found is the 1940 census records in Tennessee.

Life in the cove changed for many. In the meantime, Lost Cove families continued farming and selling produce.[59] Profit soon re-entered the mountainous community when a second sawmill was built in 1939. The 1939 sawmill was the last structure to be built in the cove. Situated up in the cove but far away from the houses, this sawmill, like Mac English's, produced pulpwood and acid wood. Mr. Bryant notes that the parts for the sawmill were hauled up the three-quarter mile mountainous trek "with a sawmill engine on a sled and a cable wire":

> The people would pull the cable up so far, and then anchor the cable down as they inched up the mountain. They would build the road in front of them as they went up the mountain. In order for the sled not to turn over, they would hold items like saws up to the edge of the sled. Men would also walk behind the sled and place sticks in the holes of the wheels so the sled would not slide back down the mountain.[60]

Lonon notes that Clifford Miller revealed to him that "he, with the help of other Lost Cove residents, had transported the sawmill into the area one piece at a time."[61] While the families worked this new sawmill every day, Swin Miller's 1938 Chevy truck transported the lumber from the sawmill to the railroad tracks. According to Lonon's book, the railroad moved Miller's truck into Lost Cove on a flat car.[62] Of course, Lost Cove's sidetrack existed before the second sawmill was hauled up the mountain. Thus, Swin Miller's truck helped the families earn more income by transporting and milling the timber.

Many tools were used in the production of timber. Tools like mallets, axes, and froes aided the workers in splitting timbers after the initial cut. Velmer Bailey made his own froe while working the mill. A froe, also called a shake axe or paling knife, helped Velmer split the wood along the grain. The froe is used along with a mallet in order to make planks and split the timber. The L-shaped tool allows workers to split wood at the exact spot they choose. The froe's handle is not as long as an axe handle and its blade is longer than an axe blade. Velmer used this tool every time he split wood.

Along with the Millers, Tiptons, Baileys, and Bryants, families such as the Coopers and Presnells also worked the mill. According to Lloyd Bailey, Mr. Harrison Cooper and his wife, Mary Ethel Shelton, moved into Lost Cove during the Depression. Mr. Cooper ran the sawmill and logging camps while his wife cooked the meals for the working men.[63] Trina Presnell Fox, who lived in Lost Cove during the 1930s, recalls that her father, Robert Presnell, worked as a machine operator at the sawmill. Her mother, Clara Young Presnell, and Trina enjoyed living in the cove. Every family in the cove welcomed them openly. Though Ms. Fox only lived in Lost Cove less than two years, she candidly remembers living next to the railroad tracks. Her family lived in I. Mac English's old house near the railroad. The door on the house is carved with detailed work. The house, built out of logs and timber from the

Velmer shows Servilla Bailey, his wife, his work from in front of their home (1952). Courtesy of Chad Fred Bailey.

sawmill, had a huge porch and a deck on the second floor.

Although the second sawmill helped the families survive, the forests would once again be depleted; by the late 1940s, this second sawmill eventually ceased to produce wood for income.

The livelihood and income on which Lost Cove residents had come to depend faded once timber resources were depleted. By late 1950, the settlement had become economically linked to the outside world, and when this link

Hosea Bailey sits in Swin Miller's 1930 Chevy truck with Isaiah and Miller boys. The logs are heading to the sawmill (1952). Courtesy of Chad Fred Bailey.

snapped, the community dwindled. Furthermore, by this time young men were leaving the settlement for the Korean War and seeking marriage in nearby towns.

Four

Moonshine in the Mountains

*When money was scarce, whiskey was like money—
an important trading commodity.*[1]
—Tom Robertson

For more than 160 years, the world outside of Appalachia has stereotyped the Appalachian mountaineer as being overly fond of moonshine, or illicit whiskey. Even in the 1860s, when Lost Cove was founded, conflict with revenuers over whiskey taxing and illicit manufacturing of potent liquor was making news throughout the country. America became enthralled with the mountaineer and moonshine. The mountain people produced millions of gallons of whiskey. Newspapers portrayed moonshine as a requirement for being Appalachian. In popular mythology, feuding always accompanied moonshining. Henry Shapiro notes that the "tendency of mountaineers to engage in feuds, and more specifically the practice of private justice through ambush or 'bushwhacking,' and the tendency of mountaineers to manufacture illegal or untaxed whiskey, had already become a part of the mythology of Appalachian otherness by 1900."[2]

In 1877, an estimated number of moonshine stills operating reached 2000 throughout the North Carolina, Tennessee, Georgia, and Virginia mountains. The distillers ran the stills at least 20 days each month with a daily output of 15 gallons. The government claimed that blockaders were costing the Treasury approximately $2,500,000 yearly and that the annual loss from moonshine equaled the internal revenue tax throughout the nation.[3]

The people of the Mountain South made moonshine mostly due to economic reasons. Mountain distillers avoided revenue taxes yet paid their land taxes with the money earned from moonshine. Some made moonshine to provide clothes and books for their children to attend school. General circumstances and specific needs for their families determined whether or not men became distillers. Others made moonshine for entrepreneurial reasons.

Old Pop—as we called him—was a moonshine maker and entrepreneur. He had his moonshine still on Upper Higgins Creek in Flag Pond, Tennessee. He made moonshine for days in the mountains, not returning home until gallons were ready. He stopped in Lost Cove often, during the steam-engine days. He stopped the train just to buy moonshine for himself and his railroad buddies. He, the engineer, and those in the caboose walked the three-quarter mile up the mountain just for that moonshine. He knew the moonshine in Lost Cove was the best. Geneva Tipton

McNabb knew every month when my great grandfather would stop for his moonshine. He said it was "the best moonshine around." He would on occasion lay down more than $50 for Lost Cove moonshine. Money back then was precious, but he liked to drink, and it often got the best of him. Camille Flett, Geneva's daughter, iterates that railroad men often stopped the trains at Lost Cove so they could purchase and distribute barrels of moonshine. Dock Tipton's family and others hauled the moonshine down the mountain to the railroad tracks so the engineers and conductors could take the moonshine to the railyard in Erwin, where they would distribute their purchases to others on the railroad and in the city.[4]

Although clichés about mountaineers, moonshine, and feuds are annoying, manufacturing illicit whiskey was an important source of income for some people in the mountains. In Loyal Durand's article, " Mountain Moonshining in East Tennessee," Durand states that to the mountaineer under economic pressure after the Civil War, moonshine brought in a greater profit than unprocessed corn since corn was of low value and difficult to transport.[5] Gordon B. McKinney states that, "in the late nineteenth century, 75 percent of all Internal Revenue officers in the United States were stationed in the southern mountains, trying to enforce the liquor tax."[6]

Prices for moonshine could reach up to $40 a gallon in the mountains. People would buy quarts to gallons just to satisfy their cravings. Tom Robertson's article "Moonshine on the Mountain" examines how making whiskey became an economic necessity in some communities. Robertson quotes Jack Hatfield: "Making whiskey was a way of life. Before the coal mines came, you either dug roots, raised a garden, or made whiskey. It was a thing of necessity, whether you were feudin' or not, you had to do it."[7]

In Wilbur R. Miller's article, "The Revenue: Federal Law Enforcement in the Mountain South, 1870–1900," Miller explains that the minority of mountaineers who practiced the complicated art of distillation with varying levels of skill and acted out of diverse motives made moonshine either for economic necessity or profit.[8]

Moonshine enabled some Lost Cove dwellers to increase their income by selling it to nearby towns or railroad men. Some dwellers made the "shine" for themselves and their families, and some traded "shine" for basic goods and medicine. Lost Cove families relied upon moonshine just like other mountain community moonshiners. Moonshine was a necessity to those in the mountains. It brought good income to families who were already struggling after the Civil War and even into the Depression era.

However, despite the clichéd equation of moonshine with mountain feuding, moonshine did not bring feuds to Lost Cove. True mountain entrepreneurs seized opportunities to sell and make moonshine to benefit themselves as well as railroad workers, lumberjacks, and miners.[9] The average moonshiner needed to be skilled, have good marketers, and have high ambitions. According to Arthur, moonshine stills "are usually located on small, cold streams, and on wild land little adapted to cultivation. Sometimes, however, stills are situated in the cellar or kitchen or other innocent looking place for the purpose of diverting suspicion."[10] Wilbur Miller states:

Four. Moonshine in the Mountains

Moonshiners usually located their still in crude log shelters near the heads of the coves or hollows formed by swift mountain streams that provided the cold water necessary for their operations. Hidden by trees or almost impenetrable mountain laurel and reached by paths known to only a few people.[11]

Since moonshine stills were hidden in the mountains of Appalachia, the families, neighbors, and skilled moonshiners protected and supported one another. In Lost Cove, every house had a spring, so almost every family made moonshine to help sustain themselves. Moonshine wasn't just made by men. Women also helped make moonshine, some even taking it over as a chore or being a scout for revenuers. When some Lost Cove men were working on the railroad, the women would attend to making moonshine, often using the moonshine as a remedy for colds and fevers. Wilbur Miller states that women were often supporters of their menfolk. Women in the communities or valleys often deterred revenuers by meeting them at the door of their houses, pretending to know nothing of their kinfolk's whereabouts. Women delayed revenuers with warnings or shouts so their husbands, fathers, or sons could escape.[12]

Geneva McNabb recounted several times that her mother, when visiting kinfolk in Erwin, sold moonshine, especially when her father wasn't available. She would make her rounds to families she knew and kinfolk. Dock, her father, often ran moonshine throughout Mitchell and Yancey counties. When he left the community to sell, her mother, Usley, tended the distillery and sold the moonshine when she visited Erwin.

In a book titled *The Second Oldest Profession: An Informal History of Moonshining in America*, Jess Carr notes that many moonshiners made agreements fighting against government revenuers. The first agreement meant that moonshiners stood together by assembling small guerrilla bands to fight off revenuers. The second scheme entailed moonshiners securing neighborhood sympathy with "silence or participation" regarding this illegal business.[13] The kinship bond held strong in the mountains of North Carolina. No tax revenuer or lawman could penetrate the support system. Because Lost Cove is situated high above the Nolichucky River in isolation, moonshining was able to thrive there.

In his book *News from Yancey: Articles from Area Newspapers* (1840–1900), Lloyd Bailey, Sr., published an article from 1898 that states:

> Revenue Agent A.E. Aiken returned yesterday from a trip through Egypt Township in Yancey County. Illicit distilling, he says, is on the decrease, and that the only place in Yancey County where the revenue law is being violated to any extent is in what is known as "Lost Cove," which section he did not visit. Lost Cove is a section that lies contiguous to both the North Carolina and Tennessee lines, neither state claiming jurisdiction as the boundary lines between the two states is not definitely known, hence the name of "Lost Cove," where the moonshiner frolics unmolested.[14]

Because of Lost Cove's isolation, moonshiners did not deal with revenuers as often as did moonshiners closer to towns such as Burnsville and Asheville, North Carolina, or Erwin, Tennessee.

The earliest accounts of moonshine distillers in Lost Cove start with John D. Tipton. Tipton was known throughout western North Carolina newspapers as the "Hermit of Lost Cove." Tipton, an evader, for over 12 years eluded all revenuers who tried to catch and entrap him. By the time revenuers found his spot of distilling, all equipment and Tipton would be far gone. But on May 26, 1887, information passed on to *Falcon Newspaper* in Elizabeth City, North Carolina, states that John D. Tipton was captured by Deputy Collector Jeff H. Hyams in Bakersville, North Carolina, on May 25. The account reads:

> Mr. Jeff Hyams, Deputy Collector, came most unexpectedly to the object of his search, John D. Tipton, the "Hermit of Lost Cove," and captured him, together with his distillery and apparatus. For twelve years Tipton has been engaged in his unlawful business, successfully eluding all efforts to entrap or catch him. The deep seclusion of Lost Cove, a wild region among the mountains in Yancey County or in Tennessee—the boundary not yet determined—affording him a sure hiding place for years. Sometimes his place of operations was discovered, and information given to the revenuer officers; but when they came out to secure the prize, Tipton had folded his tents and stolen away, distillery, and all.[15]

He was charged with distilling and fined $100. He spent four months in Buncombe County Jail beginning November 1887. Though Tipton was caught and fined in Buncombe County, his homestead of Lost Cove remained in disputed territory.

The courts often had to let distillers go if they resided in disputed territories. But disputed territories did not always allow moonshines to go uncharged either. Revenuers could not always prevent families from making whiskey or corn liquor. Mountain distillers were smart and elusive. By 1912 Lost Cove moonshiners had many a day in court, as Arthur describes:

> [John D. Tipton] was accused of having begun business by the light of the moon, as was evidenced by sundry indictments in the United States court at Asheville. His example was soon followed by others; but, whenever it appeared to Judge R.P. Dick that the alleged stills were in the disputed territory, he directed the discharge of the defendants.[16]

The boundary dispute of Lost Cove enabled the moonshine haven to keep making "shine" without disruption. Moonshiners' neighbors and family members often disrupted arrests. Additionally, Wilbur Miller notes several instances involving moonshine in which the judge, R.P. Dick, lent mercy (for reasons unknown) to the moonshine makers. In several court cases in Buncombe County, North Carolina, Judge R.P. Dick routinely suspended the sentences of moonshiners in minor cases where retailing was done:

> Dick "was known for his kindly temper" when hearing revenue cases. From 1882–1883 Judge Dick normally suspended sentences for petty revenue violators, mostly sellers rather than distillers, who paid reduced fines averaging about $20.00 instead of the minimum of $100.00 and a thirty-day jail term prescribed by law.[17]

Judge Dick's lenient views suspended an all-time high of 60 percent of cases in 1887.[18]

Though Lost Cove remained a haven from revenuer fines and arrests, the boundary line dispute would end up in litigation courts for years. Court records indicate that from 1887 to 1916, litigation cases were filed in the United States Circuit Court of Asheville, North Carolina, then again in the Supreme Court of Tennessee, in which it was settled. The dispute over a strip of land that ran along Iron Mountain to where the Nolichucky runs through the mountains and to the top of Bald Mountain only aided Lost Cove moonshiners and anyone that lived in the disputed territory.

North Carolina commissioners claimed that the trees were properly marked and that Tennessee surveyors agreed to the markers. The notes filed by Captain Gudger were deposited with the secretary of state in Raleigh, North Carolina. The filed case included Dugger v. McKesson, which held that surveyor testimony is admissible in court. The lines were improperly handled by surveyors and trees were not marked correctly. The marks on trees for state boundary lines normally were placed on the north side of the trees. If the marks were placed on the south side of a tree, the sun could fade the marks, making it hard for surveyors to determine the boundary lines.[19] While North Carolina agreed to the boundary lines, Tennessee surveyors did not agree.

The boundary line dispute would not be decided until 1916. The Supreme Court of Tennessee, in the case McCarty v. Carolina Lumber Company, determined that the United States Geological Survey conducted in 1888 was not conclusive in determining the state lines, "since the survey was without authority to establish a line, and attempted only to represent the line as it was then thought to be located."[20] The North Carolina commission ran the line without terms agreed. The McCarty case determined that the original line that North Carolina ran in 1799 established the boundary with Tennessee. Though Tennessee commissioners tried to have the lines changed, North Carolina commissioners never acted on the dispute, so the original line established became the boundary line.

The need for laws against moonshine started taking place throughout the Mountain South. Many revenuers believed that distillers needed to be forced out of the mountains. Distillers, on the other hand, ignored the revenuer and kept making moonshine. Moonshine arrests throughout the mountains increased, even though North Carolina had enacted a prohibition law in 1908, 12 years prior to the nationwide enactment.

Moonshiners are said to be industrious and patient. Moonshine making is a family business that also includes in-laws and their family. Almost every day in the mountains, revenuers busted up moonshine stills; sometimes up to four stills a day were found and axed during the late 1910s. Sometimes sons and wives were fined and arrested as well. Fines were no big deal to the average moonshine stiller. After a fine or arrest, men returned directly to the store to buy more copper or galvanized iron to build another still. The resilient moonshiner never stopped making shine for a revenuer.

Many Lost Cove men were charged with possessing whiskey, violating prohibition laws, distilling, and manufacturing whiskey. Dock Tipton eluded revenuers— just like his father did in the 1880s—through the early 1900s. Dock enlisted several of his family members, including Sam Cooper, his son-in-law, and his sons, William, Joe, and Albert. Since Lost Cove sat in disputed territory, he and his fellow moonshiners did not care if revenuers were hunting them and their stills, or if they were caught. In a June 1924 *Johnson City Chronicle* article titled "Spectacular Raid of Three Stills Made Near the State Line," three men are arrested for a big moonshine operation. Considered to be one of the largest raids ever in the disputed section, three fully complete moonshine stills were captured near the Tennessee–North Carolina line in Yancey County and not far from Unaka Springs. The operation was described as a "wholesale liquor center[21]: "Destroying the three distilleries, officers captured 1,200 gallons of beer and twenty gallons of whiskey. Dock Tipton, Sam Cooper and Perry Hughes, captured in the raid, as operators of the stills are in jail here, and will be taken to North Carolina on Thursday for trial. The raid was conducted by U.S. Revenue Officers and Sheriff S.W. Shelton of Unicoi County...."[22]

In November 1924, the same day Dock Tipton, Sam Cooper and Perry Hughes appeared before the courts in Asheville, three other men from the mountains were tried and fined. C. Clark and L.C. Rice were fined $10 for possessing whiskey, and Porter Taylor was charged for violating the prohibition act and fined $50. Perry Hughes and Sam Cooper were both charged with violating the prohibition act and were sent to jail for four months. Dock was given four months in jail and fined $100 for manufacturing whiskey.[23]

Families were often left to take care of the moonshine stills, even when the men were in jail. In a letter titled "A True Story," Albert Tipton weaves the tale of how Dock Tipton was arrested in Lost Cove. Albert, son of Dock and Uslie Hensley Tipton, brother to Geneva Tipton McNabb, recounts the big moonshine still in his house growing up. The family, including brothers, made moonshine and apple brandy day and night. There was a guard who watched over the still as well. Dock liked drinking moonshine and often began a drinking binge that lasted a month. One day Alfred and his brothers noticed seven men walking up the hill from the railroad tracks. There were nine men, with two men staying at the tracks to guard. The men were revenuers, and they searched the Tiptons' house and the land surrounding the property. Alfred explains that they found a 10-gallon keg full of moonshine and busted the keg into pieces. The revenuers continued their job and busted another moonshine still that was full of mash. Once they were finished, they arrested his father Dock.

Dock Tipton was sent to Asheville. Documents found in the *Asheville Citizen-Times* on November 7, 1924, show that Dock Tipton was fined $100 and given four months in jail for manufacturing whiskey.[24] After his father returned from jail, Alfred and his two brothers decided to make more whiskey. Albert was 12 years old when he and his brothers built their moonshine still. They chose to place the still way back in the mountains away from the settlement. They took two barrels and a still with them and built a furnace out of rocks. When they started to run the whiskey, they dragged the fire out front of the still and threw water into the furnace, so they could unload the still. Once Alfred threw the water into the furnace, the water hit the rocks and a yellow liquid came out of the rocks. The boys went home after the event and told their father. Dock told them "it was dead man's gold."[25] Some residents in Lost Cove, like Alfred, talk about gold in the mountain above Lost Cove, but no one has ever found the mine to this day. The family moved to Erwin, Tennessee, in the 1930s. Alfred never forgot about the gold he found, but he knew how to get back to it, though he died without ever going back.

In the 1930s, Swin Miller, another prominent leader in the cove was arrested for distilling. The *Asheville Citizen-Times* printed a short article titled "Large Still Is Taken by Yancey County Officers in which members of the sheriff's department capture a large still in Lost Cove." According to the article, Swin Miller was arrested in

Moonshine still of Stanley Hicks. Burton-Manning Collection, Box-23, Folder 37, Accession #25. Archives of Appalachia, East Tennessee State University.

the raid. He was charged for distilling a large quantity of beer, which was destroyed along with a half-gallon of whiskey that was seized.[26]

Some families in Lost Cove also made corn liquor. Kellner notes that "corn whiskey was distilled from fermented mash of grain containing at least eighty percent corn."[27] In Lost Cove, corn liquor was seen as differing from moonshine. Families used fruits such as cherries, blackberries, apples, and peaches to make moonshine. One person I interviewed, who wished to remain anonymous, explained that berries or sweeteners were added to moonshine but not to corn liquor, causing the corn liquor to have a strong taste that most railroad men preferred. This anonymous interviewee says that stills in Lost Cove were never hidden.[28] In Lost Cove, entire families participated in making corn liquor and moonshine. The anonymous interviewee's family helped out their father while he made it. Mr. Bryant also helped his father during the distilling process.

According to Mr. Bryant, there were at least two stills in Lost Cove. Although he acknowledged that his father made plenty of moonshine, Mr. Bryant never told me who owned the other still.[29] Mr. Bryant states that "there was one house in the cove that had a basement. Within the basement, moonshiners had a tunnel that shot out to the hollow and up a mountain to get away from the revenuers."[30]

Families were willing to work together to distill moonshine because it was a great cash crop, better than tobacco and corn put together.[31] In his article, Durand estimates the extent of moonshine production in East Tennessee for the year 1956.

Durand states that "officials of the Tennessee State Alcohol Tax Division of the Department of Finance and Taxation estimate a state moonshine production of about 1,664,000 gallons per year."[32] In 1956, North Carolina lists the illicit whiskey production at probably five or more times that of the Tennessee production.[33]

Lost Cove dwellers often sold moonshine to railroad workers and area townspeople. My grandfather Bob Johnson, who lived in Erwin and was a CC & O engineer, told me that my great-grandfather Hank S. Johnson, also an engineer, bought moonshine from Lost Cove dwellers as well as making his own. Mrs. McNabb confirmed that "Old Man Johnson" bought plenty of moonshine up in Lost Cove.[34] Since Lost Cove dwellers made moonshine, many railroad engineers, brakemen, and section workers hiked one mile or so up the ridgeline to buy the "shine." Alfred Tipton also notes in his letter that railroad workers, people from Erwin, Tennessee, and others throughout the mountains would walk into Lost Cove to buy moonshine. Moonshine during that time might sell for $40 a gallon.[35]

Since Mr. Bryant's father worked for the railroad, selling moonshine was easy and profit was plenty. The demand was high for the moonshine, which could be used for recreational or medicinal purposes. Mr. Bryant states that his father, Frank, also made moonshine to carry out and sell. Frank made 30 gallons in one setting.[36] Richard Bailey, John Miller's grandson, acknowledges that John made plenty of moonshine in his day. John and a group of men were called the "Devil Boys" because they made moonshine around Devil's Washing Bowls along the railroad tracks and state line.[37]

According to Mr. Bryant, almost everyone in Lost Cove drank moonshine. Sometimes the women drank it as medicine to lessen cold symptoms and relieve pain. According to Esther Kellner's book *Moonshine: Its History and Folklore*, "[m]oonshine was administered for numerous ailments, fevers, rheumatism, snakebite, pneumonia, and food poisoning."[38] Women even drank moonshine as a "pick-me-up" when colds, tiredness, or ills overtook them. Some even mixed it with flavors like chamomile, mints, or maple sugar and diluted it with hot water. Women looked upon moonshine as a tonic for growing children and a restorative for infants who were weak and frail.[39]

Almost every man, especially the young men, would drink moonshine just about every day. To Mr. Bryant and Mr. Tipton, moonshine was like spring water. The taste quenched their thirst. However, for these two men, moonshine running and buying became a chore of sorts. Mr. Tipton states that they walked out of Lost Cove three trips in one night just to get moonshine from people on Martin's Creek, which was at least five miles from the cove. If Mr. Bryant did not have moonshine he would walk the miles to Martin's Creek.[40] Mr. Tipton never made it to Martin's Creek one night due to drinking the hard stuff himself. Mr. Bryant and his friend Harry left him alongside Short Branch, near Unaka Springs, where he lay on the ground until Mr. Bryant and Harry returned.[41] Mr. Bryant adds that they put a rock against Mr. Tipton so he would not roll off down the mountain. When the men returned, Mr. Tipton could not believe that the men returned so quickly. Both men laughed hard after remembering their journey.[42]

When the Great Depression set in, moonshine selling allowed the families to survive.[43] Not only was moonshine a part of mountain life, but a way to make money for household goods and food. Moonshine kept Lost Cove families from living in poverty. The extra income allowed families to travel to the markets for food and see the doctors in nearby cities. While moonshine making remained hidden during the pillar years of the church, moonshine still ran through the blood of many Lost Cove men and women.

FIVE

Mountain View Free Will Baptist Church and Lost Cove School

"Free Will Baptists think that the opportunity for redemption is available to all who exercise free will to believe and practice the Christian faith...."[1]
—Howard Dorgan

Even if moonshine was made in their settlement, families in Lost Cove never strayed from religion and education. To Lost Cove dwellers, religion kept them closer to God, and the school provided the best education for their children. Both church and school blended together religious and worldly issues to expand the students' minds. For Lost Cove dwellers the church brought out religious zeal and emotional piety among the families, while the school taught autonomy and integrity. Both institutions used the same building, and the institutions augmented the social and kinship networks in the settlement. Lost Cove's combination church and schoolhouse stood on a tiny knoll high above most of the houses, and it could be seen from every house in the settlement.

In her book *Appalachian Mountain Religion: A History*, Deborah McCauley notes that "Appalachian mountain religion is one of the very few uniquely American religious traditions to which Protestantism in the United States can lay claim. It is made up of church traditions found almost entirely in the region's mountains and small valleys."[2] The Lost Cove church was of the Free Will Baptist denomination. According to Howard Dorgan, author of the article "Old Time Baptists of Central Appalachia," the establishment of the Toe River Association of Free Will Baptists was organized in 1850, at Jacks Creek Church in Yancey County, North Carolina.[3] Dorgan observes:

> Free Will Baptists accepted a doctrine of the general atonement that Christ died for all persons. Sinners receive grace by freely trusting Christ. For most Appalachian "Freewillers," that faith includes the rudiments of a creedal statement first adopted in 1916 by the North Carolina State Conference of Free Will Baptists: "We believe, as touching Gospel Ordinances, in believers' baptism, laying of the hands, receiving of the sacrament in bread and wine, washing the saints' feet, anointing the sick with oil in the name of the Lord, fasting, prayer, singing praise to God and the public ministry of the Word, with every institution of the Lord we shall find in the New testament."[4]

When the Free Will Baptist church formed in Lost Cove, the church and school functioned as two institutions but one social setting. Lost Cove's church did

Five. Mountain View Free Will Baptist Church and Lost Cove School

Lost Cove School and Mountain View Free Will Baptist Church. Courtesy of Teresa Miller Bowman.

experience several changes when it first formed.[5] The first accounts of a church being built in Lost Cove place construction around 1880. According to Lloyd Bailey, the earliest families built the church together, naming it Tipton's Chapel after a family in the settlement. In Lloyd Bailey's book, Chester Bailey, who lived in Lost Cove, recounted the names of the preachers of Tipton's Chapel. According to Chester Bailey, "Reverend Mark Wilson, Rev. Joe Ramsey, and Rev. Jim Hunter were associated with the church until the closing." The church folded around 1904. No records are found regarding why this church failed to continue.[6] A second church, named Lost Cove Free Will Baptist, was formed in 1909 by John Beam and others.[7]

When this second church joined the Jacks Creek Freewill Baptist Association in 1911, the founding members elected the Reverend Dan Miller as their pastor. Soon, church delegates including Robert Miller, Sam Miller, and W.M. Hensley represented the church at association meetings. The church remained a member of the Jacks Creek Association until 1919, when it failed to report minutes to the association. As a result, it was dropped from the association. Though no records are found regarding the church's continued operation, Lloyd Bailey insists that "the church continued to operate for some years" after it was dropped from the association.[8]

When the Lost Cove church finally resumed operations, the church became known as Mountain View Free Will Baptist Church. In 1934, 15 years after being excluded from the association, the church was again active. The members elected the Reverend Bob Miller as their first pastor. Members such as Velmer and Harley Bailey served as deacons, while Servilla Bailey worked as the clerk. By 1935, the church re-entered the association with the Reverend W.G. Honeycutt as the pastor. The church welcomed 27 members through its doors. Delegates serving the church in 1935 were sisters Bonnie Miller, Jettie Bailey, and Augustine Bailey. John Miller served as the third deacon. When Harley Bailey moved to Erwin, Tennessee, to become deacon of

Lost Cove Church members (1952). Courtesy of Chad Fred Bailey.

Five. Mountain View Free Will Baptist Church and Lost Cove School 69

Front row: Martha Miller, Carrie Bailey, Virginia June Bryant, and baby Sarah. Back row: Jason, Sam, Swin Miller, Everett Tipton, and Velmer Bailey holding baby (1930). Courtesy of Teresa Miller Bowman.

River View Free Will Baptist Church, Clifford Miller replaced Harley Bailey as deacon. Mountain View was the third and last church formed in Lost Cove.[9]

Since Appalachian culture rests on profound beliefs in the church and God, isolation rarely deterred mountain settlements from religious participation. The church instilled in families the Free Will Baptist beliefs and practices. According to McCauley, practices such as plural eldership, anointment with oil, and foot washings are characteristic of Free Will Baptists.[10] Indeed, eldership plurality, baptisms, communion, and foot washings were prominent in the church at Lost Cove. Some church members even participated in fasting.

At Lost Cove, elder plurality thrived. Elders and deacons preached and led choir practices. They counseled, helped with church budgets and collected tithes. They helped preachers share the burden of leading a church, communing with the community and even writing sermons. They were the backbone of the church, especially when preachers couldn't make the trip into the cove for church services or revivals. Since the church's inception, Lost Cove saw many preachers come and go. There were only two or three pastors that actually lived in Lost Cove through the years. When elders were called upon to preach, one community member took the helm and led services. Velmer Bailey preached many times at Mountain View Free Will Baptist Church and led prayer and Bible services for families during the week. If families couldn't make the church services, he would visit their homes. His dedication to God and community held a true testament to his work and life. He supported preachers, his church, and community throughout the years in the cove.

Baptisms occurred especially among youth in the cove. In Appalachia, great importance is placed on baptism by immersion. Baptism in "living waters" is a tradition among Appalachians that dates back to the first settlers in the mountains. Immersing the sinner in running water cleansed the soul and served as a point of entry to salvation, as well as confirmed one's place in the community. Baptisms were transformative to both those participating in the ritual and those watching the ceremony. The young baptized men and women took on new roles within the community, whether through church involvement or community efforts. The Lost Cove church did not have a baptism pool, so youth were baptized in either the river or branches within the community. Most baptisms took place in the summer and during revivals.

The Lost Cove church members participated in communion most often during foot washings. The practice did not occur every week or every month as in some mountain churches and associations. Communion was usually practiced during revivals or in services deemed necessary. The Free Will Baptist communion or the Lord's Supper became an open communal conversion experience when foot washings occurred. To many Baptists, communion cleansed the self and community as a whole, allowing church members to search their minds and hearts for salvation and purity. Communal worship practices uplifted community spirit and self-belief through grace and humility. Since Free Will Baptists have always followed the New Testament, the practice of communion and foot washings is a true testament to Jesus' teachings. For just as Jesus washed his disciples' feet, the Last Supper followed.

Lost Cove communion and foot washings occurred every six months or annually, depending on preacher involvement and attendance. In *Giving Glory to God in Appalachia: Worship Practices of Six Baptist Sub-denominations*, Howard Dorgan notes that foot washings always took place in conjunction with the annual communion.[11] Foot washings were considered to be a gospel ordinance, the same as baptisms.[12] The practice became a symbol of humility for many in mountain religion. Among some Free Will Baptists, women served as leaders but not pastors. In Lost Cove, the women of the church were leaders and were admired by the community.[13] They helped one another with everyday chores. They provided food to families, especially cooking during revivals and during funerals. Women would teach children the word of God at home and they also participated in foot washings.

Mr. Bryant notes that the men sat on one side of the church and the women on the other. During foot washings, "the men folk would take the benches in the church and face each other. The men would start at one end of the pew, and one man would wash the man in front of him. The men would go back and forth." The repetitive foot washing continued until the last man on the pew was cleansed. The men dried their feet with a towel. The women also participated in foot washings, cleansing other women's feet. Mr. Bryant's mother, Janie, always washed feet, along with his Aunt Martha and Bob Miller's wife, Emma.[14] Mr. Bryant states that "communion was held during foot washings. The members would eat flat bread and drink blackberry juice or grape juice during the Passover supper and then the members would wash the feet."[15]

While foot washings were a part of the church, being saved was evident in church members' "crying eyes and the shouting of 'amen.'"[16] Pastor Davis notes that the church held revivals every year, with families gathering in the one-room church and schoolhouse. The revivals were held during the summer months. The uplifting celebration lasted for hours. The families gathered with their kin; even outsiders came to hear preaching in the cove. While Mrs. McNabb lived in Lost Cove, she remembers little Sam Miller, who once represented the church at the associations, as a hymnal teacher. He taught singing school while the children sang gospel songs.[17]

Baptisms occurred at every revival, and families fixed meals and gathered together in the afternoons. Hymns were sung and bursts of shouting sounded out.[18] In her article "Grace and the Heart of Appalachian Mountain Religion," Deborah McCauley describes how religiosity manifested in places like Lost Cove:

> Throughout mountain religious life, there is a dominant emphasis on the purity of God-generated or God instituted emotion or religious experience. Expressive and ecstatic worship traditions—singing and praying spontaneously, shouting, shaking hands, crying, thrusting hands heavenward, even testifying and preaching spontaneously—have a very long heritage in mountain religious life.[19]

Verno Harris Davis, the last preacher to speak in Lost Cove, described the community's practice of foot washing in an interview:

> Foot washings were normally done by the preacher, or other members of the congregation who lived a life with God. You had to be a pretty good person. In other words, it was expected of you to take part. You had to examine yourself, that was the main thing. If there was anything wrong, you would ask the congregation to pray for you before you got the foot washing. That shows respect in God's word. It was nice and we enjoyed it. We had about three or four foot washings while I was up there.[20]

In 1943 Mr. Davis became ordained through the Jacks Creek Free Will Baptist Association. At first, Mr. Davis was a visiting preacher who spoke the word of God at homes of the sick and elderly. Evangelistic work was a clear calling for Mr. Davis. According to Mr. Davis, Velmer Bailey, a deacon of the Lost Cove church, asked him to preach for the church at a church conference. Mr. Davis believes that Velmer Bailey asked him because he shouted when he preached to the church when he visited. Davis laughs at his own comment.[21]

Mr. Davis' pilgrimage and teachings to the Lost Cove people left a distinct impression in the minds of the families. According to Mr. Bryant, the most prominent preacher he remembers was Mr. Davis. Mr. Davis worked for Erwin Utilities, but on Saturdays, after work, he would drive his truck from Little Bald Creek up on Spivey Mountain to Unaka Springs and walk into Lost Cove in the evening. Mr. Davis and other preachers spoke on Saturday evenings and had Sunday morning services and preaching.[22] Mr. Davis never rode the trains into or out of the settlement. By the time church dispersed, the trains had already left the station. After church, Mr. Davis ate lunch with one of the families in the cove, alternating between families each time he preached. He recalls sleeping at everyone's house as well.

Mr. Davis recalls: "I started out on foot around 3:00 p.m. I walked up and down the tracks one to two times a month."[23] The eight-mile round-trip walk never deterred Mr. Davis from preaching. His dedication to the people at the Lost Cove church and to God empowered his preaching and life. Mr. Davis' preaching, led by the Spirit, was

Velmer and Servilla Bailey heading to church services (1956). Courtesy of Chad Fred Bailey.

strong and powerful. For one to two hours, he preached in the church. Mr. Bryant acknowledges that "Mr. Davis received five cents once. He would not charge nothing. In other words if they gave him five cents, they gave him five dollars."[24]

Though Mr. Davis is one of a handful of preachers who spoke at Mountain View Free Will Baptist Church, other honored ministers from 1915 to the 1950s were the Reverend Bob Miller, the Reverend G.W. Honeycutt, the Reverend Dock Taylor, the Reverend Quince Miller, the Reverend Van Hensley, the Reverend Cecil H. Higgins, and the Reverend Elbert Wheeler.[25] Many of the preachers in the cove visited their members often, especially when they were disabled or too sick to travel to the church. The Reverend Bob Miller travelled on Saturday and Sunday after church to visit members in Pigeon Roost and Poplar. He prayed and shared bible verses and a short sermon with his members. At some point, the church in the cove was named the House of Welcome Church. The Reverend Bob Miller served as preacher during the early 1950s. When Bob Miller took a position as pastor in Marietta, South Carolina, the church hired various ministers throughout the years to serve, and many ministers from neighboring towns walked into Lost Cove once a month. Only during the last several years of Lost Cove did just one minister serve, and that man was Verno Davis.[26] According to Lloyd Bailey, the last known revival was conducted by the Reverend Clyde Fender from November 18 to 23, 1956.[27]

While revivals uplifted congregation spirits and transformed their lives in practices within the community, fasting unified the self and one's relationship with God. Fasting opened a deeper understanding of God among Free Will Baptists. It means strengthening ones spiritual life and surrendering oneself to God wholly through self and others. The heart is the sole purpose for fasting. The practice helped people

Five. Mountain View Free Will Baptist Church and Lost Cove School 73

Velmer Bailey preaching at Mountain View Free Will Baptist Church, Lost Cove (1952).

with mental and emotional problems break heavy burdens, free the sinner of addictions, bring protection to one's life against Satan, and make the heart more attentive to God.[28] Most mountain congregations practiced fasting during certain seasons of the liturgical calendar such as Lent and Holy Week. Faithful servants also fasted during Nativity or Christmas. The practice is mentioned nearly 30 times within the New Testament, which Free Will Baptists follow. But not all congregations followed the liturgical calendar.

There are no specific days or frequencies for fasting per the New Testament. Jesus assumes that all followers of Christ shall fast; therefore fasting along with giving and prayer could be practiced whenever the sinner chose to fast. One prominent leader in Lost Cove often fasted during Nativity and the lead-up to Lent.

Velmer Bailey often preached and held prayer services for Lost Cove residents. His true dedication to God and the Word of God held true to his life. Velmer's family bible documents the days and years that he fasted. While the documents state that Velmer fasted for 21 days, some entries suggest that he fasted longer. He may have eaten a meatless meal at some point during his fasting days, which suggests the traditional fasting of Christians specifically during Lent. The detailed document is described below:

1. "My first fast began December 11, 1951. Went 21 days and broke on January 10, 1952.
2. Second fast began January 11, 1953. Lasted 21 days and broke February 1, 1953.
3. Third fast began January 25, 1954. Lasted 21 days and broke February 14, 1954.
4. Fourth fast began January 1, 1955. Lasted 21 days and broke January 22, 1955.
5. Fifth fast began February 7, 1956. Lasted 21 days and broke February 27,1956.
6. Sixth fast began March 7, 1961. Went 21 days and ended March 27, 1961.
7. I was 59 years old March 19, 1961 while fasting. Praise Jesus. I am 93 years old this day February 1, 1996, VB initials."[29]

Lost Cove church members dedicated their lives to church and community. Since many men in the cove worked for the railroad, workers or families that lived along Cane Bottom would join the services at the church on occasion. Many residents accepted everyone into the church, even those who worked the railroad and were of different cultures. Once, a racially charged situation occurred in the cove's religious landscape.

According to Mr. Bryant, from the mid–1930s to late 1940s, an African American preacher who resided at the railroad camps along Cane Bottom preached to the black men working the railroad. The black preacher also worked with Mr. Bryant's father, Frank. Mr. Bryant notes that this "black preacher would walk into Lost Cove to speak with the families and eat with different families every Saturday for supper." Mr. Bryant's family ate with the black preacher many times, as did other families.[30] Mr. Bryant expresses that when the black preacher wanted to preach at the Lost Cove church, one member would not allow him to preach. Mr. Bryant could not understand why the disgruntled member did not like the black preacher, since the member worked with the black men on the railroad. But finally, after members of the church got together to talk about the situation, they let the black preacher preach in the church. Mr. Bryant believes he preached one time. He adds that "they all thought the world of him [the black preacher]."[31] Free Will Baptists are taught to be in fellowship with everyone, as with God. Though minor prejudice entered mountainous communities, there were never negative words about race relations from Lost Cove informants.

Lost Cove's church sat on a tiny knoll high above the houses, and it was seen from every house in the settlement. The church became the families' foundation, their home and fellowship house. Lost Cove families had many church gatherings during the holidays such as Christmas, Easter, and Memorial Day. In Lost Cove, community and family were united, joined together by blood and friendship.

Christmas Eve services were held at the church and families listened to the preacher talk about the birth of Christ. Candles were lit and families sang traditional Christmas hymns during the service. During the Christmas season families made cards to send to other families within the community and those members who resided outside the cove. The card presents a picture of the church with written words: Peace on Earth.

Christmas was a time for children as well. Children were given homemade and store-bought presents from their parents and grandparents. Many gifts came from Sears and Roebuck catalogs. Families gathered around the fireplace during winter and children picked some gifts from the catalog. Jim Johnson, son of Dolly Miller Johnson, states that, "one Christmas, Polly and Dolly received oranges and a box of peppermint sticks for a present. The twins cherished the box of peppermint sticks and kept the box after it was emptied just to smell the peppermint odor lingering in the box."[32]

In 1952, word of Santa coming to Lost Cove sent ripples across North Carolina. Mainstream newspapers heard about the Ninth Operation Christmas Santa and his scheduled visit to Lost Cove. Articles from Asheville to Statesville supported the planned event and the unexpected turn. On December 7, 1952, an article from the *Asheville Citizen-Times* provided the earliest information on Santa's visit.

In the article, "To Play Santa Claus," the paper announced that "Frank Edwards, a Mutual Broadcasting System news commentator will play Santa Claus to the children of Lost Cove on December 15, 1952."[33] Santa was scheduled to ride a helicopter into the cove during the annual Operation Christmas event. The yearly event provided presents and supplies to orphanages and rural youth across the state of North Carolina. Operation Christmas started in Charlotte and ended in the mountain regions at the end of that week. One photographer out of Greensboro learned of this annual event and decided to visit Lost Cove to take pictures of the children and families. His visit would be full of anticipation and waiting.

On December 18, 1952, the *Statesville Daily Record* printed a story titled "Photographer Tells of Wait." A photographer, Cletis Peacock, of the *Greensboro Daily News* visited Lost Cove on December 14 and waited patiently, along with the children and families, for the Ninth Air Force's "Operation Christmas" to drop Santa in from the skies. Peacock hiked into Lost Cove from Poplar, North Carolina. His trek took him five miles into the settlement at night. "At 10:45 pm Sunday night he reached the cove."[34] Peacock spent the night at Swin Miller's house. The weather conditions were harsh. Snow poured down and winds howled in the cove.

Mountain View Free Will Baptist Christmas card. Courtesy of Chad Fred Bailey.

The next day Yancey County Superintendent Bruce Hunter hiked into the cove to join the occasion. Around 2 p.m. on Tuesday, December 16, the children and families gathered in the church-schoolhouse and listened for any word on Santa and his helpers. By late afternoon, the battery-powered radio provided the news they didn't want to hear. Santa could not make the trip due to high winds in the mountains. One helicopter had been damaged in a wreck in Black Mountain, and a second helicopter sent had to turn around due to the storm. All the families in Lost Cove were a little disappointed but felt that Santa would come later in the week.[35]

Though Santa did not make the trip into the cove, the children visited him in Asheville later that week. On Thursday, December 18, 1952, the children travelled by train under sponsorship from the Asheville Moose Lodge, no. 781. The Moose Lodge scheduled many events for the children and guardians during their two-day trip. Two accounts in the *Asheville Citizen-Times*, titled "11 Youngsters from Lost Cove Coming to City" and "Children from Lost Cove Have Big Time Seeing the Sights of City," provide details on their visit.

The children along with six adults arrived in Asheville on December 18 around 5 p.m. The children who made the trip were: Eugene Bailey, 15; Junior Miller, 15; Homer Miller, 14; Vester Miller, 14; Isaiah Bailey, 13; Archie Miller, 10; Hosea Bailey, 8; Wayne Miller, 7; Elsie Miller, 17; Barbara Jean Miller; and Priscilla Bailey.[36] The adults included Mr. and Mrs. Velmer Bailey, Mrs. Swin Miller, Mr. and Mrs. John Miller, along with Sinclair Conley, the teacher. The youth stayed at the Battery Park Hotel in downtown Asheville. J.B. Pettit, the chair of the Moose Lodge committee, headed the schedule for the youth, along with others within the organizations.

The first event of the evening began at 6 p.m. on Thursday night. The children were supper guests at the Asheville Linen Supply Company at the Rathskeller, which is a restaurant located in the company basement. After supper, the children went to the Imperial Theater to watch a movie.[37] After the movie they returned to the hotel for the night. The next day would be an adventure-filled day full of surprises.

On Friday, December 19, 1952, the children ate breakfast at Tingles Café. From morning until noon, the children visited the Central Fire Station as guests of Chief J.C. Fitzgerald. They also took a ride on the fire trucks. By mid-morning they toured Ivey Department Store and the *Asheville Citizen-Times* building. At noon, they ate lunch at S&W cafeteria, where they were welcomed by the Reverend Nane Starnes. Immediately following lunch, the youth toured Biltmore Estates and its dairy farm, where they ate refreshments. Their fun-filled day landed them also at the Asheville airport, where some children and adults took a plane ride with Paul McMurray's A and H Flying Service.[38] Their busy day didn't end that afternoon. They still needed to visit Santa at the Moose Lodge.

On Friday evening the children attended dinner at the lodge, and the Christmas party began soon after. Santa gave out gifts and the youth were happy. Children enjoyed punch and cookies that night, along with many members of the Moose Lodge. The next day, December 20, 1952, the youth travelled back to Lost Cove. Due to the Santa's delay, Lost Cove children were able to see many sights on their visit to Asheville. Their visit opened their eyes to the outside world. Lost Cove children were supposed to see Santa in Lost Cove on Monday, December 15, yet they visited him instead. When they returned home that day, they experienced an even bigger surprise they didn't expect.

An article in the *Asheville Citizen-Times*, titled "Santa Claus Finally Arrives at Lost Cove," appeared the next day in the newspaper. Through hail and heavy rain, four men hiked into the cove to deliver presents. Sergeant Stafford Stillpass played

Train ride to Asheville (December 18, 1952). Hosea Bailey (8). Courtesy of Chad Fred Bailey.

Santa Claus that day. Sergeant Leroy Estes and Airman Second Class Roger Lupardus were his helpers, and Bruce Hunter, the school superintendent, guided them to the settlement. The four-mile hike soaked all of the men. The men had no sled to carry the presents, so all four men carried 79-pound packs of toys, fruits, and candy on their backs. The children and families in Lost Cove had no idea of Santa's visit. As Santa and his helpers walked to the church-schoolhouse, every kid in the cove hurried to meet Santa. Eight-year-old Wayne Miller jumped on Santa's lap first. He asked

Lost Cove children and parents enjoying dinner in Asheville, NC (1952). Courtesy of Chad Fred Bailey.

if Santa had his flying machine.[39] The children's visit with Santa and his helpers lasted only a few hours that day. The harsh weather prevented the airmen from staying too long. It didn't matter to the kids because the real Santa had come to see them. The following year, in 1953, Santa scheduled a second trip into the cove. Newspapers from Texas, Tennessee, and Florida wrote articles about the visit.

Articles titled "Operation Santa of Five Airmen Slowed to Walk," "Air Force Crew Delivers Presents to Lost Cove," and "Santa Moving Infantry Style" provide information on the airmen, Santa, and the gifts the children received. According to all of the articles, Sergeant Bob Johnson from Indianapolis, Indiana, played Santa that year. Johnson donned his "white beard and bright red working clothes."[40] He, along with Sergeant George J. Dacre of White Plains, New York, and three other airmen, hiked into the cove on December 20, 1953. The men carried 85 pounds of gifts to the settlement. The airmen arrived in the cove around noon that day. No one in the settlement knew that Santa was coming until he surprised them. The only way the families could have known about Santa's visit was by their battery-operated radio. Lost Cove children were not on the Operation Santa list in 1953. Since there were gifts left over, someone remembered the settlement.[41]

In the *Kingsport News* dated December 21, 1953, Sergeant Dacre talked about the trip and how the children greeted them. There were 20 anxious children who "all rushed over and greeted Santa Claus. However he said, they accepted with quiet reserve the gifts of toys, clothing, watches, food, candy, nuts, fruit, and a battery radio."[42] When presents were handed out, one of the children, 10-year-old Billy Bailey, opened his gift quickly. He received a BB gun, with which Dacre said he immediately "displayed typical mountaineer accuracy." A photographer took pictures of the occasion. Some of the flashbulbs were lying around the floor when Billy "picked them off one after the other with one shot apiece."[43]

The children and families enjoyed Santa's visit. The families did not see Santa after 1953. There are no articles or information found in newspapers that report a visit to the cove again. The 1952 and 1953 Santa visits were memorable and exciting for the families. Other family events would occur throughout the ending years.

Every year families gathered together to commemorate Decoration Day or Memorial Day. This community effort united all families and friends throughout the surrounding settlement and their families elsewhere. In order for the graves to be presentable, the families would spend days fixing up the graves, cleaning the headstones, cutting the grass, and placing new spring flowers on the graves. The families took care of their loved ones even after death. Their dedication and love passed down from generation to generation.

Betty Bryant Peterson remembers visiting her Uncle Frank and Aunt Jane during Decoration Day. Her family, which included her father, Jim, and mother, Naomi Howell, and nine siblings, travelled on the train from Poplar at 11 a.m. and stayed in the cove until 2 p.m., when the Lost Cove train carried them back to Poplar. Betty recalls walking up the path and seeing the Millers, Bryants (her Uncle Frank and cousins), and Baileys present at the decoration. Families placed wreaths on the gravestones.[44] Even after the families left Lost Cove, the tradition continued. Today, Lost Cove residents still commemorate their lost loved ones. Some families still hike into Lost Cove, placing flowers upon their loved ones' graves. The cemetery is pristine, even now.

While revivals and services inspired the congregations, burials also played an important role in the mountainous community. Every family that lived in Lost Cove buried a family member in the cemetery. The hidden cemetery sits high on a knoll above the once thriving settlement, situated in a woody area close to the Swin Miller house and near Wiley Tipton's property. The pristine site rarely shows overgrowth.

In *Death and Dying in Central Appalachia: Changing Attitudes and Practices*, James K. Crissman states that most burial grounds or cemeteries were situated on a high place so water could not seep into the graves and disturb the departed.[45] Crissman adds that mountain people buried their beloved ones on a mountain or hill because "they felt that in death as in life they would want to look over their beloved mountains."[46]

According to Mr. Bailey, his two brothers, a grandmother, and some cousins are buried in Lost Cove.[47] Mr. Bryant's grandmother and grandfather, Arch and Sindy Miller, are buried there as well. Mrs. McNabb states that her grandfather John D. Tipton and his wife, Caroline Peterson Tipton, are buried in Lost Cove. Along with her grandparents and her uncle Everett T. Tipton, the gravestones date back to the late 1800s. There are at least 25 graves in Lost Cove Cemetery. Some graves are marked with a family member's name, but many families used plaques or stones to mark their loved ones, including children.

In the early 1900s, children often died from pneumonia, tuberculosis, and influenza in the United States. The CDC states that "children under five accounted for 40 percent of all deaths from these diseases."[48] Many children's graves are not identified

Five. Mountain View Free Will Baptist Church and Lost Cove School

in the cemetery. Children died at birth or around the age of two. Others died in their teens or at the age of 21. Mr. Bryant once said that typhoid had entered Lost Cove in the earlier years. On the Find a Grave website, two children's names appear in the cemetery that are not marked: Baby Girl Tipton and Otis Tipton. The dates state that Baby Girl Tipton was born on March 1, 1914, and died the same day, while Otis Tipton's birth and death dates aren't provided. Baby Girl Tipton is Geneva Tipton McNabb's sister. Information on the website states that her parents were Dock and Usley Hensley. Otis Tipton is George and Gusty Bailey Tipton's son.[49]

Nola Tipton is the daughter of Wiley and Hester Price Tipton. She died around the age of two years. While the gravestone places her birth in 1917 and her death in 1918, the Find a Grave website gives her birth and death dates as February 22, 1916, and October 27, 1918.[50] Nola is an aunt to Geneva Tipton McNabb and sister to her father, Dock. Research shows no known death certificate for Nola.

A small plaque for Donald Miller sits in the cemetery near Bonnie Miller. Donald is the baby son of Clifford and Hazel Bailey Miller, according to the Find a Grave website. In Clifford Miller's obituary, there is no evidence that shows Donald to be their son. Donald is said to have died on the day of his birth. Donald would be the nephew to Bonnie Miller, and his plaque sits on the backside of her grave. The headstone of Bonnie Miller, a teenager, shows that Bonnie was only 16 when she passed. The North Carolina certificate of death states that Bonnie Miller, daughter of John Miller and Huldie Webb Miller, died of tuberculous meningitis on June 3, 1938. She was 16 years old. Doctor Cooper from Relief, North Carolina, tended to Bonnie from May 19 through June 3, 1938. She died the last day he attended to her.[51] Kris Hawkins Rosalina shares a story about Bonnie Miller. Her father, Jack Hawkins, brother-in-law to John D. Miller, was witness to Bonnie's funeral. The train brought Bonnie's coffin to Lost Cove, and Jack, along with others, helped carry Bonnie's small coffin up the mountain for service and burial.[52]

One grave in Lost Cove shows Calvin Coolidge Miller, son of the Reverend Robert Miller and Emma Bryant. Coolidge was 18 years old when he died from abdominal pulmonary tuberculosis on February 15, 1943. He would've been 19 years old two weeks later in March. W.H. Tanksley signed the death certificate and had seen Coolidge from January 7 through January 22, 1943. Tanksley notes that Coolidge was alive the last day he saw him. On the death certificate John Miller is named as informant.[53]

Britt Bailey is also buried in the cemetery. The 1940 United States census records show that Britt and his mother, Jettie (Jettia), resided in the Ramsey Township. His mother's age was 52, and he was 22 at the time of the census. His estimated year of birth was 1918. Velmer Bailey was one of Britt's older brothers. Britt died at the age of 22. He passed on October 10, 1940, from an unknown illness, according to an article in Lloyd Bailey's Toe River series: "Funeral services were conducted by Reverend Cecil Higgins. Burial was in the Tipton Hill cemetery in Mitchell County where a large number of relatives and friends were gathered to pay a last tribute at the ceremonies."[54] Though Lloyd Bailey places Britt's burial at Tipton Hill Cemetery, no grave marker or death certificate is to be found on Britt Bailey in Tipton Hill. Other family members with grave markers as stones include Roy Guthrie's mother and brother.

Roy Guthrie, James and Trula Bryant's son, states that his mother died when he was three years old. Roy had two brothers, Richard and Odell. He and Richard went to live with Mary Lee Guthrie, his father's sister, in Sugar Creek, North Carolina, after her death. His brother Odell went to live with his aunt. Mr. Guthrie's mother died from tuberculosis. His brother Odell died at the age of 18 months from spinal tuberculosis. The two are buried side by side at the Lost Cove cemetery. Their burial is designated by two stones side by side behind John D. Tipton's gravestone.[55]

There are several Tipton family members that are buried in Lost Cove. Wiley Tipton, son of John and Caroline Peterson Tipton, lived in Lost Cove until his death in 1934. Wiley is further discussed in the family section. His grave sits next to those of his parents.

Russell Tipton is the son of Wiley and Hester Price. Russell was born on April 13, 1914, in Lost Cove. Russell worked for the Civilian Conservation Corps (CCC) camp. The CCC worked young, unemployed men from ages 18 to 25 during the Great Depression. According to the website History.com, the CCC gave millions of young men jobs on environmental projects throughout the country. Developed under Roosevelt's New Deal, the CCC became a successful program that helped shape the national and state parks today.[56] Russell worked for the CCC camp in Brevard, North Carolina, for 20 months. Russell died at the age of 21. His death occurred in Brevard, North Carolina. His death certificate shows that on April 2, 1936, Russell died from a fracture at the base of his skull. He wrecked his car on East Main Street in Brevard. His car hit a telephone pole and he was ejected. He died 11 days before his 22nd birthday.[57] The funeral was held in Lost Cove on Sunday April 5 and the Reverend W.G. Honeycutt of Burnsville presided over the service. Russell's headstone lies next to Wiley's in the cemetery.

Other known graves include Augusta Bailey and Jettie (Jettia) Bailey. In the 1920 North Carolina census, Augusta is listed as seven years of age. The census lists the name as Augustis not Augusta. Her estimated year of birth is 1913. Augusta does not appear in the 1940 census with Jettie (Jettia) and Britt Bailey. Jettie Bailey was buried next to Augusta in the Lost Cove cemetery. Jettie moved into Lost Cove after her husband, William, passed from typhoid in 1919. Her estimated date of birth is 1888. The 1920 census shows that she was 32 years of age and supporting children Velmer, Chester, Elva, Harley, Augustis (Augusta), Britt, and Orvil. Jettie lived in Lost Cove until her death in 1948. More information on Jettie is provided in the Bailey family section.

For many years, Lost Cove residents buried their own people by relying on one another. Each family participated in burial practices just as they helped with the birth of children. When children and adults died, families helped build caskets, brought flowers and food, and even sat with the body so animals wouldn't interfere with the burial. Help would come from youth as much as adults. Mr. Bryant's grandmother, Sindy Miller, died one evening, and they buried her three days later. Before the burial, young people would sit up and watch the deceased person's casket, because animals would show up and get into the grave.

Crissman notes that sitting up with the dead was a matter of protecting the body from cats, rodents, and insects.[58] Cats weren't the only reason why families kept watch over the coffin. Sitting up with the dead also occurred out of respect for family

Lost Cove Cemetery (2007). Photograph by the author.

members who lived outside of the community. Since some family members lived far away, and telephones were unavailable, families had to wait for others to receive word of a death.[59]

The people who died in Lost Cove were never embalmed. Burials days depended upon the weather. If someone died in the winter, it would take the men at least three days to bury them because the ground was too hard. Crissman explains that the men were responsible for digging the graves. Male neighbors and friends helped because it was a part of their "community duty."[60] According to Mr. Bryant, the graves were eight feet deep.

Russell Tipton gravesite (2007). Photograph by the author.

Left: **Wiley Tipton gravesite (2007).** *Right:* **Bonnie Miller's tombstone, daughter of John and Hulda Miller (2007). Photograph by the author.**

The men would dig a four-foot square hole, then grade it down six inches, then dig another four feet.[61] Mr. Tipton adds that "when they started to cover the grave up, they would lay boards across the casket to stop the dirt from caving in on the casket."[62] This technique also prevented the dirt from accelerating the decay of the burial receptacle and corpse, as well as keeping animals from unearthing the corpse.[63]

After the burial was complete, the families would gather at the deceased person's home. Food was brought by extended family members and neighbors. This act of kindness lifted a burden off the family of the deceased. Visitation at the family home lasted for hours and sometimes days. Neighbors and members of the extended family often recalled fond memories of the deceased. Burials brought out communion and fellowship throughout the mountainous community.[64]

Before the days of funeral homes, Appalachian coffins were often made by relatives, neighbors, and carpenters in the community.[65] Velmer and Chester Bailey, both carpenters, often built the caskets for families in Lost Cove. Mr. Bryant notes that the Baileys would use oak wood for the caskets. Oak trees grew abundantly in Lost Cove. The wood was sturdy, durable, and popular among high-status mountain people.[66] Mr. Bryant also states that John Miller and Velmer Bailey made the headstones for the deceased.[67] Only one gravestone in Lost Cove is made of marble. Since John D. Tipton was a Union soldier, his headstone was made by the Veterans Administration. Most of the headstones are limestone and granite. The Baileys used tools such as chisels and picks to carve the headstones. Several graves are hand inscribed. Other headstones, made later in the twentieth century, are inscribed by funeral businesses in Erwin, Tennessee, or Burnsville, North Carolina. The deceased were treated with care and love by their families and extended families.

There is no undergrowth on the hill where the cemetery lies, only sunshine peeking through the trees, piercing the headstones. Though death was a part of life,

life in the cove flourished through the youth and schoolhouse. Mr. Bryant notes that the one-room building had desks on one side and pews on the other.[68] Of course, spring water flowed outside the building, there was an outdoor toilet (or "privy" as Mrs. McNabb calls it), and a big wood stove provided heat for the school and church during winter months.[69] In the steeple of the one-room building, a bell summoned children as well as church members into the church. While no information is found regarding the establishment of the school, Alderman notes that some of Lost Cove teachers were Bob Holliday, Royce Brinkley, Carl Young, John Hensley, Faye Miller, and Sinclair Conley, the last teacher in Lost Cove.[70]

Some information on the earlier teachers in Lost Cove is genealogical in nature. No information is documented on Bob Holliday. On the other hand, Royce Brinkley grew up on Jacks Creek in Yancey County. He was the son of Charles and Sally Peterson Brinkley. Jacks Creek is only 30 miles from Lost Cove. His mother Sally could have been a relative of Caroline Peterson Tipton, who was married to John D. Tipton, one of the first to arrive in Lost Cove. By 1940 Royce was 27 years old and living in Illinois. Carl T. Young grew up in Ramsey Township. His father was Don Young and his mother was Margaret Peterson. Carl Talmadge served in World War I and married Pansy McCurry in 1912. Since their mothers had the last name Peterson, both Brinkley and Young may have taken the schoolteacher job due to family connections. Since all the families in Lost Cove were distantly kin to one another, their lineage probably played a role in them taking on the responsibility of teaching at the school. While further research is needed, their mothers' maiden names provide some evidence and link to Lost Cove's families.

Another teacher, John L. Hensley, is the son of Will Love Hensley and Linnie Hensley. He grew up in Bee Log in the Egypt Township of North Carolina, which is close to the settlement. No marriage records are found on John, yet one document states that he was widowed. According to the 1940 census, he was 42 years old and lived with his mother. When he died in 1984, his death certificate indicated he was a retired teacher. There is no information on how he obtained the teaching position in Lost Cove, but his last name may have some connection to families in the cove. The teachers in Lost Cove often stayed with families through the week and would return home on the weekends.

Geneva McNabb remembers that in 1924 her teacher was a man named John Howell. Mr. Howell would stay in the cove all week with her Aunt Hester and Uncle Wiley Tipton.[71] Mrs. McNabb adds that "ABC's, writing, and figuring were subjects in second grade." She also states that "the children did more in that one room school than they did in a bigger school." Her oldest sister was told that she knew more than students did in high school.[72] Since most teachers boarded with families such as the Tiptons and Millers, their teachings helped the students learn about the outside world, and, in return, the outside world came to this little mountain school. John Howell's brother Baird Howell also taught in the cove during the 1940s. Baird grew up in White Oak Flats and is Betty Bryant Peterson's uncle. According to Betty, Baird walked into the cove on Sunday and stayed with Velmer Bailey and his family during the school week. He often visited their home before he walked into the cove.[73]

The only known female teacher to enter Lost Cove was Faye Johnson Miller. Mrs. Miller began her career teaching in Lost Cove after she graduated from Cullowhee

Carl Young, teacher, with school children. Front row: Kenneth Tipton, Hazel Bailey, Maude Howell, Polly Miller, Ulis Miller, Dolly Miller, Bonnie Miller, and Everett Tipton. Back row: Leona Howell, Britt Bailey, Phil Miller, Arvil Bailey, and Clifford Miller (1931). Courtesy of Teresa Miller Bowman.

Teachers College, which is now Western Carolina University. Faye Miller grew up in Bee Log, North Carolina, which is in the Egypt Township of Yancey County, not far from Lost Cove. She was the daughter of Virgil and Stella Howard Johnson. She was the oldest of seven children.

In the late 1940s Faye entered Lost Cove by train with two Yancey County school officials and hiked up to the settlement wearing high heels. In an article from Don Haines, Faye describes her first experience in the cove:

> The first thing was to find me a family to stay with during the week because teachers didn't have their own house. When we went up to the first house, they refused to accept me. I found out later it was because I was wearing makeup, which marked me as being too proud. Next they took me to Velmer Bailey's house, and they said they'd take me.[74]

Velmer Bailey's family housed many teachers in Lost Cove. She taught students through the eleventh grade. She soon gained trust with her students and community and taught for several years at the school. Her life as a young teacher changed when she met and married Ulis Miller of Lost Cove. They moved to Erwin after they were married. She did travel back to teach several times in the 1950s when the last teacher grew ill and when he had obligations with the Board of Education. When she did substitute teach, Faye hiked into the cove with her daughter Teresa.

Teresa Bowman, Ulis and Faye's daughter, visited Lost Cove several times when her mother taught school. Teresa recalls that in 1956 she and Faye hiked the railroad

Five. Mountain View Free Will Baptist Church and Lost Cove School 87

Lost Cove School (1957). Courtesy of Chad Fred Bailey.

tracks from Unaka Springs on a Sunday afternoon. Teresa says that it was a long walk for a three-year-old, and Isaiah Bailey and other young men met them at the bottom of the settlement on the railroad tracks. Isaiah carried little Teresa up the long, windy mountain road to the settlement. The pair stayed in the house of Chester and Carrie Bailey during the school week.

Faye Miller standing near entrance to Lost Cove, ca. 1953. Courtesy of Teresa Miller Bowman.

    While her mother taught classes, Teresa read books. Teresa adds that several school children gathered books from the closet for her to read during class time. Teresa mentions that the desks were nailed to the floor and desks were attached to each other front to back. There were at least 10 students in the schoolhouse during Teresa's visits into the cove. Teresa remembers that during her visit, families and school kids celebrated her third birthday at the school. Teresa was born on October

27, 1953, just in time for Halloween. Families presented her with gifts and a cake. Party hats were made and drinks were served. Pictures were taken just outside of the schoolhouse steps, and a table displayed her cake and a pumpkin decorated with a party hat.[75]

Faye taught students through the 11th grade. One of the oldest students was Isaiah Bailey, and he walked to Poplar during his last year of school to attend 12th-grade classes. Faye had books for every grade level at the school. She used state-issued books and taught students at at least five different grade levels. She remembers how sometimes there would be just one student per grade at the school. Since students were in the different class levels, teaching was a demanding task. Her books lay out on her desks and students completed their assignments once she finished teaching their level. As soon as she taught one grade, she moved on to the next student. When classes ended on Friday, Faye and Teresa hiked back to Unaka Springs. Faye's experience as a teacher would not end in Lost Cove. She worked as a substitute teacher for many years in the Unicoi County School System. Faye substituted in Lost Cove for one of the most prominent teachers that any student can remember: Sinclair Conley.

Sinclair Bell Conley was born in 1882 to Lafayette (Fate) Conley and Elizabeth (Betsy) Byrd. The family lived on Jacks Creek in Yancey County. Mr. Conley's background education is astounding. In an article from the *Asheville Citizen-Times*, readers learn that Mr. Conley graduated from Wake Forest College and Rochester Theological Seminary and taught psychology and education at the University of Florida and the Oklahoma Baptist University at Shawnee. Mr. Conley also served as dean of Biltmore (now Asheville-Biltmore Technical College) from 1927 to 1933. From 1939 onward, Mr. Conley returned to his family's farm in Jacks Creek and taught at the elementary schools of Halls Chapel, South Toe, Burnsville, and Pensacola, and the high schools at Bald Creek and Bee Log.[76] After retiring, he accepted the position at Lost Cove School in the early 1950s.

Lost Cove students standing on school steps (1956). Courtesy of Teresa Miller Bowman.

When Conley accepted the position at Lost Cove, traveling to and from the settlement became a weekly chore. Mr. Conley entered the cove by train on Mondays. Several accounts reveal that Conley boarded the train at two different places. Each week he would park his car at the railway siding in Poplar, where he boarded the train to the Lost Cove siding.[77] According to Robert H. Fowler, staff writer for the *Greensboro Daily News*, Mr. Conley "rides the train every Monday to Lost Cove station and hikes to the home of Rev. Bob's brother, Swin Miller, where he boards and rooms until Friday."[78] Isaiah Bailey adds that "Conley would ride the train from Huntdale to Lost Cove and leave out on Friday afternoon."[79] He returned to his farm on the weekends to work. Mr. Conley never slowed down. He even taught Sunday school at Boring's Chapel Methodist Church.[80]

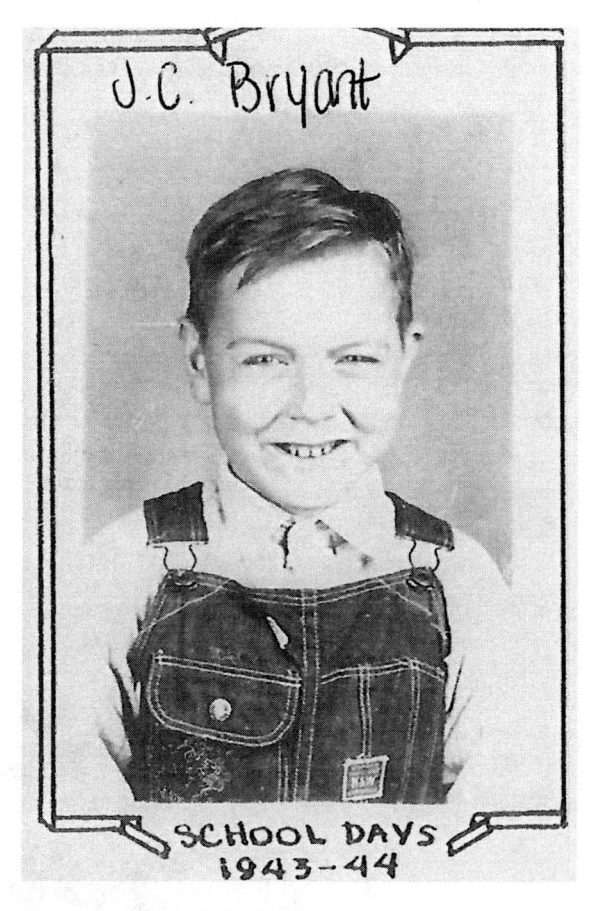

J.C. Bryant school picture (1943–1944). Courtesy of Regina Cornett.

According to Mr. Bailey and Mr. Bryant, Mr. Conley was a great teacher. In Haines's article, Ulis Miller, a student of Conley and former resident of Lost Cove, states that "Mr. Conley was an excellent teacher and very strict."[81] Though Mr. Conley taught beyond his retirement age, the students in Lost Cove learned about the world and about community. Mr. Conley was a Democrat and worldly gentleman who taught the students about life and school subjects. Even though families in Lost Cove were Republican, Conley was well respected. According to Fowler, Mr. Conley "draws on his schooling in education, religion, and psychology to teach the fifteen pupils and help them overcome the disadvantages of being cut off from the outside world."[82] Mr. Conley told Fowler, "I try to teach them life and not entirely books."[83] Mr. Conley loved his students. In the *Asheville Citizen-Times* article he states that "I've got here some of the brightest students I have ever had anywhere. They are eager to learn."[84]

The *Greensboro Daily News* reported that the Lost Cove school teaching hours were "Mondays 2:00 to 4:30 p.m. and Tuesday through Friday from 8:00 a.m. to 4:00

Five. Mountain View Free Will Baptist Church and Lost Cove School 91

Lost Cove children celebrating the third birthday of Teresa Miller Bowman, middle (1956). Courtesy of Teresa Bowman.

p.m."⁸⁵ With the grade level in Lost Cove ending at seventh grade, Mr. Conley taught students up to eleventh grade. This meant that Yancey County did not have enough funding for the Lost Cove School; however, Mr. Conley kept teaching the students up to eleventh grade. He bought the students above seventh grade their books for the school year. Mr. Conley knew that the students needed an education, so he bought the books in order for students to stay in the Lost Cove School.

Mr. Miller remembers that Mr. Conley "is given credit for establishing a high school curriculum in the cove, having the foresight to know that a seventh-grade education would soon be insufficient."⁸⁶ Hosea

Teresa Miller Bowman with schoolgirls for her third birthday (1956). Courtesy of Teresa Miller Bowman.

Five. Mountain View Free Will Baptist Church and Lost Cove School 93

Mr. Conley teaches Hosea, Priscilla, Elsie, and Miller boy a geography lesson with the globe (1952). Courtesy of Teresa Miller Bowman.

Bailey still has his report cards from his days at Lost Cove School. His seventh grade report card identifies Faye Miller as his homeroom teacher and C.B. Bennett's name is on the report card as well. From 1955 to 1956, Hosea excelled in Health and Art classes. The following year, his eighth grade report card shows he excelled in every subject. He made all A's and B's with Sinclair Conley as his principal.

While Mr. Conley made sure the students were educated, the pupils also had fun playing during recess and after school. Isaiah states that they "would play games like baseball, football and softball."[87] Mrs. McNabb remembers playing ball and tag as well.[88] Even though playing ball helped the pupils remain kids, education enabled them to look forward to high school.

During Mr. Conley's teaching years, the outside world saw how Lost Cove children enjoyed the outdoors. Youth were captured at their best, laughing and having fun in their everyday life. Velmer Bailey even built a homemade wooden riding car for his sons Hosea and Isaiah. The boys along with their friends rode the car down the hills and road in the community. The toy, made to look like a skateboard but 10 times bigger, hauled up to three boys on the ride. Velmer made the toy out of sawmill

Opposite: Lost Cove Church and school building at recess. Sinclair Conley, the 75-year-old school teacher, stands on the steps in his suit and tie (1952). Courtesy of Chad Fred Bailey.

Sinclair Conley reading to Hosea, Elsie, and Priscilla (1952). Courtesy of Teresa Miller Bowman.

wood and steel rods. Hosea and others were able to steer the ride with their feet. An article out of the *Oakland Tribune Parade* states that several other boys— Homer, Wayne, and Junior—built the "cart" by themselves out of logs and nails.[89] There is no factual information that the three boys built their own cart. If they did, they built the cart by direction from Velmer. Of course, the Bailey and Miller boys had to stop the car somehow.

Five. *Mountain View Free Will Baptist Church and Lost Cove School* 95

Kids taking a break from playing baseball. Hosea Bailey with the baseball bat (1952). Courtesy of Chad Fred Bailey.

Priscilla, Hosea, and friends (1952). Courtesy of Chad Fred Bailey.

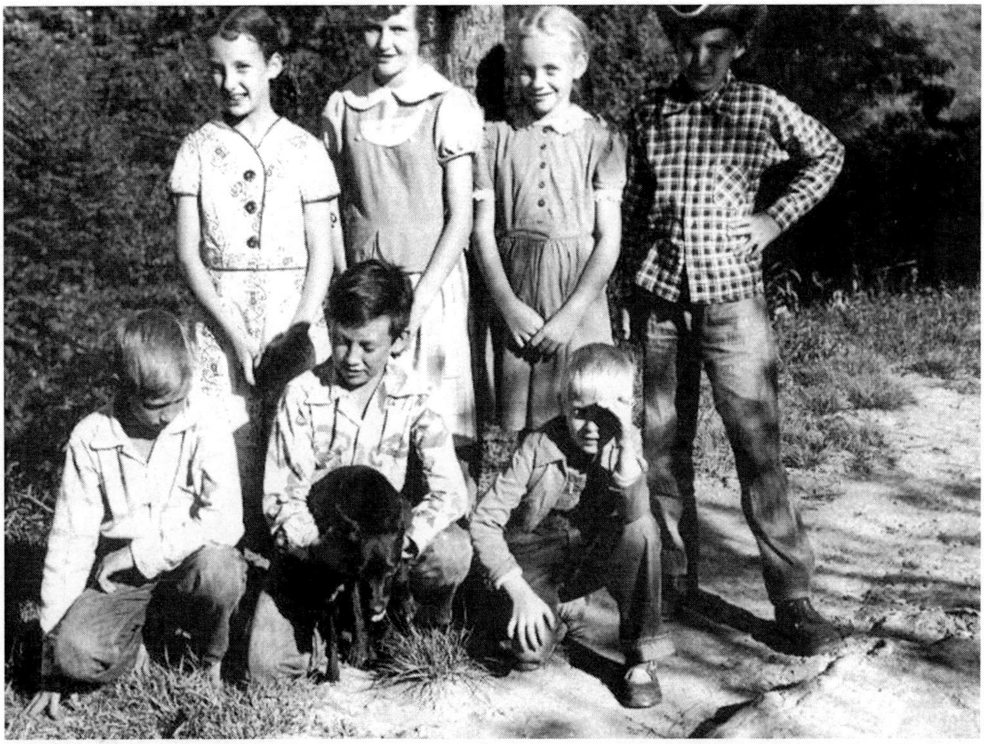

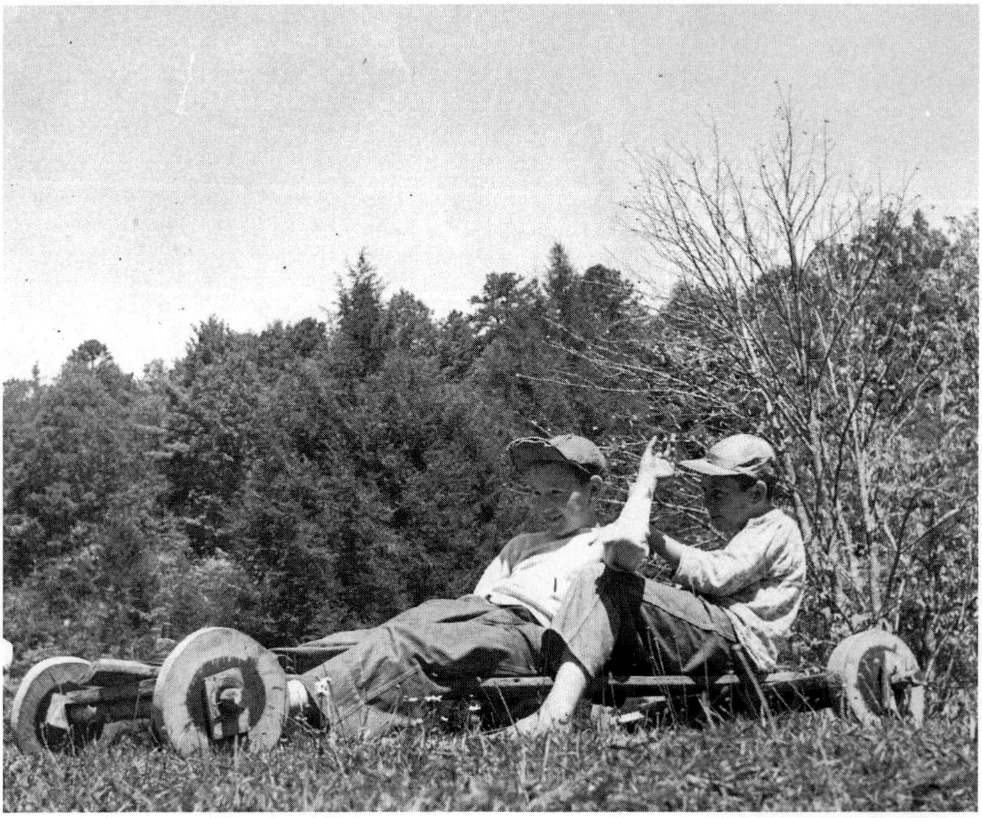

Five. Mountain View Free Will Baptist Church and Lost Cove School 97

According to Hosea Bailey, the cart had a lever that he could pull to stop the car. Velmer used a wire and wooden lever that would press the wire into the back wheels of the cart.[90] The cart would go really fast and race down the hills. During the later years, Conley taught around 11 to 15 students.

While Mrs. McNabb lived in Lost Cove, the number of students reached around 15. As Lost Cove grew during the 1930s and 1940s, the student population grew. Mr. Bailey states that "at one time he could remember 32 kids at school in different grades."[91] The student population decreased in the late 1940s and

Hosea Bailey on handmade car (1960s). Courtesy of Chad Fred Bailey.

Hosea sits on entry rock to Lost Cove near railroad tracks (1960s). Courtesy of Chad Fred Bailey.

Opposite: top, Priscilla, Hosea and other Lost Cove children (1952). Courtesy of Chad Fred Bailey. *Opposite: bottom,* Hosea and Isaiah on Velmer Bailey's homemade riding toy (1952). Courtesy of Chad Fred Bailey.

1950s. Attendance in the one-room school dwindled to 11 students.[92] By 1950, the improved roads and transportation in Yancey County enabled the school districts to consolidate the public schools. Education in North Carolina became an economic issue.[93]

According to the Yancey County Historical Association, "most of the smaller schools had been closed and their students sent to consolidated units. The smallest school (serving about a dozen families) was Lost Cove." The consolidation meant that students in Lost Cove needed to attend high school elsewhere in the county. For the students in Lost Cove, those students who wanted to continue their education in high school had preparations to make in the neighboring towns. The association states that "the county paid room and board in the Bee Log area. Conley expresses that the hike to Bee Log was twenty miles and sixteen to Tipton Hill School."[94] They walked "out of the cove each Sunday afternoon and returned the next Friday afternoon."[95] In the early 1950s, Mr. Bailey attended the Bee Log School until his family moved out of Lost Cove.

Since students attended the high school some 20 miles away, Mr. Conley taught only a few elementary children in the Lost Cove School. As the years rolled on, the population in Lost Cove dwindled due to the state economy, denial of a road, the discontinued passenger trains, and the depletion of timber. The economic and political changes reshaped society in the community. As families separated from their land, family connections and personal character began to reshape. New living patterns and surroundings emerged. Lost Cove's families began to deal with the new arrangements, and soon they were found walking the train tracks out of their once thriving town, a town that offered security and autonomy. To them, Lost Cove embodied a "sense of place and self." Today, the only sign left of the church and schoolhouse is the concrete steps where the building once stood. Two houses still stand, and a handful of chimneys can be seen scattered throughout the community.

Six

Families

*The cove was actually one large extended family, bound together
by myriad ties of both kinship and a common past.*[1]
—Durwood Dunn

When we think of Lost Cove, we think of the families. Why did they live in this isolated settlement? Who were they and where did they come from? Where did they reside after they left their home? Where are they now? From its inception, Lost Cove families shared several common interests: land, place, and kinship. The ties enabled families to survive, prosper, and share common ancestry, experiences, and values. The isolated community, first discovered by Morgan Bailey, provided a suitable environment for John D. Tipton's family, the Millers, the Bryants, and other families. In this chapter, three purposes meet. The first is to help the reader unfamiliar with Lost Cove have some sense of the families who lived there. Then, the reader will discover where some residents are buried, and where some live today.

In the article "Family, Land, and Community," Patricia Beaver points out that "kinship and family in the rural mountain community are a highly valued and central part of life."[2] To Lost Cove residents, kinship and family bound together by place and land connected each individual. As Eller once wrote,

> Land held a special meaning that combined the diverse concepts of utility and stewardship. While land was something to be used and developed to meet one's needs, it was also the foundation of daily existence giving form to personal identity, material culture, and economic life. As such, it defined the "place" in which one found security and self-worth. Family, on the other hand, as the central organizing unit of social life, brought substance and order to that sense of place. Strong family ties influenced almost every aspect of the social system, from the primary emphasis upon informal personal relationships to the pervasive egalitarian spirit of local affairs. Familism, rather than the accumulation of material wealth, was the predominant cultural value in the region, and it sustained a life-style that was simple, methodical, and tranquil.[3]

In Lost Cove the relationship between families centered on kinship. The ideal settlement, with plush rolling hills and bountiful trees, strengthened their ties to land and place. These determined families sought a meaningful life, full of stability, connectedness, individualism, and culture. Families shaped families. The spiritual and emotional growth encountered strife and hardships, yet these families survived through thick and thin. Their sense of place and individuality allowed them to survive, even though the outside world interfered with their lives. I hope the reader understands why Lost Cove was "their land," and "their home." The families always wanted to return; they believed they would once again live a sustainable and resilient life in the settlement. The families listed below are those that lived in Lost Cove at some point.

The Baileys

There were many Bailey families living in Lost Cove throughout the years. The families were the first to enter and the last to leave the settlement. Almost every man worked as a farmer, dedicating his life to working the land, tending crops, sustaining apple orchards, working the mills, and raising animals for food. Their simple yet significant life in the Appalachian Mountains provides a glimpse of the bond between land and family.

Stephen Morgan Bailey was a farmer. The family tale states that he bought Lost Cove with a rifle and $10 bill from a Native American. According to the 1860 Agricultural Census in Yancey County, North Carolina, Morgan produced Indian corn, tobacco, peas, and potatoes and had dairy cows, working oxen, and swine.[4] When Bailey entered Lost Cove, he brought his wife, Rebecca Deyton, with him. North Carolina's 1860 census records list Morgan and Rebecca's children as Cordelia (11), Joseph Mannon (9), Sarah Ann (6), Wilson C. (5), and Zeb V. Bailey (1).[5] The 1880 Yancey County census lists Morgan Bailey (55) and wife Rebecca (53), along with son John Wesley (18), and daughters Louvadia (14), Martha (7) and Mary (6), as residents of Ramsey Township. ("Louvadia" was actually Lovada, named after Morgan's mother.) While it is reported that Morgan and Rebecca had seven children, the census records show that eight children were accounted for by 1880. The older children of Morgan and Rebecca— Cordelia, Joseph, Sarah Ann, Wilson, and Zeb—are not mentioned in the 1880 census. They all would have been in their twenties by 1880.

Cordelia is listed as the oldest of Bailey's children. In the 1860 census she is 11 years old. Her estimated date of birth is 1848. She is 22 years old in the 1870 census and lives in Poplar, North Carolina, along with her father, mother, and siblings. Records indicate that she used Mary as her first name instead of Cordelia in the 1870 census. Information discovered shows that Cordelia married John Smith of Mitchell County. The 1940 census records indicate that she then lived with her sister, Lovada, and her son Simpson in Bradshaw Township. Further research shows that Cordelia died on January 18, 1941, from apoplexy, a stroke. Mr. W.L. Byrd signed as informant on her death certificate. The record indicates she was a widow and 88 years of age.[6] Joseph, the second oldest child, moved to Tennessee during his life.

Joseph was born around 1849. The Yancey County census records of 1850 state he is one year old. The exact date of birth is not known. The 1870 census list Joseph as 20 years old and living in Poplar with his family. By 1880, Joseph is not listed in North Carolina census records. He would have been around 30 years of age. Joseph moved to Unicoi County between 1880 and 1900. In 1900 the Tennessee census shows Joseph as head of household in Unicoi County. He is listed as Manning Bailey (53) and is married to Jane (47). They have three children: Anna Liza (13), Morgan (10), and John Wesley (6). Manning and Jane Morris married on December 20, 1879, at the Unicoi County Courthouse. The matrimony was witnessed by J.C. Roberts and signed by the Unicoi County clerk, J.B. Erwin. Joseph Mannon (Manning) Bailey died on May 28, 1920, at the age of 70. He was buried in Martin's Creek Cemetery on the south end of Unicoi County, known as the Lilly Dale Community. Jane was buried in the cemetery as well. The graves are unmarked.

Two children—Sarah Ann and Wilson C.—can't be accounted for after 1870. There are no marriage or death certificates to be found. The 1870 census put Sarah Ann Bailey at 17 years old. Sarah, along with her mother and father, lived in Poplar, North Carolina. Her estimated year of birth is 1853. If she married someone, her last name would have changed, making it harder to track down information about her life after 1870. Wilson C. Bailey is 16 years old in 1870. His year of birth is 1854 or 1855. Wilson's information is not found in any war documents including pensions and enlistments. Wilson may have used his middle name in later census records. In the 1870 census, there were three more children listed with Morgan and Rebecca: Zebulan (Zebulon Vance), 14; John W., 10; and Lovada, age four.

Zebulon's estimated year of birth is around 1856. While the 1860 census states that he is one year old, he should have been four at the time of the census. There are no records of Zeb in the 1880 North Carolina census. He is documented in the 1900 census, living then in Ramsey Township in Yancey County. Zeb married Hannah Jane Wilson around 1875. In the 1900 census he is listed along with wife Hannah and six children: William (18); Morgan (16); Jane (14); Peggie (12), whose her first name was Maggie; Calvin (9), whose first name was John; and Sam Bailey (6).[7] Zeb is listed as a farmer. He is listed in the 1920 census in North Carolina also. By 1940, Zeb and his family had moved to Unicoi County. Zeb was buried alongside his wife in Martin's Creek Cemetery in Unicoi County. Zeb and Hannah lived with their son Sam and his family. Zeb was buried in the same cemetery as his brother, Joseph Manning (Mannon). Hannah died in 1947 at the age of 83. Zeb died in 1950 at the age of 93. While he lived in Yancey County, it is safe to say that he lived in the Lost Cove area. Some of his children were buried in North Carolina and some in Unicoi County.

According to the 1880 census, John Wesley Bailey was 18 years old; his estimated year of birth is 1862. In the census he was listed as Wesley and as living in Yancey County with his father and mother. His younger sisters Louvadia (Lovada), Martha and Mary were also living in the house. Wesley was a laborer. His brother Joseph Mannon named his son after John; the two have the exact same name. There are no records indicating if John Wesley ever married or when he died. Research conducted shows no indication of his residence in the early 1900s.

Louvadia (Lovada) was 14 years old at the time of the 1880 census. Her estimated date of birth is 1865 or 1866. Lovada lived in Poplar Township in 1900. Research shows that she married Samuel Johnson of Mitchell County. She was widowed and had four children: Simpson, Robert, Peter, and Millard. There are no other records indicating her marriage to Samuel or any death records. Lovada lived with Simpson, her oldest son, in 1930. They resided in Mitchell County in Bradshaw Township. In 1940 she was 73, and her sister Cordelia Smith lived with her and Simpson. Cordelia Mary Bailey Smith was the oldest of Morgan and Rebecca's children; in 1940 she was 86.[8]

Information on the two youngest children, Martha and Mary, is scarce. While both girls lived with their parents in Poplar, North Carolina, at the time of the 1880 census, there are no records on their marriages or where they may have lived and no death certificates. In 1880, after the census records were documented, Rebecca Deyton Bailey died at the age of 53. She was buried next to her husband Morgan in an unmarked grave in the Bailey Cemetery in Relief, North Carolina. After Rebecca's death, Morgan married Susan Catherine Weatherman. Morgan and Susan never had any children together. Morgan died on April 1, 1889, and was buried in the Yellow Jacket John Bailey Cemetery in Relief next to Rebecca, his first wife. His second wife, Susan, was buried in Wickliffe Cemetery in Salina, Oklahoma.

Morgan Bailey and Rebecca are in the family cemetery next to his father and mother, John and Lovada Bailey. The cemetery is located near the Toe River. The cemetery is secluded and sits high on the mountainside. The only marker is a white sign that sits near the road. No cars can climb the trail. The cemetery dates back to the Civil War and was restored by descendants of John Yellow Jacket Bailey in 2002. The cemetery has a wrought iron fence surrounding the graves. The cemetery is sloped, and years of erosion have exposed the tombstones to deterioration. There are at least 27 graves at the site. John and Lovada's stone reads:

> Here lie Yellow Jacket John Bailey, son of Ansel and Elizabeth Bradley Bailey, pioneer from Little Kings Creek in Wilkes Co. now Caldwell, and wife Lovada "Lovey" Ray, daughter of Hiram and Elizabeth Cox Ray.
> In 1834 he deeded 100 acres to the commissioners and created the county of Yancey. Bailey Square in Burnsville is named after him. Their children Elmira Honeycutt, Ansel (to GA), Martha "Patty" Tipton Cooper, Hiram (to TN), Morgan (B. here), Rev. Garrett (to TN), Thomas (B. here), John, Margaret "Peggy" Tipton, Temperance "Tempy" Hughes Bennett, Lovia Louisa Briggs (to TN), Jefferson (Union Soldier), Martin Luther (D. young), Addison Crusoe (D. young), Elizabeth Bryant, Liza Jane (B. here, D. young), Calvin, Aaron, Sarah Garland (to GA), Curtis are buried alongside them in the cemetery, along with other family members, for a total of at least 27 graves.[9]

Morgan Bailey's children lived in Lost Cove throughout the years. The earliest accounts indicate that some of the children resided in Lost Cove even after Morgan and Rebecca passed away. Through the years Lost Cove men were farmers and laborers in Ramsey Township, which includes Lost Cove and Poplar. One of the earliest accounts of grandchildren living in the cove comes from William Bailey and wife Jettie.

William N. Bailey, the son of Zebb Bailey, grandson to Morgan Bailey, owned a general store in Poplar, North Carolina, just south of Lost Cove. He married Jettie Hedrick in 1901 in Yancey County. Jettie was the daughter of Mack Daniel and Sarah Adkins Hedrick. Her family lived in Lost Cove during the early years. William and Jettie had eight children: Velmer (1902–1997), Chester (1903–2002), Elva (1906–1994), Harley (1909–1986), Walter (1913–1918), John Orville (1917–1992), Britt (1918–1940), and Augusta, whose birth and death is unknown. William was also a logger, and Jettie ran the general store. When William died in February 1919 of typhoid, Jettie sold the general store and moved to Lost Cove because some of William's brothers lived there. William was buried in the Bennett-Barnett cemetery in White Oak Flats,

"Yellow Jacket" John Bailey Cemetery (2020). Photograph by the author.

North Carolina. William's father, Zebb, son of Morgan, and mother, Hannah Wilson Bailey, were buried in Erwin, Tennessee, at Martin's Creek Cemetery. This cemetery is one of the oldest cemeteries in Erwin.

According to the 1920 census for Ramsey Township, Jettie was living in Lost Cove with seven children. One of her children, Walter, is not mentioned in the census. Instead the name Augustis is listed. There are always discrepancies dealing with census records. Chad Bailey, son to Hosea and grandson to Velmer, William and Jettie's oldest child, Augusta and Elva were the only girls born to the couple. The children of William and Jettie were prominent leaders in Lost Cove throughout the years and until its demise.

Velmer Bailey, the oldest, was born on March 19, 1902, in White Oak Flats, North Carolina. The community sets along the Pisgah National Forest on the back side of Lost Cove, close to the Sioux community in North Carolina and the Spivey Mountain community in Tennessee. Velmer was a carpenter by trade and a deacon as well. He married Servilla Harris in October 1931 in Erwin, Tennessee. The Reverend Ealy Billings conducted the ceremony. They both lived in Lost Cove, where Velmer often preached at the Mountain View Free Will Baptist Church. He also logged during his days in Lost Cove as well as farmed. Velmer was known to have the best apple orchard in Lost Cove. His apple trees produced apples even into the early 2000s in the cove. Schoolteachers would often stay in his and Servilla's home during their week of teaching at the school, which was also the church.

Stephen Morgan Bailey tombstone (2020). Photograph by the author.

Velmer and his family were the last to leave Lost Cove. Velmer left the inscription on the wall behind the pulpit of the church/school: *School closed forever at Lost Cove, December 17, 1957. Sinclair Conley, 75 years old. Last revival conducted by Clyde Fender, November 1956. Last Sunday school, November 26, 1957. Very sad.*[10] The family walked out of Lost Cove on January 1, 1958. The family moved to the Lamar community in Washington County, Tennessee. Velmer and Servilla had seven children who grew up in Lost Cove: Okie (1932–2005), William (1934–1934), Earl (1935–1935), Eugene (1938–1997), Isaiah (1940–), Hosea (1944–), and Priscilla (1945–).

Servilla died on August 25, 1995, in Jonesborough, Tennessee. Velmer died on March 24, 1997, just five days after his 95th birthday. They both were buried in the Maple Lawn Cemetery in Jonesborough, Tennessee. Okie Bailey, the oldest child, died on August 19, 2005, in Au Gres, Michigan. He was married for 52 years to Helen and had three children: Teresa Agan, Darrell, and Ron. Both William and Earl Bailey were buried in Lost Cove Cemetery; they died the same day they were born. Eugene Bailey died on May 10, 1997, in Jonesborough, Tennessee. Eugene married Janevieve and had three sons: Victor, Christopher, and Timothy. Isaiah Bailey resides in Erwin, Tennessee, along with his family. Isaiah married Nellie Lynn Barnett on September 16, 1960. They have a daughter, Angela. Hosea married Linda, and they have twins, Chad and Brad. They live in Jonesborough, Tennessee. Priscilla Bailey Knode, the youngest of the children, resides in Jonesborough as well. The photos of children in this book are provided by Chad Bailey, son of Hosea Bailey.[11]

Chester and Carrie Tipton Bailey had two daughters and one son-in-law. Chester was a carpenter and employed by the Clinchfield Railroad. He worked on the railroad during the Lost Cove years. Since there was a side rail at the bottom of the Lost Cove entrance from the railroad, Chester, as well as other Lost Cove men, worked the rails from Erwin to Poplar for the Clinchfield. He and Carrie Tipton were married on March 24, 1923, in Unicoi, Tennessee. After leaving Lost Cove, Chester and his family made Erwin their home in 1955. Their daughter Hazel and her husband, Clifford Miller, live in Erwin, and Virginia Dare "June" Bryant moved to Lapeer, Michigan. Chester was a member of Unaka Springs Free Will Baptist Church. His wife, Carrie, passed away on December 22, 1993. Chester died on December 29, 2002, and he and Carrie were both buried in the Evergreen Cemetery in Erwin, Tennessee. While Velmer and Chester were two prominent men in Lost Cove and in this book, there were other children of William and Jettie who lived in the cove as well.

Elva married Joel Worth Tipton, a native of Poplar, North Carolina. Joel was the son of Joseph and Biddie Cooper Tipton. His family resided in Mitchell County. Elva and Joel lived most of their married life in Erwin, Tennessee. They were married on February 10, 1923, when Elva was 19. They had five children: Leonard, Barbara, Betty, J.R., and Lynda Tipton. This information was provided by Gale Ratliff, granddaughter of Elva. Joel passed away in 1981 at the age of 88. Elva passed away in 1994 at the age of 87.[12] Both were buried in Evergreen Cemetery in Erwin, Tennessee.

Harley Bailey was born in Lost Cove on April 9, 1909. He married Mamel (Mabel) Tipton on April 28, 1930, in Unicoi at the age of 21. Wiley and Hester Tipton, Mamel's parents, were in attendance at the ceremony. The Reverend James Deyton officiated.[13] Mamel (Mabel) is the oldest child of Wiley and Hester. Harley and Mamel both grew up in Lost Cove. Her parents were one of the earliest families in the cove. Joseph Bailey, grandson of Harley and Mamel and great nephew to Velmer, provided detailed information on Harley's life. The pair had three children: Louise, Edwin Yates, and Dean Bailey. Louise and Dean were born in Tennessee, while Edwin's birth was in North Carolina. The family lived in Unicoi County but returned to Lost Cove in the early 1930s before Edwin was born. Edwin was the only child of theirs born in Lost Cove. Edwin Yates Bailey was born April 20, 1933. Harley and his family lived in the cove for several years. As a child, Edwin and his family took the trains to Erwin to shop and visit family and friends.[14] By 1940, the family moved back to Erwin before Dean's birth. The 1940 census lists Dean as one year old.

After moving to Erwin, Harley worked at the Spar Mill Road mica grinding mill under the Erwin Feldspar Corporation. He ran machinery that ground down rocks from the mines in North Carolina. Harley and Mamel (Mabel) were buried in Evergreen Cemetery. Harley passed away in January 1986 at the age of 76. Mamel passed away in March 1999 at the age of 88. Their oldest child, Louise, married Kenneth Adkins and resides in Erwin. The couple has one child: Judy Adkins Sorenson. Edwin married Jennie Lee Witcher in Erwin. The couple has three children: Joseph, James, and Terry. The Reverend E.Y. passed away at the age of 80 on May 16, 2013. Jennie

Velmer Bailey family walking back from church: Hosea, Velmer, Priscilla, Servilla, Isaiah, and Eugene (1952). Courtesy of Chad Fred Bailey.

Six. Families 107

Lee still lives in the couple's homestead on Chestoa Pike. The youngest child, Dean (Roland) Bailey, lives in Erwin and is married to Linda.

John Orville Bailey was two years old according to the 1920 North Carolina census. His estimated year of birth is 1917. The 1930 census records show no evidence of John Orville or his mother Jettie in either North Carolina or Tennessee. He would have been 13 at the time. Research does show that Jettie still lived in Lost Cove during the 1930s and until her death in 1948. Tennessee marriage records show that on March 26, 1939, John Orville married Bertha Lee Norton in Unicoi County. John Orville was 22 years old at the time of his marriage. The county clerk, J.T. Chandler, signed the document, and the Reverend Stephen O. Redacre presided over the ceremony.[15] The pair had two sons and two daughters: John, Dan, Margaret Bennett, and Faye Foster. John Orville died on November 27, 1992, after a lengthy illness in Unicoi County. He was 75 years old. John was a World War II navy veteran and retired from General Motors in Michigan after 30 years of service. He went to church at Riverview Baptist Church in Erwin, Tennessee.[16] John was buried in the Roselawn Memorial Park in Carter County, Tennessee.

While some of William and Jettie's children lived long lives, several of the children died at early ages. Walter Bailey was born in 1913 and died at the age of five. Records indicate that he died from lobar pneumonia on September 20, 1918. S.J. Cooper witnessed the death certificate in Relief, North Carolina. Walter was buried in the Bennett Cemetery in the Upper Pigeon Roost area of Mitchell County.[17] Jettie and Britt are listed in the 1940 census records for North Carolina. They lived in Lost Cove in 1940, and Jettie was 52 while Britt was 22. Lloyd Bailey's book says that Britt was 21 when he died. Birth records are always estimated; Britt's birth should be around 1918. This article provides at least a suggested date for when Britt was born. There are plaques in Lost Cove Cemetery with Britt's and Jettie's names on them. Also buried in the cemetery was Augusta "Gustie" Bailey Tipton.

Augusta Bailey's date of birth is unknown. There are several discrepancies within the census records during the 1930s. Judging from census records, marriage certificates, and Augusta's burial in Lost Cove, it seems she

Family photograph: Velmer and Servilla holding Priscilla with Isaiah, Hosea, and Eugene (1940s). Courtesy of Chad Fred Bailey.

did marry George Tipton in Unicoi County on April 7, 1934. George was 26 years old, and Augusta's age is not shown on the marriage certificate. The county clerk, J.T. Chandler, signed the certificate and the Reverend H.T. Wright held the ceremony.[18] The pair had two children during their marriage: Hillard and Shirley Jean. Augusta died sometime before 1940. The 1940 census for Unicoi County lists George and both his children. He was widowed and lived with his father, Sam, and mother, Sarah. George was 33 years old. Augusta was buried in the Lost Cove cemetery. A small tin plaque displays her name. George was buried in the Evergreen Cemetery in Erwin. After Augusta passed away, he went on to marry Myra Emma Walker, his second wife, in 1941.[19] Their oldest child Hillard lived in the cove until the age of 20. He worked for the sawmill and drove a

Servilla and Priscilla (1952). Courtesy of Chad Fred Bailey.

Hosea and Isaiah Bailey on front porch steps (1952). Courtesy of Chad Fred Bailey.

truck for his uncles. Hillard left the cove in 1955 and moved to Detroit to work for General Motors. He married Lois Ann Bradford in 1987. He returned to Erwin after he retired. He died in 2001 at the age of 66. He was buried in the Roselawn Memorial Park in Carter County. His daughter Shirley Jean may have married Joseph B. Stout, but no other information is found.

The Bailey family remains the most prominent family in Lost Cove. Generations of family members resided in the cove from its inception to the end. Morgan Bailey found a piece of heaven above the Toe and Nolichucky rivers. His children, grandchildren, and great grandchildren survived and thrived in the isolated mountains for decades. Their resilient nature and love of land enabled generations to experience life in a community untouched by chaos and outsider persuasions.

The Tiptons

The second of the prominent families living in the cove were the Tiptons. Documents indicate that some family members were distillers and farmers. Wiley, Jr., and Isabel—Isabella Whitson Tipton—were farmers, and Wiley also preached as a Free Will Baptist minister in Mitchell and Yancey counties. John D. was the oldest child, and he had five younger siblings: David, Margaret, Sidney, Camilla E., and Sarah A. John D. and David were born in Kentucky, while their siblings were born in North Carolina. Before 1860, Wiley and Isabel moved to Yancey County because her parents lived there. By 1860, records show, his siblings included Cozey, Harrison, and Marcus.[20] Their children and some of their grandchildren lived in the cove until the 1950s. Their first child, John, became a well-known figure within the community and beyond.

According to the 1860 census, John was 24 years old and a farmer in North Carolina. He was married to Mary Caroline Peterson Tipton, who was 22. Caroline's estimated year of birth is 1838. They married on January 19, 1860, in Yancey County, and clergyman Samuel Hensley officiated.[21] John and Caroline lived close to his parents in the Red Hill Township. Caroline's parents, the Reverend Moses and Mary McKinney Peterson, lived in Jacks Creek Township in Yancey County. The Reverend Moses helped form Free Will Baptist churches in the mountains of western North Carolina. John and Caroline welcomed their first son, Moses, named after Caroline's father, in 1860.

When John entered the North Carolina Third Mountain Infantry in 1864, he, along with Morgan Bailey, began a new journey of life in the North Carolina mountains. Their regiment traveled through eastern Tennessee and western North Carolina, raiding Confederate posts and camps. John was gone when Caroline gave birth to their second son, Wiley. They named their son after John's father and grandfather. Caroline raised both boys in Lost Cove along with the Bailey families.

By 1880, the Yancey County census for the Ramsey Township district, in which the community of Lost Cove was located, listed John D. Tipton (42) as a distiller and his wife, Caroline Peterson Tipton (42), as keeping house. The Tiptons had six sons and one daughter listed: Moses (20), laborer; Wiley (16), laborer; Sidney (14); Thomas (10); Lawson (10); Doctor Landon (Dokter) (7); and Naomi (3), the youngest.[22] We know that John and Caroline lived in Lost Cove during the 1880s.

In Lloyd Bailey's book, Lost Cove's church is called Tipton's Chapel during the 1880s, but evidence through deeds shows that John did not acquire land in Lost Cove until 1902. There is evidence that John sold 50 acres of land close to Lost Cove to Reuben Peterson. Peterson paid $80 for the land. The land, which lay close to Peterson's store in Poplar, was Ansel Bailey's old tract and ran near the Johnson and Cooper lines. The church name could derive from Wiley Tipton, John's father, since he lived near John and Caroline, and he was a clergyman. Did John's father and family already live in the cove? Many believe that John came into the cove because of Morgan Bailey's insistence. John's occupation as distiller kept him traveling through the mountains even after his service ended with the infantry. Many documents portray him as the "Hermit of Lost Cove," due to him evading the law continuously and his well-hidden stills.

John and Caroline were buried side by side in Lost Cove Cemetery. Caroline passed away on December 25, 1910, at the age of 73. John died on May 14, 1920, at the age of 82, yet he could have been older. According to the death certificate, John died from cystitis or prostatitis, conditions characterized by chronic pelvic pain and urinary symptoms that affect the bladder or prostate.[23] Thomas Tipton was the informant. Caroline's death isn't documented in any death records. Some of their children stayed in Lost Cove and raised their own families, while others moved away to neighboring Erwin.

Moses was born on January 22, 1860. He married Linda Jane Justice on May 16, 1894, at the age of 34 in Yancey County. Linda (Lindy) was 23, and the ceremony was administered by minister E. Peterson. Three people witnessed the marriage.[24] Linda was the daughter of Jacob and Rebecca Roberts Justice of Bee Log, North Carolina. The community lies just 24 miles from Lost Cove. Linda's date of birth was June 7, 1871. Census records show that Moses and Linda lived in Poplar in Mitchell County during the 1910s. They had one child, John Russell, who was born on November 9, 1903. By 1920 the family had moved to Erwin, Tennessee. Moses was 59 and Linda 50. Their son John, named after his grandfather, was 16. Little detail is given on Moses' occupation as a salesman and life in Erwin. On the other hand, his death certificate provides specific details about his demise.

Moses was buried in Erwin, Tennessee, at the Tipton cemetery #3. He died on July 23, 1924, at the age of 64. His death certificate shows that Moses, a merchant, died from a knife wound that he received in a fight with a drunken man.[25] Dock Landon Tipton, Moses' brother, is named as informant. While the death certificate doesn't state who killed Moses, the Find a Grave website says that his brother, Thomas, killed him. While there are no documents to support this claim, he did die from a knife wound during a fight. Geneva Tipton's daughter Camille Flett states that her mother told her that Moses died at the hands of a Webb man.[26] His wife, Linda Jane, was buried in Martin's Creek Cemetery in Erwin, Tennessee. She passed away in 1955. Moses and Linda's son John Russell joined the Company K Infantry in Tennessee. John Russell was buried in the Golden Gate National Cemetery in San Mateo County, California. He died at the age of 63 on March 16, 1967.[27]

John and Caroline's second son, Wiley Tipton, was born on May 30, 1864. John joined the North Carolina mounted infantry less than one month after Wiley's birth. According to the census, in 1880 he was 16 years old and a laborer. He lived in Lost Cove with his parents. In the summer of 1893, Wiley married his first wife, Margarett Bennett. Justice of the Peace C.R. Byrd married the couple in Yancey County. The couple had two witnesses, a Mr. Whitson and Sal Hughes.[28]

Margarett was the daughter of Archibald and Vianna Tipton Bennett from Ramsey Township. Sometime before 1899, Wiley and Margarett either divorced or she died. There are no records that indicate either. Wiley did go on to marry a second wife.

He married Hester Price Tipton on December 17, 1899, at the county clerk office in Erwin, Tennessee. W.S. Tucker issued the marriage license.[29] Hester Price's date of birth is said to be July 2, 1881, but her tombstone gives the year 1879. Some documents estimate her date of birth as 1884 as well. Hester's birthplace is said to be Erwin, yet there are no records indicating her parents' names. In 1900, the married couple lived in Erwin, but they moved to Lost Cove before 1910. The 1910 census records incorrectly indicate that Wiley and Hester had five children, when they actually had four: Maggie (9), Isaac (7), Carrie (5), and Grace (1). Maggie and Carrie were born in Tennessee, while Isaac and Grace were born in North Carolina. The pair also had a hired boy in the household. His name was Wilson Adkins, and he was 19 years of age in 1910; he may account for the "fifth" child noted by the census. Census records indicate that Wilson's occupation as driving a team and working on his own account under the Tipton household, but in 1920 Wilson Adkins was not listed with Wiley Tipton's family. There are no records indicating his residence, marriage, or death.

The 1920 census for Yancey County (Ramsey Township) shows that Wiley was 56 years of age and Hester 39, and notes that they had seven children, four girls and three boys: Madge or Maggie (19), Isaac D. (17), Carrie (14), Grace (10), Mabel also named Mamel (8), Russell (5), and Everett (1). The census records do not document three additional children: Callie, Nola, and Kenneth. This is due to Callie's death at one year old and Nola's death at two years of age, before the 1920 census. Callie was buried at Unaka Springs Cemetery in Erwin, Tennessee, near her mother, Hester. No records indicate her cause of death. Her sister, Nola, died at two years and eight months due to amyloid liver disease. Nola was buried in Lost Cove Cemetery.[30] Kenneth was born in 1922, so he would not have been counted in the census.

Wiley and Hester owned over 100 acres in Lost Cove, land that his father had deeded to him. Their eldest, Madge, married Hampton L. Woodby on March 7, 1921, in Unicoi County. She was 21 years old. Hampton Woodby was a World War I veteran. The 1930 census records do not list Madge and Hampton together. Her father, Wiley, and mother, Hester, had four children living with them in 1930, along with Madge (Maggie) and three of her children. They all lived in Lost Cove. Four years after the census, Wiley died at the age of 67. He was buried in Lost Cove Cemetery next to his mother and father. The death record states that he died from unknown causes on October 6, 1934.[31] Hester lived for 38 more years. She died in 1972. She was buried at Unaka Springs Cemetery in Erwin. Madge and Hampton moved to

Colorado by 1940. They had four children: Helen, J.E., Mildred, and Madlyn. Madge died in 1998 at the age of 97. She was buried in the Rock Island National Cemetery in Rock Island, Illinois. Her husband, Hampton, was buried in the Mountain Home National Cemetery in Johnson City, Tennessee.[32]

Isaac D., born on November 11, 1902, was the second child of Wiley and Hester. The 1930 census records do not show Isaac in North Carolina. Records indicate that he may have moved to Erwin by 1930. Research shows that Isaac may have married Maggie Bennett Tipton in Erwin around 1930. They both are listed in the 1930 and 1940 Unicoi County census on the Asheville Highway. Records indicate that he worked in the pottery industry. Their marriage lasted 13 years before Maggie died in 1943. The death certificate lists Isaac Tipton as informant and Maggie's parents as Charles I. Bennett and Julia Boone Bennett. He remained in Erwin for a while until he moved to Florida. Isaac D. married his second wife, Juanita Ambrose Tipton, on April 5, 1987.[33] He was 85 years old when he married Juanita. Isaac died on March 6, 2000, at the age of 97 in Jacksonville, Florida. His obituary says that he retired from the International Brotherhood of Operative Potters. His second wife, Juanita, died in 1996. Both were buried in the Evergreen Cemetery in Erwin.

Carrie married Chester Bailey in Unicoi County on March 24, 1923. Chester grew up in Lost Cove. He was the son of William and Jettie Hedrick Bailey and great-grandson to Morgan Bailey. They lived in Unicoi County at the time of the 1930 census, but moved to Lost Cove due to the Depression. With many family members living in the cove, their family was taken care of by relatives. The couple had two children, Hazel and Virginia. Hazel was 17 in 1940 and Virginia was 14. Hazel met her future husband, Clifford, in Lost Cove. They married in 1941. Clifford was the son of John and Hulda Webb Miller. Clifford and Hazel moved to Erwin after their marriage. Hazel and Clifford had three daughters and one son. Clifford passed away in 2012 at the age of 95. Hazel still lives in their home on Chestoa Pike.

Carrie and Chester's youngest daughter, Virginia "June" Bryant, was born on March 16, 1926, in Erwin. She married Harvey T. Bryant in Spartanburg, South Carolina, in 1944. Virginia and Harvey moved to Michigan. The couple had two children, Joan and Harvey. Joan married Joe Maas, and they had two children. Harvey married Bonnie, and they had two children. Harvey Sr. died in 1987 in Michigan. Virginia died on August 23, 2017, at the age of 91. The couple were buried in Flint, Michigan. Hazel and Virginia's parents were buried in Evergreen Cemetery. Carrie died in 1993 at the age of 88. Chester died in 2002 at the age of 99.

Grace was born in 1909. In 1920 she was 10 years old. Grace grew up in Lost Cove until she moved to Erwin. On December 7, 1927, she married William Clifton (Bill) Britt in Unicoi County. The Reverend Zeb Ledford presided over the ceremony. Grace was 18 and Bill was 21.[34] Bill was the son of Frank and Dorah (Dora) Price Britt of Erwin. He was my great-grandmother Alice Britt Johnson's brother. At the time of the 1930 census, the couple had one child, Betty Jo (1). By 1940 the pair lived in Newell, West Virginia, and a lodger, Harvey Chitwood, lived with them. Bill and Harvey were both listed as garage mechanics. The records do not mention Betty Jo. She lived in Unicoi County with her grandparents Frank and Dora when the 1940 census was taken. She was 11 years old.

When they moved home, Bill became an auto mechanics teacher at Unicoi County High School in the late 1940s. Grace and William divorced at some point. Research shows no death certificate or gravestone for Grace M. Tipton Britt. She may have remarried later. William married his second wife, Edna Bowling, and had one son. Bill died on June 22, 1998, at the age of 92. He was buried in Jobe Cemetery in Erwin. Grace and William's daughter Betty Jo Britt Barber lives in Cumming, Georgia. She is 90 years old.

Mabel (Mamel) Tipton was 18 years old according to the 1930 Yancey census. She still lived with her father and mother in the cove. In April she married Harley Bailey in Erwin. Harley was the brother of Chester, and son of William and Jettie Bailey. The couple resided in Lost Cove during the 1930s. Her father, Wiley, died in 1934. Mamel helped her mother tend to the farm and home. The couple left the cove in the late 1930s. By 1940 they lived in Unicoi County. Harley worked as a hoister in the spar mill. They had three children: Louise (9), Edwin Yates (6), and Dean or Roland (1). Mamel and Harley were buried in the Evergreen Cemetery.

After Wiley died in 1934, only two children remained in Hester's house: Everett Talmadge and Kenneth Tipton. Everett was 20 years old and Kenneth was 16. Everett was a laborer for the CCC camp. He helped build roads and trails with the Camp Cordell Hull unit in Unicoi at the age of 17. He worked for almost two years and discharged in June 1940. He enlisted in the United States Navy soon after and served aboard the USS *St. Louis*. He served for only six months due to an injury. The Navy discharged him in January 1941. Everett married Thelma Buchanan on March 20, 1943, in Unicoi County. He was 24 years old and she was 19.[35] They moved to Johnson City from Erwin in 1962. They had three children: Russell L., Saundra, and Everett Kyle. Everett died on April 24, 1995, at the age of 75. He and Thelma were buried in the Evergreen Cemetery in Erwin.

Kenneth, the youngest child, lived in Lost Cove in the 1940s with his mother. Born in 1922, Kenneth married Marie Tinker on October 30, 1942, in Washington County, Tennessee, with Joe M. Strother as M.G. (Minister of the Gospel).[36] Marie was the daughter of William and Mae Bell McCoury Tinker. The couple resided in Erwin, Tennessee, and had one daughter, Claudia Marie Tipton Humphries. Kenneth worked for NFS (Nuclear Fuel Services). He passed away on May 20, 1987, at the age of 64. Marie passed away on December 17, 2004. They were buried in Evergreen Cemetery in Erwin.

The third child of John and Caroline, Sidney, born between 1865 and 1867, resided with John and Caroline at the time of the 1900 census in Poplar Hollow Township in Mitchell County. Sidney was named after John's brother. He was 35 years old and listed as a divorcee and day laborer in the household. We know that John purchased land in Lost Cove in 1902. Did Sidney live with them in Lost Cove? By 1910, Sidney was not counted in the census with John and Caroline. There are no documents, neither marriage nor death certificates, on Sidney. The last known document is the 1900 census.

The twins, Thomas and Lawson, are 10 years old according to the 1880 census records in Yancey County. Their estimated year of birth is 1869 or 1870. By 1900 both men are at least 20 and are not living in the household with John and Caroline. In

1910, census records indicate that Thomas Tipton lived in Poplar Hollow and was married with two children. His wife, Julia Edwards Tipton, was 35; his boys, Burnie (Bernie) and Joseph, were 16 and 7, respectively. Thomas worked as a laborer for the railroad.[37] Thomas and Julia married on March 14, 1894, with Mr. Cooper as justice of the peace. Records indicate that Thomas's uncle, Samuel Tipton, and Samuel Bailey were witnesses for the couple.[38] In 1920, the family lived in Ramsey Township, which includes Lost Cove. He was a farmer. They lived in the cove along with his brothers Wiley and Doctor.[39] At some point, the family moved to West Virginia. Thomas worked at a lumber company. Research indicates that Thomas died on August 31, 1946, in McDowell County. Julia (Judie) died in 1927 of tuberculosis in Poplar, where her parents lived. Both of their children, Bernie and Joseph, died in West Virginia. Bernie died in 1964 and Joseph in 1937.

Thomas's twin, Lawson, was named after Caroline's brother. There are no records of Lawson after the 1880 census. Research indicates that he may have lived in Unicoi County in 1900, but no marriage or death records provide further information on Lawson. There was one child that lived in Lost Cove with his children for many years. The sixth child of John and Caroline liked to gamble and distill.

Doctor Landon Tipton is Geneva Tipton McNabb's father. Doctor's date of birth should be around 1873, but other records give his birth date as February 22, 1867. He was seven years old according to the 1880 census records. Dock was a distiller like his father, John. Dock married Usley Hensley Tipton on July 29, 1898, in Unicoi County, with E.W. Akard as minister.[40] Usley was the daughter of Logan Hensley and Elizabeth Tipton. They resided in Erwin during the 1900 census. He lived with his wife, Uslie (Usley), and daughter, Dora B., who was one year old. By 1910, the family moved to Lost Cove. The census indicates that Dora, then 10, had siblings Ethel (9), William R. (6), Joe H. (4), Dockie (Lockie) (2), and Albert (just born). The census indicates that Dora, Ethel, and William were born in Tennessee, while Joe, Dockie (which should be Lockie), and Albert were born in North Carolina. Dock is listed as a farmer.[41] The 1920 census shows that by then three more children had joined the family: Wiley, 7; Edney (Edna), 5; and Jeneva (Geneva), 3. Their grandfather John D. lived with them in Lost Cove, and he was listed as 84 years old. There was also one more person living in the household: Dock's father-in-law, Logan Hensley.

Dock and Usley lived in Lost Cove for many years. Dock farmed his land. Like his brother Wiley, Dock had over 100 acres of land that his father deeded to him. Dock also made moonshine like his father John D. Geneva explains that moonshine kept the family fed when money made from crops couldn't support the family. Dock liked to gamble also, but he always took care of his family. Dock and Usley had one more child, a daughter, on March 1, 1914, but she died the same day. She was buried in Lost Cove Cemetery. No name is given on the death certificate. All of Dock and Usley's children married. Dock worked at a sawmill as a lumberman. He lived in Unicoi County for 15 years before he died. Dock died at the age of 84 on November 25, 1951, of heart failure due to cardiovascular hypertension. Bill Tipton is the informant on the death certificate.[42] Usley passed away on March 4, 1963, from heart failure. Usley was 83 years old. Dora Honeycutt is the informant for the certificate.[43] Dock and Usley were buried in the Evergreen Cemetery in Erwin.

The oldest child, Dora, born in October of 1899, was 21 years old when she married Frank D. Honeycutt in Erwin on July 24, 1920. P.W. Emmert was the justice of the peace for the ceremony.[44] Dora and Frank had three children: Fred, Ruth, and Ralph. Before 1940, the pair divorced, and the three children lived with Dora and her parents, Dock and Usley. Dora was 40 years old, Fred was 18, Ruth 17, and Ralph 14. The family, along with Dora's sister Geneva, lived in Unicoi County. Geneva indicates that the family moved to Unicoi County during the late 1930s. Dora lived with her parents most of her life. She cared for them until the day they died. Dora passed away on July 28, 1972, at the age of 72 and was buried in the Evergreen Cemetery.

The second oldest child, Ethel, was 20 years old at the time of the 1920 census. Her date of birth is April 3, 1901. Her first name is Callie, but census records list her as Ethel as well. There are two entries for her in the 1920 census records: one in the household of her father and mother in Lost Cove and one in the household of Henry Clay Hampton in Unicoi County. They married on May 21, 1918, in Unicoi County. P.W. Emmert was the justice of the peace. Clay was 20 years old and Ethel was 18.[45] By 1930 Ethel and Clay had six children: Opal (11), Ruby (9), Pearl (7), Hallen (5), Gladis (3), and Rex (1). They lived in Unicoi County, and Clay's mother, Annie, lived with them. By 1940, the pair had four more children: Jesse (7), Jean (5), Annalee (3), and Phyllis (1).[46] Clay worked as an oil house manager for the railroad in Erwin. Clay died on July 15, 1957, at the age of 68. He was buried in Evergreen Cemetery. Ethel lived to be 92. She died on January 20, 1994, in Erwin. She was buried next to Clay.

William, Dock and Usley's first son, was born on May 21, 1904. He was 15 at the time of the 1920 census and lived in Lost Cove during his early twenties. In 1935, William (Bill) married Myrtle Riddle Tipton on May 11. The Reverend J.S. Scott held the ceremony.[47] Myrtle was the daughter of Thomas and Eliza Riddle. The couple resided in Unicoi County until their death. The pair never had children. William died on May 17, 1987, at the age of 82. Myrtle died on October 17, 2003, at the age of 93. The pair were buried in Evergreen Cemetery.

Herman Joe Tipton was born on March 23, 1906, in Lost Cove. He was 13 according to the 1920 census. He lived in Lost Cove until the late 1930s with his family. Herman married Suze Belle Phillips in 1930. Belle's family lived in the Ramsey Township. She was the daughter of Samuel Cornelius and Nellie Higgins Phillips. While he lived in Lost Cove, Herman worked for the railroad section gang. In 1940 the couple lived in Unicoi County. They had three sons: Wayne (8), Franklin D. (3), and Ronald (under 1). Herman worked as a foreman at the feldspar mill.[48] The couple had three more children after 1940: Leon, Patricia, and Kyle. Herman passed away on December 20, 1990, at the age of 84. Belle died on March 4, 2004, at the age of 94. They were both buried in Evergreen Cemetery.

The fifth child, Lockie Lee, was 11 years old in 1920. Her date of birth was March 25, 1908. In 1932, she married Victor Banner in Unicoi County. She was 24 years old and Victor was 21. J.S. Scott was the minister.[49] Victor was the son of Benjamin and Sarah Banner. They lived in Erwin and had five children: Aileen and Wahaeetah (Juanita), 6; Harmon, 5; Louise, 3; and Lillian, under one. Victor's mother, Sarah, also lived with them. Victor worked as a laborer at the feldspar plant.[50] They did have three more children after 1940: Jean, Marvin, and Melvin. During their marriage, they moved to

Baltimore, Maryland. Lockie died on March 15, 2005, and was buried next to her husband Victor at the Cedar Hill Cemetery in Baltimore.

Albert Tipton was nine years old in 1920. His date of birth was April 1, 1910, in Lost Cove. By 1930, Albert lived in Rock Lick District in Buchanan County, Virginia. He was 20 years old and lived at the house of Harry F. Ramsey. Albert worked for the railroad as a laborer. He is listed as a boarder along with 17 other people.[51] On August 17, 1935, Albert married Mandy (Amanda) Buchanan in Unicoi County. By the time of the 1940 census, Albert and Mandy had two children, Raymond (2) and Robert (2). He worked at the feldspar plant as a laborer.[52] On October 2, 1943, Albert enlisted into the army. He enlisted at Fort Oglethorpe, Georgia. Albert served two years in the army and was released on August 13, 1945.[53] Albert was buried in the VA Cemetery in Johnson City. He died on January 1, 1983. Amanda passed away on November 30, 2003, and was buried in the Evergreen Cemetery.

Wiley, the youngest son, was born on November 6, 1912, in Lost Cove. He was seven years old in 1920. According to Camille McNabb Flett, Wiley worked for the CCC (Civilian Conservation Corps) along with her father, James McNabb, during the 1930s. Wiley and James were in Company 1461 out of Cosby, Tennessee. The company organized in May 1933 at Fort Oglethorpe, Georgia. Wiley was only 20 years old when he began work for the CCC. He worked as an assistant leader with his company. During their time in the company, Wiley and James worked in Tremont, Tennessee, which helped develop the National Park Service in the Great Smoky Mountains.[54] The camp sits near Meigs Mountain below Lynn Camp Prong Cascades. The company started out with 172 men, and within a year only 58 remained. Wiley and James left the company in 1938.

Wiley entered the army on April 1, 1940, in Honolulu, Hawaii. He enlisted with the 13th Field Artillery at the age of 27.[55] There seems to be a discrepancy about when he actually enlisted. Another document states he enlisted on May 17, 1941, at Fort Oglethorpe, Georgia. His occupation is given as semiskilled blacksmith, forgeman, and hammerman.[56] If Wiley enlisted in Hawaii in 1940, he may have been discharged before he reenlisted in 1941. In November of 1941, Wiley was released from the army. He would return in January 1942 and serve until August 1945. Before Wiley enlisted in 1941, he married Charlotte Ingram in Unicoi County on February 22, 1941. Charlotte's father, Ike Banner, was present, and J.E. Saws presided as the justice of the peace.[57] Charlotte was the daughter of Isaac and Mamie Banner from Unicoi County. Wiley became her second husband. During their marriage, Wiley and Charlotte resided in the Martin's Creek area of Erwin. After the war, Wiley worked for P.C. Cooper Construction as a heavy equipment operator. Wiley and Charlotte never had children together. Charlotte already had three children when they married. Charlotte passed away in 1999. Wiley lived to be 94 years old. He died on March 18, 2007, in Erwin. They both were buried in the Evergreen Cemetery.

The two closest girls of Dock and Usley, Edna Mae and Geneva, would be inseparable in their later years. Edna Mae was born in Lost Cove on May 12, 1915. Edna and the youngest, Geneva, were close. Geneva said Edna often took care of her during their years in Lost Cove. They both had chores, and Edna often aided Geneva. After the family moved to Unicoi County, Edna married John Carl Robbins in Sullivan

County on November 28, 1937. They were married by H.H. Massengill, justice of the peace.[58] He was 35 years old and Edna was 22. John was the son of James Calvin and Omilda Sonora Corvin Robbins of Virginia. John Carl and Edna met in Erwin. According to the 1930 census, he lived in the household of his brother-in-law, James J. Jessie. John and Edna never had children. They lived in Florida during the 1960s, and Edna became a National Shuffle Board Champion and was inducted into the Hall of Fame in 1967. John Carl died in 1971. Edna returned to Erwin and lived next to her younger sister Geneva. Edna died at 101 years old on June 7, 2016. She was the last surviving child of Dock and Usley. She and John were buried in Evergreen Cemetery.

The youngest child, Geneva, was born in Lost Cove on September 8, 1918. Her parents let Doctor Cooper, who delivered her, name her. Geneva loved growing up in the cove. When her family moved to Erwin, Geneva lived with her father and mother and her oldest sister, Dora, and her family. She was 21 years old according to the 1940 census. James H. McNabb is listed as a U.S. Army private in the 1940 census. He was stationed in Sausalito, California. He previously was stationed in the Philippines. He was 26 years old in 1940.[59] On March 8, 1943, Geneva married James Harry McNabb in Unicoi County. Fred Booth, justice of the peace, held the ceremony.[60] James was the son of Robert and Bessie Harris McNabb. He grew up in Erwin. James served in the World War II, and in the Korean conflict as a 1st Lieutenant with the HQ Company 3 Medium Tank Battalion. The couple had three children: Eldora Lee "Pug," James Wiley, and Tammy Camille. Harry died on October 11, 1971, and was buried in the Jobe Cemetery in Erwin. Eldora and Camille both live in Erwin. Geneva lived to be 92 years old. She died on January 11, 2011. She was buried in Evergreen Cemetery. Harry and Geneva's son Jim died on December 21, 2011, after a courageous battle with cancer.

The last child of John and Caroline, Naomi (Omie or Oma), was born on June 26, 1877. In 1880, according to census records, she was three years old. Naomi doesn't appear in the census records in 1900. In 1910, she is listed in the house of Samuel Cooper of Ramsey Township. Naomi (Oma) was 32 years old in 1910, and Samuel was 45. He was 13 years older and was born in 1867. Samuel Cooper was the son of Archibald and Mary Cooper. Naomi was Samuel's second wife. He had two children: Martin and Clarisa. Samuel's first wife, Mary Jane Bennett, died from complications in childbirth with their daughter Clarisa just six months after her birth. Samuel married Naomi Tipton in 1898. The 1900 census records indicate that Sam lived with his two children in Ramsey Township along with his first wife, but Mary Jane died in 1897. Could Jane Cooper be Naomi in the 1900 census? In 1910, deeds acknowledge that Sam and Naomi lived in Lost Cove. The pair had five daughters, two sons, and a hired boy: Martin (17), Clarsey (Clarisa) (13), Zellie or Donzella (12), Moses (10), Hattie (6), Caroline (4), Mary (3), and William Price (20).[61] Sam was a farmer and hired William to help tend his farm and livestock. Even though Sam was a farmer, he distilled moonshine just like Naomi's father, Dock Landon.

The pair lived near Drip Rock Spring, which sits near the southwest line of Lost Cove. By 1920, they lived in Unicoi County and had four more children in the household. Edward (9) and John (7) were born in Lost Cove, while the two youngest, Pansy (5) and George (2), were born in Tennessee. Naomi was 43 years old when she died on February 8, 1921. She was buried in Martin's Creek Cemetery in Erwin. After her death, Sam continued to live in Erwin and raised his children. He was caught in 1924 for distilling whiskey and beer along with Dock Tipton and Perry Hughes. He served four months in the Buncombe County jail. At the time of the 1930 census, his household included the four youngest children: Edward (19), John (17), Pansy (14), and George (12). Also in his household was Dovie (Donzella) Cooper (32), one of his oldest children.[62] She lived in the house so she could help raise her siblings. Sam died on May 31, 1937, in the home of his brother William Cooper. He was buried in Martin's Creek Cemetery. Many of their children—including Private Martin; Clarisa and her husband, Samuel Price; Moses and his wife, Nell Cooper, and son, Theodore; Hattie; Edward; and John D—were buried in the same cemetery. John D's brothers and sisters lived in the cove until they married.

David was the second oldest son of Wiley and Isabel. His estimated year of birth is 1841 or 1842. He was 19 years old according to the 1860 census. David helped his father on the farm. He served in the Civil War with the North Carolina Third Mounted Infantry along with his brother John and Morgan Bailey. David served in Company D with the infantry. In his Civil War documents, David is listed as a deserter beginning in November 1864. The records show that he carried with him one Ballard Rifle when he left.[63] David did return to duty on May 1, 1865. He married Sophrona Caroline Hopson before 1866. She was the daughter of George and Lila Stanley Hopson of Mitchell County. The family lived in Lost Cove before they moved to Bakersville, North Carolina, in the Harrell section. David filed for his pension in June 1882. He and Sophrona had four sons and three daughters: Marion H, James, Emma, Sidney (after his brother), Mack, Theba, and Loretta.[64] The family moved to Roan Mountain before the 1900 census. David died on October 4, 1904. Sophrona (Frona) filed for his pension on her behalf on October 24, 1904. She lived to be 84 years old. Sophrona died on February 5, 1929. The couple were buried in Roan Mountain.

Wiley and Isabel's oldest daughter was Margaret. She was born in 1843 and was 17 years old in 1860. Margaret married John Garland on August 16, 1860, and Samuel Hensley was the Minister. John was the son of William and Rebecca Garland of Yancey County. According to the 1870 census the pair had four children: Wiley, William, Delilah Emeline, and Abby Ann (Isabel). The family resided in the Red Hill District of Mitchell County. John is listed as a farmer.[65] By 1880 the couple had four more children: David, Sidney, Missouri, and Marcus.

There are some discrepancies when the couple is listed in the 1910 census records. Records indicate that they lived in John Phillips and Malissa Garland's home, but they did not have a child named Malissa or Melissa, so these records may be unreliable. Research shows that neither of them appears in the 1910 census as head of household. John Samuel died in 1916 at the age of 81. Margaret passed away only six months later on July 2, 1917, at the age of 73. They both were buried in the Old Garland Cemetery in Red Hill.

The third son of Wiley and Isabel was Sidney. Sidney was born around 1844–1845 in Kentucky. Sidney was 14 years old according to the 1860 census. He was 20 years old when he enlisted in the North Carolina Third Mounted Infantry in Burnsville on June 4, 1864. Records list him as a farmer. He was assigned to Company A in the infantry.[66] After his service, Sidney returned to Lost Cove. He married Lyddey Margaret Bennett on March 4, 1866, in Yancey County.[67] Margaret was the daughter of Uriah and Eliza Deyton Bennett. Margaret may have been related to Rebecca Deyton, Morgan Bailey's first wife. By 1880, Margaret was the head of her own household with children John D., Malissa, and Kinsey Tipton. Records show she was widowed, which could mean they divorced. There is no information on when Sidney died or where he was buried. Margaret married Richard Riddle in 1883. She died in 1907 and was buried in the Bennett-Tipton Cemetery along with son John D.

The second oldest daughter of Wiley and Isabel was Camilla Emeline. Her estimated date of birth is May 15, 1846. Camilla is listed as 12 years old in the 1860 census, but her age would actually have been 14. She married James Lawson Peterson of Jacks Creek when she is around 19 years old. Lawson was the son of the Reverend Moses and Mary Polly McKinney Peterson. According to the 1870 census the couple lived in Jacks Creek and had three children: Charles, Mary, and John D.[68] Lawson was a farmer while Camilla tended to the children and home. By 1880, the pair had added three more children to the home: Margaret, Elizabeth, and Naoma. There should be two more children in the home: Tina Caroline and Mary Lucinda. The couple had five more children before 1894: Moses, Reuben, Minnie, Cora, and Sarah. Before 1920, they moved to Unicoi County. Lawson died in 1923 and Camilla died in 1927. They both were buried in Peterson Cemetery.

Sarah Ann was the third daughter of Wiley and Isabel. She was born around 1849. She was 18 years old when she married Cornelius Nick Bryant in 1867. Nick was the son of Thomas and Sophia Bryant. According to the 1880 census, the couple had five children: Emaline, Samuel, Jane, Sidney, and Missouri. They lived in Red Hill District in Mitchell County. Sarah Ann had two more children: Kimsey and Alice. She died within one year after Alice's birth at the age of 34. She was buried in the Old Garland Cemetery in Red Hill. Nick married Sara Slagle after Sarah Ann's death. He died in 1904 and was buried in the same cemetery.

The youngest daughter was Cozey, also named Kezia or Keziah. Cozey was born around 1853–54. She was seven years old in 1860 and was named after her Aunt Wiley's sister. She was only 18 years old when she married Robert Vance Honeycutt on January 3, 1870, with Mr. Adkins as minister.[69] Vance was the son of Ezekiel and Mira Honeycutt of Jacks Creek. At the time of the 1880 census the couple had five children: Lawson, Elizabeth, Mahle, Margaret, and Mira. By 1900, the pair had three more children: Nora, Ebyan, and Emil. Vance was a farmer and Keziah was a housekeeper. During their marriage, the couple had around 16 to 18 children. Some of the children are mentioned twice, but the couple may have named a new child the same as the sibling if the child passed away at an early age. Other children include Betsy, Elmira, Amy, Hester, Alice, Ancil, Emma, and Clayton. There are two children named Amy and Betsy may be a nickname for Elizabeth but no records confirm. By 1920 the couple lived in Poplar, along with their daughter Emma and her two children. The couple moved to Unicoi County around the 1930s. On January 2, 1932, Keziah died from pneumonia at the age of 77, just one day before she and Robert were to celebrate their 63rd anniversary. Her death certificate gives her name as Kezar rather than Keziah.[70] Robert died on October 20, 1943, from cancer. The couple were buried in the Tipton-Griffith Cemetery in Mitchell County. The youngest two children of Wiley and Isabel were Harrison and Marcus.

Samuel Harrison was born around 1854. He was 16 years old at the time of the 1870 census. He lived in his mother's household, and his brother Marcus lived with them. His father, the Reverend Wiley, died before the 1870 census. Samuel married Martha Anne Garland of Mitchell County before the 1880 census. Martha Ann was the daughter of Chrisenberry and Elizabeth Betsy Whitson Garland. According to the 1880 census, Samuel and Ann had two children: Isabel, named after Samuel's mother, and Charles. Samuel was a farmer. By 1900, the pair had added seven children to the household: Betty, Marcus, Louisa, Christopher, Lawson, James, and Luther. Isabel lived with the family and she was 84 years old. The family lived in Red Hill.[71]

By 1920 Samuel and Ann had only one child in the household along with a daughter-in-law: Lawson and Rettie (Loretta) Beam Tipton. Samuel lived to be 73 years old. He died on February 16, 1928, from pneumonia with a contributory factor of influenza. Samuel was buried in the Tipton Hill Cemetery in Mitchell County.[72] Martha lived five more years and died at the age of 75. She was buried next to her husband. The last child of the Reverend Wiley and Isabel would move to Unicoi County.

Marcus Tipton was born on March 25, 1858. He was 22

Wiley Tipton family: Hester Price Tipton holding Russell, Grace, Mamel, Ike, Carrie, Maggie, and Wiley (1930). Courtesy of Joseph Bailey, son of Harley Bailey and Mamel Tipton.

Front row: Mamel Tipton Bailey and Huldie Miller. Second row: John Miller and Louise Bailey Adkins. Far left: Roland Bailey. Center: Edwin Bailey, ca. 1940s. Courtesy of Joseph Bailey.

years old at the time of the 1880 census, and his mother, Isabel, lived with him and his wife. Marcus married Prudence Massengill in 1879. They had six children by 1900: Ezekiel (19), Samuel (15), George (11), John (9), Sarah (7), and Jane (5). Marcus and his family lived in Red Hill and he was a farmer.[73] Sometime before 1910, Prudence passed away. There is no information on her death. The pair had two more children, Pearl and Gracie, before 1910. When the 1910 census was taken Marcus, now called Mark, was listed in Unicoi County along with his new wife and family. By 1910 Marcus was married to Mary Stanley of Mitchell County. Mary was only 25

Harley Bailey and Mamel Tipton Bailey with Louise, Roland, and Edwin, early 1950s. Courtesy of Joseph Bailey.

Dock Landon Tipton family: Usley pregnant with Geneva, Wiley, Dora, Lockie, Ethel Tipton holding Edna, Bill, Albert, and Herman (1920). Courtesy of Camille McNabb Flett, daughter of Geneva Tipton McNabb.

Dock Landon Tipton family: Ethel, Dock holding Herman, Dora, and Usley holding Bill, ca. 1920s. Courtesy of Camille McNabb Flett.

Dave Tipton and his wife, Zettie (Rosetta) Piercy (1940). Courtesy of Jeff Bryant.

in 1910, while Marcus was 52 years old. Marcus was a farmer while his two sons, George and John, worked at a lumber mill.[74] Marcus died three days after his birthday on March 28, 1938. He was 80 years old and was buried in Martin's Creek Cemetery. Mary would eventually marry her second husband, George Edwards. Mary died in 1962 and was buried next to Marcus. Marcus and Prudence's children married and had their own children. Several moved to Virginia while others stayed in North Carolina and Tennessee. Samuel, the second oldest child of Marcus and Prudence, lived in Lost Cove along with his wife, Sara Jane Beam, and children through the 1920s and 1930s.

Samuel Harrison is named after his uncle and great uncle. He and Sarah Jane had two children recorded in the 1910 census: King David and George. Both of the boys were born in Lost Cove. Sarah was the daughter of William and Harriett Bennett Beam from Mitchell County. By the 1920 census the couple had five more children: John, Ferrell, Sherman, Hobart, and Dock. Samuel and Sarah were home farmers. The couple had four more children after the 1920 census: Mack, Ruby Mae, Robert, and Henry. By 1940 the family lived in Erwin. Sarah died in 1946 from cervical cancer. She was buried in the Erwin Cemetery. Sam married Jane Buchanan and she had one child Chester, from her first marriage. Jane died at the age of 32 in 1947. After she died, Sam married her sister, Sindy. Samuel died on September 15, 1968. He was buried next to Sarah, his first wife. Most of Samuel and Sarah's children were delivered by a midwife in Lost Cove or in Poplar. Their children lived in Lost Cove until they married or decided to move away.

Geneva Tipton McNabb and her husband, Harry (1950). Courtesy of Camille McNabb Flett.

Samuel and Sarah's oldest son, King David, was born on June 20, 1905. David lived in the cove until he married Rosettia (Zettie) Piercy in May 1928. Zettie was the daughter of Herbert and Hattie Bailey Piercy of Limestone Cove. The couple lived in Erwin and had five children in 1940, according to census records: Homer, Juanita, Dixie Lee, Dora Lee, and Lillie. Their first daughter, Magdalene, died at the age of six and was buried in the Erwin Cemetery. During their marriage, the couple had six more children after 1940: David J., Bonnie, Diane, Robert, Ronald, Dorothy, and Darlene. Dave worked for the spar mill as a machine operator. Eventually he worked for the Clinchfield Railroad and retired. Zettie died in 1978 at the age of 67. Dave passed away on October 2, 1984, at the age of 79. The couple were buried in Martin's Creek Cemetery, where many of their relatives from Lost Cove were buried. Their daughter Dixie Lee married J.C. Bryant from Lost Cove. David's brother George lived in the cove for many years and married a Bailey descendent.

The second oldest son, George, was born on March 3, 1907. George married Augusta Bailey in 1934 in Unicoi County. Augusta was the daughter of William and

Jettie Bailey from Lost Cove. The pair was married for only six to seven years before Augusta died. According to the 1940 census, George was 33 years old and lived in Unicoi County with his parents. His two children with Augusta, Hillard and Shirley Jean, also lived in the household. George married Myra Emma Wilson Walker in Tennessee in 1941. The pair lived in Erwin and never had children. George died in 1955 and was buried in the Erwin cemetery. Augusta died before 1940 and was buried in Lost Cove.

The other children of Sam and Sarah's were not born in Lost Cove nor did they reside in the cove. John Calvin was born in Buladean, North Carolina. He married Dorothy Mae Thomas and had five children: Johnny Edward, Steven, Johnny Reb, Janice, and Willa Dean. Ferrell was born in Yancey County. He married Elizabeth Shelton, and the couple had three daughters: Patsy, Nellie, and Betty. Sherman Glenn was born in Poplar, North Carolina, with the help of a midwife. He married Mabel Clara Garland and they lived in Unicoi County. Hobart was only seven years old when he died in 1924. Dock Tipton married Ollie Gillis in 1938. They moved to Maryland after his service in World War II. Mack was born in Poplar and lived in Erwin after his World War II service as a combat infantryman. He married Lillian Hazel Tipton and had two daughters, Doris and Karen.

Ruby Mae was born in Erwin. She married Aaron Jack Frost and had two children: Billie Jean and Magdalene. Robert married Mary Tilson and they had one daughter, Sarah Betty. Henry was the last child of Sam and Sarah. He married Pansy Nadine Edwards in 1950. He served in the army and moved to Oregon.

Generations of the Tipton families lived in Lost Cove from the 1860s through the 1950s. With the Reverend Wiley Tipton and Isabel as the patriarch and matriarch, their children and grandchildren, along with their nieces and nephews, lived in Lost Cove for nearly 80 years. Their eldest child, John D. Tipton, lived in the cove his entire life as a Union soldier, farmer, and distiller. The Tiptons raised their children without ever wanting for anything. The families thrived in the settlement by distilling, working for the railroad, and working in the sawmill. The Tipton family documents will remain secured in the Archives of Appalachia at East Tennessee State University. Their story is finally told through their granddaughter Geneva and other family members.

The Millers

The third prominent family living in Lost Cove was the Millers. The Miller family resided in the Ramsey Township as early as 1860. The patriarch, Hiram Miller, and matriarch, Martha Patsy Bennett, had four sons and one daughter according to the 1880 census: Archable (15), Nancy (13), James (8), Jason (7), and Samuel (6). Their oldest, Archibald (Arch), is the earliest Miller to live in Lost Cove during the early 1900s. There are no deed records in the Yancey County registry that indicate how Arch Miller acquired his Lost Cove land.

Arch Miller married Lucinda (Sinda or Sindy) Hedrick before 1890. There are no marriage records on file. Lucinda Hedrick was the daughter of Mack Daniel Hedrick and Sarah Adkins. Both sets of parents lived in Ramsey Township. Almost every Miller homestead in Lost Cove lay near the schoolhouse and church. Their homesteads were close to the sled road that was used to haul crops to the Poplar store. Arch Miller, his children, and his grandchildren lived in Lost Cove until the community's demise.

In 1900 Arch (28) and Sindy (24) had five children: Robert (9), John (8), Swin (3), Jane (6), and Martha A. (5).[75] By 1910, the pair had added three more children to their family: Samuel (9), Claude (6), and Nathaniel (2). Arch worked as a farmer and raised cattle and crops to support his family. According to 1920 census records, the Miller family also included a grandson named Albert who was over one year old. The 1940 census lists Arch as 75 years old and Sinda as 67. There was one child living in the household with them, Samuel (38). Arch and Sam are listed as farmers. Arch and Lucinda lived in the cove until the day they died. Arch died at the age of 81 on February 12, 1947. Lucinda died on November 30, 1950, at the age of 84. They both were buried in the Lost Cove cemetery. Their oldest son, Robert, became a preacher. He was not in the household at the time of the 1910 or 1920 census. Before 1910, Robert became the head of his own household.

Robert "Bob" Miller was born between 1887 and 1890. He married Emma Bryant Miller on December 6, 1907, in Yancey County. J. Ramsey, a Free Will preacher presided over the marriage. Sam Cooper and Nora Lewis were witnesses at the ceremony.[76] Robert was 20 years old and Emma was 18 when they married. Emma Bryant was the daughter of J. Waitsel Bryant and Naomi (Omie) Tipton. Her mother was not the same Naomi as John and Caroline's child. Naomi was Joseph Tipton and Edith Cooper's daughter.

The couple appears in the 1910 census records along with a son, John, who was one year old. Records indicate that in 1918 Emma had a second child, Causa Irene or Kanza Arline, born on May 31, 1918. At only three months and twelve days Causa Irene died. The death certificate explains that the child had not been in good health since birth. She died on September 13, 1918. The informant and undertaker on the death certificate was J.W. Bryant, Emma's father.[77] By 1920, they had two more children: Carmon (Carmen) (7) and Esta (3). Robert (Bob) worked as a laborer on the railroad section gang along the Toe and Nolichucky rivers. Before the 1930 census, two more children had been added to the family: Samuel (10) and Coolidge (6). The family also had Harley Bryant, Emma's brother, in the household. Harley was 19 and worked at the American Bemberg Corporation in Elizabethton, Tennessee. Robert (Bob) became a preacher sometime before 1930. He once served as a delegate for the Lost Cove Free Will Baptist during the 1910s.

Bob and Emma are listed in Unicoi County in the 1930 census. Sometime after the census, the family moved back to Lost Cove. Emma Bryant Miller died on July 18, 1931, from "recurrent sarcoma in the right inguinal region." She is diagnosed in June 1931 by Dr. R.H. Crawford at Rutherford Hospital, North Carolina."[78] She was 42 years of age and John Miller, her son, was the informant. Emma was buried in Swingle Cemetery in Unicoi. After her death, the reverend returned to Lost Cove.

It was 1934 when the church re-formed after losing its charter in 1919. The members elected the Reverend Bob Miller as their preacher. Bob preached for one year at the Mountain View Free Will Baptist Church before the church members hired the

Reverend W.G. Honeycutt. Some of their children remained in Lost Cove while others moved to Unicoi County.

John David was the oldest child of Robert and Emma. John was born on September 17, 1908. He was named after his mother's father and was born in Lost Cove. John is listed as 11 years old in the 1920 census records for Ramsey Township. Ten years later, he lived in his father's house in Unicoi County. On September 20, 1932, John married Pearl Rebecca Hawkins in Unicoi County. Justice of the Peace J.D. Woodward presided over the ceremony.[79] Pearl was the daughter of Sam and Sallie Hawkins of Unicoi. She was born in High Point, North Carolina, but her family moved to Unicoi before the 1930 census. She was the second oldest daughter and had six siblings. John worked in Elizabethton at the American Bemberg Corporation, the rayon mill. Kris Hawkins Rosalina, niece to Pearl and John, recalled that John built the post office in the town of Unicoi and the couple resided next door to the building through the 1960s.[80]

On June 3, 1940, Pearl had a baby boy named Richard Roy Miller. Richard was born in Elizabethton, Tennessee. On October 16, 1940, just four months after Richard was born, John registered for the service. John was 32 years old when he registered and Alice Buchanan of the Unicoi County Register's office was the signee on his card.[81] Tragedy occurred the following year when Richard died on July 23, 1941, from meningitis B or influenza.[82] Between 1941 and 1968, John divorced Pearl and remarried. Pearl died on August 29, 1965, at the age of 54. John died three years later on July 12, 1968, at the age of 59. He had a heart attack. All three were buried in Swingle Cemetery in Unicoi.

The second child, Carmon, was born on June 24, 1913, in Lost Cove. He was seven years old at the time of the 1920 census. In 1930, Carmon was 16 and listed in the home of Bob and Emma. Two years later, at just 18 years old, Carmon married Maude Honeycutt on May 10, 1932. The Reverend Zeb Ledford presided over the ceremony. The Reverend Bob was the witness.[83] Carmon and Maude had a son, Billie Jack, sometime in 1934. Just 11 months after Billie Jack was born, Carmon passed away at the age of 21 on May 21, 1935. He died of pulmonary tuberculosis. His father, Bob, was the informant on the death certificate.[84]

Esta was the only daughter of Robert and Emma. She was born in Lost Cove on July 3, 1916. She was 13 and in Unicoi County in 1930. In 1940, Esta Ada was 23 years old and worked for Southern Pottery, where she hand painted dishes and plates. Her initials EAM are still found on pottery today. Esta married Percy Arrowood on January 13, 1944.[85] They married in Washington County, Tennessee. Percy was the son of Jerry and Louise Arrowood. His parents were from Kentucky, but he was born in Wisconsin on June 13, 1919.

In an interview, Betty Bryant Peterson recalled Percy and Esta visiting their family home along White Oak Flats. She says many families in the cove came to visit the Bryants since her father, Jim, worked for the railroad section gang and her Uncle Frank lived in the cove. Betty's mother, Naomi, made a huge dinner for the family. That night the weather turned and the snow started falling. The Arrowoods could not walk back into the cove, so they stayed with the Bryants for one week. The snow was so high that no one could travel anywhere.[86] Percy and Esta lived in the cove during the early years of their marriage.

According to Teresa Miller Bowman, her Uncle Bob Miller baptized Percy during a June revival in the cove. Percy was baptized in Devil's Creek around 1949. Before Percy married Esta, he enlisted in the army in Milwaukee, Wisconsin, in 1941. The pair moved to Wisconsin during the mid–1950s. They had six children: Ronald, Ginny, Linda, Paul, Phillip, and Stanley. Ronald Arrowood was the only child born in Erwin. He died at the age of 50 in June 1993. His siblings still live in Wisconsin. Percy died on May 10, 2001. Esta lived to be 99 years old. She died on April 30, 2016, just two months short of turning 100. The couple were buried at Bent Cemetery in Bryant, Wisconsin.[87]

The third child, Samuel J., was born on March 8, 1920, in Lost Cove. Doctor S.J. Cooper delivered Sam. He was 10 years old according to the Unicoi County 1930 census. There are no census records on Sam in 1940. He registered for the army at the age of 21 on July 1, 1941, in Unicoi County. John Miller, his brother, is his contact on the card. Sam's home address is the CCC Camp 1455 at Cordell Hull in Limestone Cove.[88] On February 20, 1946, he enlisted at Fort Oglethorpe, Georgia. He was single and worked in the Medical Administration Corps in Hawaii. He served in the army until June 30, 1951. After Sam left the army he resided in Erwin. He never married. Sam J. died at the Oteen Veterans Administration Hospital in Asheville on July 18, 1955, at the age of 35. His death certificate states that various factors caused his death. He had severe tuberculosis, which he battled for five years, as well as a right frontal cystic brain tumor. L.E. Newman, M.D. attended to him from June 15, 1953, until his death.[89] Sam may have received his injuries during World War II when he was stationed in Hawaii. His services were held at his brother John's house in Unicoi, and Father Mulhearn of St. Mary's Catholic Church in Johnson City conducted the interment. Sam was buried in Swingle Cemetery along with his mother, brother, nephew, and sister-in-law.

The youngest child of Bob and Emma, Calvin Coolidge, was born in Washington County on March 21, 1924. According to the 1930 census he was six years old. After his mother died in 1931, the family moved into Lost Cove. The 1940 census lists Coolidge's age as 16. He lived with his father and stepmother, May. Coolidge also had three half siblings: Elsie (5), Junior (3), and Homer (under 1). Coolidge lived to be only 18. His obituary in the *Johnson City Press* says that he died in Lost Cove at the home of his father on February 15, 1943. He died from pulmonary tuberculosis. He was buried in Lost Cove Cemetery. The Reverend Carl Osborne conducted his funeral service.[90]

During the mid-1930s Bob married his second wife, May (Mafrie) Edwards, in Yancey County. She was the daughter of Bert (Burton) and Minnie Edwards. The couple had six children during their marriage: Elsie, Junior (Ray), Homer, Everett, Dean, and Archie. The family continued to live in Lost Cove during the 1940s. Besides being a preacher, Bob also worked as a timber laborer at the Lost Cove sawmill. Their son Dean lived to be only one month old. Dean died on February 28, 1948, of no known causes and was buried in the Lost Cove cemetery. In 1952, the Reverend resigns three months after becoming the pastor again at the Lost Cove church. He preached his last sermon on August 17, 1952. Bob became a preacher in South Carolina after he left Lost Cove. The family lived there for a while before they moved to

Millville, New Jersey, in 1968. Mafrie died in 1995 and was buried at the Greenwood Memorial Park in Vineland, New Jersey. There is no information on Bob's death or where he was buried.

The second child of Arch and Lucinda was John. John was born sometime in October 1891 or 1892. He was 18 years old at the time of the 1910 census. He helped his father, Arch, on the home farm as a laborer. According to the 1920 census, he lived with his parents and siblings. He is listed as 25 years old but was actually 28. John married Hulda Webb on April 24, 1920. They were married in Red Hill Township. She was 27 and he was 29. Justice of the Peace J.P Garland conducted the ceremony and Steve Collins, Isaac Stevens, and Tilda Garland were witnesses to the marriage.[91] Hulda was the daughter of Clingman and Joann Garland Webb of Red Hill Township. Hulda was born on January 5, 1887. She was a few years older than John when they married, yet the marriage records state that she was younger. There are some discrepancies in census records regarding John and Hulda.

The 1920 census indicates that Hulda Webb was widowed, but Bernie, her first husband, did not die. The pair divorced before 1916. She was 26 years old and listed as a general farmer and head of her household. The records do not indicate that John was in the household. He is listed in his parents' house at the time of the 1920 census. Hulda had four children according to the census: William (10), Frank (9), Clifford (3), and Fieldon Webb (8½ months).[92] Teresa Miller Bowman states that "Hulda was married to a Whitson man before she married her Uncle John. She has three children with Whitson: Isaac, Leah (Leona), and Frank."[93] The records are inaccurate when it comes to the children from her first marriage and her children with John. It is surprising that John is not listed with Hulda in the 1920 census since all the children have last name Webb, and Clifford and Field's last name should be Miller.

When the 1930 census was conducted, the pair had seven children in their household: Clifford (14), Field or Phil (13), Bonnie (8), twins Polly and Dolly (5), Eulas or Ulis (2), and Ada (11½ months). John was a laborer at odd jobs and his home was valued at $300.[94] Richard Bailey, grandson to John and son of Polly Miller, states that "John is a tall man with broad shoulders. He often drinks his coffee in a saucer" like many ole timers in the Appalachians.[95] Drinking coffee out of a saucer cooled the drink faster. The technique derives from eighteenth-century Victorian society. In an interview with James Johnson, son of Dolly Miller, James (Jim) recalls that his grandfather was a blacksmith, a jack of all trades. John worked also for the railroad and the CCC camps. He owned a big barn in Lost Cove and had an ox. Jim says that John loaned out his tilled fields for crops to other families within the cove.[96]

All of their children were born in White Oak Flats before the family moved into Lost Cove in the late 1920s. By 1940 the younger children were in their teenage years and Clifford and Phil were in their early twenties. John Miller's stepchildren were old enough to have families of their own in the 1940s.

Hulda's oldest son, Isaac Whitson, enlisted in the army at Fort Benning, Georgia, in 1945. He married Nadine Anders in Alabama. Isaac retired from the United States Army and NASA. They had two children: William Earl and Betty Sterling. Ike had two stepdaughters as well: Betty Phillips and Willa Dean Riley. He passed away in 1989 at the age of 83. He was buried in the Roselawn Gardens of Memory in

Decatur, Alabama. Her daughter, Leona, married Charlie W. Phillips. They had two sons and four daughters: Jim McGee, Nick, Mrs. Jack Allen, Mrs. Junior Butler, Kate, and Ada Sue Phillips. Leona died at the age of 49 in 1959. The couple were buried in the Cherry Grove Cemetery in Jonesborough. The third child of Hulda and Burnie lived in Mitchell County throughout his life. Frank married Mildred Talley Whitson in Red Hill. The couple had four daughters and two sons: Mrs. Cecil Peterson, Mrs. Arvel Peterson, Mrs. Gus Peterson, Mrs. Claude Frye, Boyd Whitson, and Dairse Whitson. Frank also had two stepdaughters and three stepsons: Mrs. Charles Garland, Mrs. Ernest Yelton, Larry Miller, Roger Dale Miller, and Terry Miller. Frank died at the age of 72 in Spruce Pine. He was buried along with Estella Horton Whitson at Peterson Cemetery in Mitchell County. The children of John and Hulda lived in the cove until they moved to Unicoi County.

According to the 1940 census John was a farmer and his son Phil helped on the farm, while Clifford was a cook for the section gang on the railroad. Clifford was born on November 7, 1916. He was 23 years old at the time of the census and lived with his parents and five siblings. Clifford met Hazel Bailey in the cove. He married her at the age of 24. Hazel was seven years younger. Hazel was born on December 21, 1923. Her parents, Chester and Carrie Tipton Bailey, were a prominent family in the settlement. Clifford and Hazel moved to Erwin after their marriage but moved back to the cove during the Depression years. According to Jim Johnson, Hazel worked under the Works Progress Administration as a professional photographer during the Great Depression.[97] The organization, part of the New Deal, employed millions of people in the public works projects of constructing roads and buildings. The couple eventually moved back to Erwin in the early 1940s and Clifford worked for the Clinchfield Railroad as a track foreman. The couple lived in Unaka Springs in the early years of their marriage and then resided on Chestoa Pike. Clifford was one of the founding members of Unaka Springs Free Will Baptist Church along the Nolichucky River. The pair had four children: Hilda J., Wanda, Jacqueline Laws, and Clifford Joseph.

The oldest, Hilda J., was born in 1943 and died on April 20, 1982, at the age of 39 from a lengthy illness. She was buried in the Evergreen Cemetery. Wanda Marie was born in 1946 and unexpectedly passed away at the age of 65 on January 9, 2011. She also was buried in Evergreen. Daughter Jacqueline married Michael Laws and has one daughter India. Michael passed away from leukemia. Jacqueline lives on Chestoa Pike in Erwin. Clifford lived to be 95 years old. He passed away on February 11, 2012, and was buried in Evergreen. His wife, Hazel, is 97 years old and lives in Erwin with her son Clifford. Her daughter Jacqueline lives next door. Hazel is still full of life and memories.

Phil, the second oldest son, is listed in the early census records as Fieldon and Field. He was born on May 22, 1918. Phil was 21 in 1940 and lived with his parents in Lost Cove. He enlisted in the army on February 24, 1942, at Fort Jackson in Columbia, South Carolina. Phil served in the South Pacific and the Marshall Islands and served on the USS *Unicoi* while stationed in the Philippines. On leave from the war, Phil married Ira Birchfield in Unicoi County on February 27, 1943. Phil was 24 years old and Ira was 20. Justice of the Peace Fred Booth signed the marriage license for the couple.[98] Ira was the daughter of Sam and Ollie V. Birchfield from Carter County. She was born on June 2, 1922. She had two siblings, a sister and a brother. After serving his term in World War II, Phil returned home and eventually moved to Flintville, Tennessee. Phil worked for the Tennessee Wildlife Resources Agency, where he served as superintendent of the State Fish Hatcheries in Flintville and Erwin. In 1976 Phil moved back to Erwin and worked for the hatchery until his retirement. The couple never had children. Phil and Ira were members of Southside Freewill Baptist Church in Erwin. They were married for 65 years before Ira passed away at the age of 84 on January 30, 2007. Phil died at the Unicoi County Memorial Hospital on July 9, 2008. He was 90 years old. They were laid side by side in Evergreen Cemetery.[99]

Bonnie Miller was the oldest daughter of John and Hulda. Bonnie was born on June 2, 1922. Her birthday was the same day as her mother's. Bonnie was eight years old at the time of the 1930 census. She only lived to be 16. She became sick on May 1, 1938. Doctor S.J. Cooper, who delivered many children in the cove, visited Bonnie due to her sickness. Dr. Cooper tended to Bonnie from May 19 through June 3, 1938. She died one day after her birthday from tuberculosis meningitis.[100] Two and one half years passed after Bonnie was born and the couple welcomed twin girls.

Dolly and Polly Miller were born on November 22, 1924, in White Oak Flats. According to the 1940 census the girls were 15 years old. The pair were inseparable throughout their whole lives. From sleeping in the same bed to living in New Jersey, the two were best friends. Jim, Dolly's son, tells several stories about the twins and their life in the cove. The girls enjoyed school with Carl Young as their teacher. During recess, Polly played baseball with the other kids and Dolly often went to pick apples in the orchards. The twins ate their lunch along with the other children on top of the hill. Polly sometimes traded her food with her siblings to get out of chores like collecting water for the family. The pair even made potato babies from hollowed out potatoes stuffed with mud. They placed diapers on the potatoes as if they were dolls.[101] The girls lived in Lost Cove until the early 1940s.

When the girls reached their twenties, they moved to Spartanburg, South Carolina, to help the United States in the war effort. Dolly moved first and Polly moved later because she could not live without her sister. The pair worked sewing tents for war supplies. Dolly met Kenneth Leroy Johnson during his training in Spartanburg. Kenneth was training at Camp Croft for the army infantry. Two weeks into their relationship they married in South Carolina. Kenneth was born on October 29, 1926, in Villa Park, New Jersey, to Ernest and Leeoata Johnson. He entered the army on February 16, 1942, in Belmar, New Jersey.[102] Kenneth and Dolly moved to New Jersey soon after his training ended. Dolly worked in the International Ladies Garment Workers Union for over 40 years. The couple had four children: Ronald, James, Kenneth, and Barbara. Kenneth worked as a truck driver for Jersey Coast Freight Lines for 25 years. Their children grew up in New Jersey. Kenneth passed away in 1987. He was buried in the Atlantic View Cemetery in Manasquan.

In 1988 Dolly returned to Erwin to live. Her oldest son, Ronald, married Sue Frick. They had one son, David, and one daughter, Jennifer. Ronnie passed away in a motorcycle accident in Erwin in July 1993. He served during the Vietnam War in the Navy. He was buried in the same cemetery as his father. James Johnson married Joy Lynn Huemer and they had two children, Jessica and Joshua. They live in Neptune, New Jersey. The pair travels to Unaka Springs every summer to live in their second home, which once belonged to Chester Bailey, Hazel Miller's father. The house sits across the road from Unaka Springs Hotel. Dolly's son Kenneth lived in Unicoi and her daughter Barbara lived in Erwin. Barbara Lynn married William Henry Jernee in New Jersey. They had four daughters: Debbie Holley, Diane Jernee, Christine Harris, and Joanne Hollenback. Dolly's sister Polly moved later to New Jersey in 1945.

Polly Ann married Harley Richard Bailey. The pair lived in Spring Lake Heights and divorced in 1968 in Unicoi County. The pair had three children;: Joyce, Kathy, and Richard. Polly was active in her children's lives. She served on the PTA and Little League Auxiliary and worked on the election polls for over 30 years. Polly often visited Unicoi County during the summer months to see her brothers. She purchased the old Unaka Springs Free Will Baptist Church in the late 1980s. Joyce, the oldest child, married Gregory Collins in 1980. The couple live in Wall, New Jersey. Her middle child, Kathy, married Stephan Pollard. They had one daughter, Rebecca Stanuszek. She also had three stepchildren: Stephen, Sarah, and Jennifer. Kathy passed away in 1999. The youngest child, Richard, married Jane Taylor and lives in Fredericksburg, Virginia. Richard travels to Erwin every summer and lives in the Unaka Springs church his mother purchased in the 1980s. John and Hulda's youngest son, Ulis, lived a life of service to God, his country, and his county.

Ulis was born in White Oak Flats on May 27, 1927. He was 12 years old at the time of the 1940 census. Ulis lived in the cove until 1947. He enlisted in the army in Fort Oglethorpe, Georgia, on July 19, 1945. He was 18 years old and registered in Unicoi County.[103] Ulis served in Italy during World War II. Teresa, their daughter, states that Ulis met her mother, Faye, at a June revival in Lost Cove. Faye often stayed with Carrie and Chester Bailey when she taught during the week.[104] They married in Unicoi County in 1949. Faye was the daughter of Virgil and Stella Howard Johnson from Bee Log, North Carolina. After the war, Ulis worked in Erwin at NFS as an accountant. In 1966 he became an ordained minister. He preached at several churches in the county. He served as secretary to the Jacks Creek Ministers Association and wrote a book titled *History of Jacks Creek Association*. He devoted many of his years to serving Unicoi County as a commissioner from 1986 through 2002. Faye worked for Morrill Motors for many years and worked for the Unicoi County School System as a library/office assistant and substitute teacher until she was in her eighties. Ulis and Faye had one daughter, Teresa. She was born October 27, 1953. When Teresa was little, she traveled several times into Lost Cove so her mother could teach. In 1956, the students and community celebrated her third birthday in the cove. Teresa married Doug Bowman from Erwin on August 31, 1974. Teresa and Doug have two daughters, Julia and Lindsay. Ulis and Faye lived long lives in Erwin. Ulis passed away on June 29, 2015, at the age of 88. Faye passed away three years later on July 23, 2018, at the age of 90.

The youngest child of John and Hulda was Ada. Ada was ten years old at the time of the 1940 census. She was born on May 26, 1929. Ada lived in Lost Cove and was a member of the church until her death. She lived in Unicoi County and never married. Ada died on March 19, 1948, at the age of 18 following a six-month illness. She was buried in the Evergreen Cemetery. The third child of Arch and Sinda Miller was a prominent member of the cove community.

Swin Miller was born on June 19, 1898, in Lost Cove. He was a construction laborer according to the 1930 census. He was 29 years old and lived with his parents. By the time of the 1940 census he was married to Martha Garland. Swin was 42 years old and Martha was 48. Martha was the daughter of David and Sara Garland and born in Mitchell County. Swin was Martha's second husband. She was married to John M. Howell at the time of the 1930 census. They divorced before 1940. Swin and Martha lived happily in the cove until the end of the community. Swin owned one of the two trucks that hauled goods and timber to and from the railroad, as well as the apples from orchards within the cove. He worked in the cove's sawmill and as a community leader. Martha was a great cook and had plenty of food on her table for others in the community. Swin and Martha often boarded Mr. Conley, the teacher, throughout his teaching days in the cove. Many newspaper articles in the 1950s illustrate the lives of people in the cove, and Swin and Martha are often talked about in the articles. When the community dissolved in the late 1950s, the pair moved to White Oak Flats. Swin passed away on April 4, 1970, at the age of 71. Martha passed away seven years later in March 1977 at the age of 81. The pair were buried in the White Oak Cemetery in Yancey County.

The first daughter of Arch and Sindy Miller was Jane. Jane was born on January 6, 1894. She was 17 years old at the time of the 1910 census and lived with her parents in Lost Cove. On December 21, 1917, Jane married Frank Bryant. Frank was the son of J. Waitsel and Oma (Naomi) Tipton Bryant and brother to Emma, Bob Miller's first wife. Frank and Jane married in Lost Cove with the Reverend L.H. Griffith of Free Will Baptists conducting the ceremony. John Miller, Sid Deyton, and Tom Garland were witnesses to the marriage.[105] According to the 1920 census, Frank and Jane had three daughters: Della (8), Naoma (2), and Anna (under 1). By 1940, the pair had Kermit (22), Trula (20), Harvey (18), Dola (16), Zola (14), and J.C. (10).[106] Frank was a farm and construction laborer in his early years. He did work for the Carolina, Clinchfield, and Ohio in the 1940s. All of Frank and Jane's children were born in Lost Cove. Jane passed away on August 1, 1972. Frank lived to be 82 and passed away on October 15, 1980. They both were buried in the Evergreen Cemetery. Jane and Frank's children lived in the cove until they married or left for the service.

The oldest child, Della, was born in 1912. She does not appear in the 1930 census records with the family. She was 19 by then and married Billie Peterson in Unicoi County in 1928. Della and Billie had two children according to the 1940 census: Euphratie (9) and Betty Ann (under 1). The family lived in Poplar and Billie worked for the railroad section gang.[107] Della died on May 19, 1971, at the age of 60. The couple had more children: Phyllis Morris of Bristol, Dorothy Dowlin of Pennsylvania, and Robert Peterson of Erwin. Euphratie died at the age of 22 in 1953. Betty Ann passed away in 2013. Della was buried in Peterson Cemetery in Mitchell County, North Carolina.

Naoma was born February 23, 1917. She was named after her grandmother. She married John H. Morgan on August 25, 1939. Naoma (Naomi) and John are listed in the 1940 census in Washington County, Tennessee. The couple had one child, Barbara J. (3). Barbara is Naoma's stepdaughter. John worked for the Works Progress Administration as a road project laborer.[108] Naoma worked as a seamstress for many years at Industrial Garment in Erwin and at Bemberg in Elizabethton. The couple resided in

Johnson City. John died in 1973 and was buried in the Evergreen Cemetery. Naoma lived to be 83. She passed away on September 2, 2000. She was buried next to John in Erwin. Her stepdaughter, Barbara Carrico, lives in Elizabethton.

The oldest son of Jane and Frank was Kermit. He was born on September 26, 1919. He was 21 according to the 1940 census and lived with his family. He enlisted at Fort Bragg in 1941. Kermit married Frances Baxley after his service in the army. Frances was the daughter of Mr. and Mrs. Robert Baxley. The couple had two sons: Phil and Robert. They divorced, and he married Mildred Viola. The couple had one daughter together, Hazel Miller Fowler. The couple lived in Fort Payne, Alabama, during their marriage. Mildred died in 1987 and Kermit died on October 11, 1998. The couple were buried at the Walker's Chapel Cemetery in Dekalb County, Alabama. Phil and his wife live in Alabama. Robert died in June 2015 in Johnson City. Hazel lives in Alabama.

Trula Mae Bryant was born on April 2, 1922. She was 20 years old according to the 1940 census and lived with her parents. Trula met Arrie Lee Guthrie in Lost Cove during the timber years. Arrie Lee, along with his father, worked in the cove at the sawmill. His father, Doke, built timber homes throughout western North Carolina. Arrie Lee was the son of Doke Henry and Mary Lee Hyatt Guthrie from Forks of Ivy in Buncombe County, North Carolina. He was born in Haywood County in 1911. Trula and Arrie Lee married around 1938. The pair lived in Democrat, North Carolina, during the early part of their marriage. The couple had three boys: Richard Marvin, Roy Lee, and Marna Odell. Richard was born in Sugar Creek on January 22, 1940. Arrie Lee registered for the draft in October 1940 in Buncombe County. When Arrie was training for the service, Trula and the boys stayed in Lost Cove at her parents. Roy was born on July 2, 1941, in Lost Cove and was delivered by Lizzie Howell. Odell was born in Newport News on June 23, 1943. The family lived in Virginia for a few years since Arrie Lee worked in the shipyards.

Trula Mae did not live to see her children get older. She died on November 9, 1944, from tuberculosis at her father's home in Lost Cove. She was only 23 years old. Trula Mae was buried in Lost Cove Cemetery. Roy Lee was only three years old when she dies. He states that both he and Richard went to live in Sugar Creek with their grandmother, Mary Lee Guthrie. Odell went to live with their aunt due to his sickness. Roy and his brother Richard traveled back to Lost Cove many times until the age of seven.[109] Odell lived to be only 18 months old. He died on December 20, 1944, at St. Joseph's in Asheville from tuberculosis meningitis. He was buried next to his mother in Lost Cove. Arrie Lee died in 1966 in Washington, D.C. He was buried in the Antioch Baptist Church Cemetery in Democrat, North Carolina.

The oldest son, Richard, married Peggy Jones and they had two daughters and four sons: Pam, Tina, Bruce, Randy, Roger, and Stevie. Richard worked for the Truck Air in Asheville. He was only 49 years old when he died in 1981. He was buried in the same cemetery as his father. The only surviving son is Roy Lee. Roy Lee enlisted in the army and trained at Fort Knox in advanced armor tank training. He served in France and Germany from 1960 to 1963. He married June Carolyn Garrison in 1963. The pair lives in Barnardsville, North Carolina. Roy Lee and June have five children: Janet Lynn, Donna Lee, Lester Lee, Elizabeth Elaine, and Tammy Beatrice. Their children all live in North Carolina. Many Lost Cove men enlisted in the armed forces after they reached 18. Trula Mae's brother Harvey will leave the cove for the Navy.

The second oldest son, Harvey, was eighteen years old at the time of the 1940 census. He was born on June 13, 1923. Harvey married Virginia "June" Bailey in Spartanburg, South Carolina. Harvey served during World War II in the U.S. Navy. He served from December 1942 to November 1945. He received several medals while serving. Harvey and Virginia moved to Lapeer, Michigan, and started a family. They had a daughter and son. He worked for the Chevy Metal Fabrication Company until he retired. Harvey passed away on June 6, 1987.[110]

Dola or Dula was born on February 27, 1927. She was 16 according to the 1940 census. She married James Baxley before 1947. The pair had a child, Walter Delee Baxley, in November 1947. Dula

Arch and Sindy Miller (1930). Courtesy of Teresa Miller Bowman.

John and Hulda Miller (1952). Courtesy of Teresa Miller Bowman.

Six. Families   135

Miller family (1957). Courtesy of Chad Fred Bailey.

Hulda Miller with Bonnie holding Maude, and Clifford (1920s). Courtesy of Jim Johnson.

Faye, Ulis, and Teresa Miller (1958). Courtesy of Teresa Miller Bowman.

divorced James and married Harry R. Hensley. She filed for divorce in 1964. Dula worked in the Leon Ferenbach Company for more than 30 years. The company is a textile yarn spinning mill. Dula died on May 8, 1997, in Johnson City at the age of 70. She was buried in the Monte Vista Memorial Park.[111] Walter married Barbara Sue Conner. They lived in Gray. The pair had two children, Tammy Walters and Michael. Walter passed away on October 13, 2012.

Zola was born June 15, 1929. She was 14 years old at the time of the 1940 census.

Ulis Miller with Polly, Dolly, Clifford, and Phil (1980). Courtesy of Teresa Miller Bowman.

Zola married Burnie Tipton from Mitchell County. He was the son of Charles and Maude Higgins Tipton. Burnie was a World War II veteran. The couple lived in Erwin and Burnie was the operator of Burnie's Trim Shop, where he works until 1988. They had two children, Charles and Penny Tipton Proffitt. Zola died at the age of 50 on May 22, 1980. Burnie lives to be 72. He dies on April 15, 1997. They both were buried in the Evergreen Cemetery.

J.C. was the youngest child. He was born on July 31, 1932. During his life in the cove, J.C. helped many of

Jane Miller Bryant and J.C. (1950). Courtesy of Regina Cornett, J.C. Bryant's granddaughter.

his relatives make moonshine and sold the shine to many people in Erwin. J.C. left Lost Cove in 1952 to serve in the Korean War. J.C. completed his training at Fort Jackson, South Carolina. He served with the 14th Infantry as a rifleman and came home on leave in October 1952. J.C. married Dixie Lee Tipton in 1955. Dixie Lee was the daughter of Dave and Zettie Piercy Tipton. She was related to John D. Tipton. The couple resided in Erwin. For his service in the army, J.C. was awarded the Korean Service Medal with two bronze stars, a Combat Infantry Medal, a Purple Heart, a United Nations Service Medal, and a Good Conduct Medal. After his service duties, J.C. worked at Morflo as a painter. The pair had four children: Kathy Ann, Randy David, Marcella, and Jeff. Dixie Lee died on March 28, 2018, at the age of 81. J.C. lived for two more years after Dixie Lee. He died on June 20, 2020. His honorable life and stories throughout this book provided important information on the lifeways of the families in the cove. J.C. had close relationships with all his aunts and uncles in the cove, especially his Aunt Martha.

J.C. Bryant, Joan Carol, and nephew at school (1938). Courtesy of Regina Cornett

Martha Ann Miller, the youngest daughter of Arch and Sindy, was born on August 11, 1895. According to the 1920 census she was 21 and lived with her parents. By 1930 she lived in the household of James Jasper Hensley. James was the son of James Crawford and Rebecca Lewis Hensley. He had three children from a previous marriage when they married: Della, Monroe, and Crawford. The pair had three daughters and three sons together: Violet, Nettie, Pearl, William, Shelby, and Quinton. At the time of the 1940 census they lived in Ramsey Township.[112] James died in 1966. Martha Ann (known as

Jane Miller Bryant (1960). Courtesy of Regina Cornett.

Left: Roy Lee Guthrie and brother Richard (1940s). *Right:* Roy Lee Guthrie (1960). Courtesy of Roy Lee Guthrie.

Annie and Annia) died on January 2, 1968, in Burnsville. Both were buried in the Fender Cemetery in Bee Log. Most of their children live in Delaware, while one lives in Erwin and the other lives in Relief.

Arch and Sindy Miller's two sons Samuel and Claude lived short lives. Samuel Miller was born on June 14, 1901. He lived his entire life in Lost Cove with his parents. He was a farmer. Samuel lived to be only 45 years old. From November 12 to November 28, 1946, Dr. Cooper attended to Samuel in the settlement. He was diagnosed with tuberculosis. He passed away on November 28. He was buried in Lost Cove Cemetery.[113] Claude is 15 years old according to the 1920 census. He was born in the cove on May 16, 1904. Claude worked for the railroad section gang during his life. Claude lived to be 26 years old. From February 1 to March 31, 1930, Dr. H.D. Mills attended to his illness. He was buried in Swingle Cemetery in Unicoi with several of his relatives.[114]

The last child of the Miller clan was Nathaniel. He was born in 1909. The 1930 census lists him as 21 years old. Miller resided in the cove his entire life as a farmer. He married Ruby Hughes on August 21, 1938, in Yancey County. She was the daughter of Ollie and Florence Hughes. At the time of the 1940 census, the couple had one son, Vester (under one). He was born in 1939. The couple would have two more children: Barbara J. was born in 1942 and Eddie was born in 1944. "Nat" only lived one more year after Eddie was born. He died on June 8, 1945, in the cove. Dr. Moody from Erwin attended to his illness of dropsy for four months prior to his death.[115] He was 37 years old. "Nat" was buried in Lost Cove Cemetery. The funeral was held at Lost

Dolly Miller Johnson (1952). Courtesy of Jim Johnson, Dolly's son.

Cove church with Mr. Ed Wheeler preaching. Son Vester died in 1990 at the age of 50. Barbara and Eddie both passed away before their mother. No information is found on their deaths. Ruby eventually married again. She passed away at the age of 77 in 1998.

The Miller family and Bailey families were the last to leave Lost Cove. Their close kinship and community ties held deep through the years of the settlement.

Many Miller families all moved to Unicoi County, settling there until the day they departed this world. Their pure determination and skills led them to live a self-sufficient, happy life in the cove. No family member wanted to leave.

The Coopers

There are only two Cooper families that lived in Lost Cove: Samuel and William Harrison. The two families are not related. Samuel Cooper and his wife Naomi Tipton lived in Lost Cove during the earlier years of the community. Naomi's parents, John and Caroline, were prominent in the community. Samuel was a farmer and distiller. The couple had five daughters and two sons: Martin, Clarissa, Zellie or Donzella, Moses, Hattie, Caroline, and Mary. Naomi was Samuel's second wife. They lived in Lost Cove as early as 1910. By 1920, they lived in Unicoi County and had four more children in the household: Edward, John, Pansy, and George. The family is discussed further in the Tipton section.

The second Cooper family lived in the cove during the Depression years. According to Lloyd Bailey, Sr., William Harrison Cooper was born on September 13, 1905, in Bee Log, North Carolina. His parents were Marcus C. and Isabel Elizabeth Edwards Cooper.[116] He had three siblings. The family lived in Ramsey Township. Harrison is not listed in the 1930 census with his parents. He married Mary Ethel Shelton from English, North Carolina, in 1926. Mary was the daughter of Elbert and Ruth Hampton Shelton. According to the 1930 census, the couple had one child, William Reese. Harrison and Mary moved to the cove to work in the logging camp.

Harrison was a known logging man, who worked at several logging camps in Swain and Haywood counties in western North Carolina. Harrison ran the logging camp in Lost Cove while Ethel cooked. When the pair entered Lost Cove they lived near the sawmill. Ethel cooked every day for the workers. She was known to be a great cook. Harrison's duty at the sawmill was sending milled lumber down the mountain siding so the workers could load the lumber on the train. When the family left Lost Cove, Harrison took his prized pig with him. The couple had one more son in 1941, Wade Hampton. After Lost Cove, the family moved to Burnsville. Their son Reese died in a car accident in 1949 in Erwin. Wade married Willa Rae Blankenship Taylor in 1988 and lives in Candler. Ethel died on June 24, 1983, in Asheville. She was buried at the Cooper Ledford Cemetery in Yancey County. Harrison lived to be 80 years old. He died in 1985 and was buried in the same cemetery as Ethel.[117] Wade is owner of Cooper Enterprises in Asheville. While Harrison and Ethel did not live in the cove long, they have many memories of their life there.

The Bennett Family

The Archibald Bennett family is the only Bennett family to live in Lost Cove. Archibald and his wife Vianna or Vienna Tipton Bennett lived in the cove in the earlier years. Arch enlisted with the North Carolina Third Mounted Infantry on the same day as Morgan Bailey and John D. Tipton. He served in the same company as well. The infantry also lists Arch as AWOL on the same day as John D. Tipton. Since Company F had the most deserters, research shows he may be the friend that John D. left with in December 1864. The infantry fixed his records in 1877, which include his pension benefits and his desertion. The infantry reinstated his status so he could receive his pension.

According to the 1880 census, the couple had five children: Margaret (12), Rebecca (10), Naomia (8), Joseph (4), and Phebe (2).[118] Arch is listed as a farmer. The couple had one more child, Zeb. The oldest daughter, Margaret, married Wiley J. Tipton, son of John D. and Caroline, in 1893. The couple stayed married for just a few years. No information is found on Margaret's remarriage or death certificates. The couple never had children. Margaret's father, Arch, died in 1893. He was buried in the Haun-White Cemetery in Unicoi County. The second child, Rebecca, married Nathanial T. Aldridge in 1892. The couple resided in Carter County and had six girls. Rebecca was widowed by the time of the 1940 census. She died in 1944 and was buried in the Highland Cemetery next to her husband Nathanial.

The oldest son, Joseph, married Hannah Higgins in Unicoi County in 1909. The pair lived in Yancey County and had one son together, William. By 1920 the couple lived in Unicoi County with William, Arch, George, and daughter Irene. By 1930, two more children had been born: Max Hardin and Jack. Joe lived to be 91 years old. He died in Bristol, Virginia, and was buried at Evergreen Cemetery. His wife Hannah died in 1962 and was buried next to him. There is no information on daughters Naomia and Phebe or son Zeb. Naomia was born around 1873, and Phebe and Zeb were born in 1878. Research indicates all three may have died at birth. While the Bennetts lived a short life in the cove, the bond with John D. Tipton and family will survive through historical records.

The Hedrick Family

Mack Daniel and Sarah Adkins Hedrick lived in Lost Cove as early as 1866. During the Civil War, Mack served with the Confederates in Company G, 29th Regiment of North Carolina until 1865, when the regiment surrendered. His affiliation with the Confederate company may have caused tension among some of the families within the cove, especially the Baileys and Tiptons, since several of the men served in the Third Mounted Infantry. If there were tensions within the families that small division does not stop two of his daughters from marrying two prominent men in the cove, while the others moved away.

According to the 1870 census Mack Daniel was a farmer. He was the son of Charles and Lydia Whitson Hedrick, and his wife, Sarah, was the daughter of Rickles and Alice Tabitha Bryant Adkins. Between 1864 and 1898, the pair had nine children: Mary J., Lucinda, Nancy, James, Rickles Rex, Martin, Dorothy, Jettie, and Robert. Research does show that at least three of their children lived in the cove for many years.

Two of the Hedrick sisters, Lucinda and Jettie, married two of the prominent men in the cove. Mack and Sarah's daughter Lucinda (Sinda or Sindy) was born

Six. Families 143

in Lost Cove around 1866. There is no definite day of birth. Lucinda married Arch Miller from Lost Cove before 1890. The family resided in the cove until their deaths. Lucinda and Arch were buried in Lost Cove Cemetery. Their family information is found in the Miller section. Lucinda's younger sister Jettie met William Bailey in the settlement during her younger years. Jettie was born in 1881. At the time of the 1900 census, Jettie Hedrick lived in the household of Peter Peterson and his family in Hollow Poplar Township in Mitchell County. She was 18 years old and within the next year she would marry William Bailey. Jettie is also listed in the census with her parents that same year.

In 1901, Jettie married William Bailey, son of Zebulon and Hannah Jane Wilson. William was the grandson of Lost Cove founder Stephan Morgan Bailey. When William died in 1919, Jettie remained in the cove with her children. More information on their children is placed in the Bailey section. Jettie died in Lost Cove in 1948. She was buried in the cemetery. Her husband William was buried in the Bennett Cemetery in Pigeon Roost. Jettie's brother Rex owned land in Lost Cove.

Deeds indicate that in the early 1930s Rex Hedrick owned land near Wiley and John D. Tipton. Rickles Rex Hedrick was born on March 26, 1875. He was eight years old according to the 1880 census. 1910 records indicate Rex lived with his parents and was 34 years old.[119] Rickles married Sarah Whitson two years later at the Burnsville Courthouse on August 2, 1912. He was 37 and she was 26. Justice of the Peace J.D. Warrick signed the certificate, and the couple had three witnesses: John McCourry, Ed Warrick, and A. Adkins.[120] Sarah Ann was the daughter of Jason and Hester Finettie Adkins Whitson. Rex Hedrick and Sarah's family lived in Lost Cove until the early 1940s. The couple had four children according to the 1920 census records: Horace, Trula, Ed, and John. The pair added one more daughter, Sadie, to the family in 1921. His mother, Sarah Adkins Hedrick, died on July 20, 1923, and was buried in Hughes Cemetery. Less than a year later Rex's wife Sarah Ann died, on March 7, 1924. Sarah Ann Whitson Hedrick was buried in the Whitson family cemetery. After his mother's death, his father Mack lived with his family. Mack was 88 years old at the time of the 1930 census. In early December 1930, Mack died. He was buried next to his wife Sarah Adkins.

Rex left Lost Cove sometime after the 1940 census. He moved his family to Marion, North Carolina, and lived until the age of 85. Rex died four days after a cerebrovascular accident on September 23, 1960. His son Ed Hedrick was the informant on the death certificate.[121] Rex was buried in the Whitson Cemetery near his parents. The other children of Mack and Sarah Ann moved from the family homestead to counties nearby.

One child, Mary Lavada Hedrick Howell, is not mentioned in the early census records. Mary Lavada was born on March 1, 1866. She may be the oldest child named Mary J. since there are no records after the 1880 census on Mary Jane. Mary Lavada is listed under Sarah's genealogy records, but she is not mentioned in her father's records. Mary Lavada married Samuel Peter Howell and the couple lived in Unicoi County. They had six sons: Sherman, Frank, Jeff, Robert, Bernie, and Edgar. Their oldest son, Sherman, married Lizzie Huskins Howell. Lizzie was a midwife and often delivered children born in Lost Cove during the 1920s and 1930s. Mary Lavada died in 1958 at the age of 92 years old. She was buried in Swingle Cemetery in Unicoi County along with her children and husband. There is no information on Nancy Hedrick. She is not mentioned after the 1880 census. She may have married, but there are no marriage records or death records on her. Dorothy Hedrick was born in April 1878. She also appears as Dartha in the 1900 census records and Dortha in a birth record. Dartha, 22, is listed with her parents in Yancey County in the 1900 census records. After 1900, her name disappears in the records. There is one record that indicates that Dortha had a child named Charles B. Brackins in Yancey County on October 20, 1915. She was married to William Brackins. After that the family disappears. Research shows no death certificates for any member of the family.

Other children, like James, Martin, and Robert, do not have any connection to Lost Cove through deeds or interviews. James (Jim) Hedrick married Amanda Whitson in 1908. Amanda was the younger sister to Sarah, Rex's wife, and daughter to Jason and Finettie Whitson. The couple had six children: Ida, Deckard, Dolph, Clayton, Joe, and Burnie. Martin Alexander lived in Unicoi County during the 1920s. He married Lina Peterson, and the couple had three children: Mack, Mary Jane, and Sylvester. Robert "Bob" Isaac Hedrick was the youngest son, and he married Hammy Whitson, daughter of Jason and Finettie. Bob served in World War II with Company 156 Depot Brigade. The couple had four children: Ray, Glen, Pansy, and May. While only three of Mack and Sarah's children resided in Lost Cove, they all were well known through documents, deeds, and through the interviews. Lucinda and Jettie both lived in the cove until their deaths, while Rex moved his family after 1940.

The Howell Family

The earliest accounts of a Howell family living in Lost Cove tell of John M. Howell. John Melvin was the son of Ezekiel and Mary Howell. John was born on May 2, 1871. He was one of eight children. The Howells lived in the Ramsey Township during the 1880 census. At the time of the 1910 census John lived with his wife, Olivia (Ollie), and two children, Mattie and Ethel. His father also lived with them. Olivia was the daughter of John W. Bailey and Naomi Mary Brinkley. John and Olivia were married less than seven years. Olivia Bailey Howell was 34 years old when she died in October 1916. She may have died from complications from a birth. Records indicate that a child was born on Septembers 25, 1916, and died. Olivia was buried in the Howell-Randolph Cemetery in Yancey County.

Within six months after Olivia's death John married Martha Garland in March 1917. The 1920 census records indicate he had two more children with Olivia before her death, Russell (7) and Kate (5).[122] His second wife, Martha Garland, is the daughter of David and Sara Garland of Mitchell County. The 1930 census includes grandchildren in his household, but before 1935, John and Martha were divorced. Martha married her second husband, Swin Miller, in Lost Cove, while John married Valiria (Valerie) Hughes in 1935. John and Valerie had a daughter named Bettie. John no longer lived in Lost Cove after their divorce, but Martha and Swin remained. John died on December 26, 1943, in Unicoi County. He was buried in the same cemetery as Olivia.

John's oldest daughter, Mattie, was 25 years old according to the 1930 census. She lived with John and Martha in Lost Cove. Within the household were Mattie's children: O.B. (6), Maudie (4), and Millard Garland (2). Mattie was a widow. Records indicate that she married Tom (Thomas Garland) in Unicoi County in 1920. Tom died in 1928 at the age of 30 from a knife wound. He was buried at Martin's Creek Cemetery.

Mattie Howell eventually married Dave Wilson of Unicoi County. The couple had several children. Mattie died in 1995 at the age of 91. She was buried next to her second husband, Dave, in Evergreen Cemetery. Mattie's sister, Ethel, married Sedgie Berlon Tynes in Alabama in 1970. She died in 1999. Russell married Nola Wilson in 1933. Russell died in Virginia in 1977. Kate married William Templin in Georgia in 1942. Kate was buried at Fort Benning Georgia. She died in 2006.

The Presnells

Robert K. Presnell and his family lived in the cove during the late 1930s. Robert served as Yancey County sheriff from 1932 to 1936. According to the 1930 census, Robert and Clara had two children, Trina (13) and Clarence (9). After his term as sheriff ended, he moved his family to the settlement so he could work at the sawmill. Robert was the machine operator. His family lived in Mac English's house next to the railroad long after English left the cove. The family lived in the cove for only a few years and then moved back to Burnsville. The couple eventually had another child, Betty. Clara died in 1964 and Robert died in 1976. They were both buried in the Newdale Presbyterian Church Cemetery in Yancey County. Their daughter Trina married Arnie Fox. The pair had two daughters, Sandra and Lisa. Trina died in 2012 at the age of 99. She was buried in the Holcombe Cemetery along with her husband. Son Clarence married Irene Buchanan. They resided in Burnsville. Clarence died in 1998 and his wife passed away in 2005. They were buried in the same cemetery as his mother and father. The youngest, Betty Jean, married Guy Helms. They live in Virginia. The Presnells enjoyed their short time in the cove bonding with the Baileys and Millers.

Every family in Lost Cove represents determination and resiliency. Their kinship, values, and beliefs reflect true Appalachian culture. Many families relied upon one another to survive in the isolated community. Interaction with the outside world depended upon food, work, and family connections to others living outside the cove. Each family always believed that they would return to the community and that is why many houses still held furniture and other belongings. Appalachian families will always pass down stories of their childhood and generation after generation will remember their ancestors.

Seven

The End of a Community

"Give me the mountains where the best things are free,
Where the paintings of nature are wide and high
With canvasses stretching almost to the sky."[1]
—George W. McCoy

The Lost Cove settlement allowed families to thrive and flourish from the 1860s until the late 1950s. Self-reliance and determination were key characteristics in family life. Three prominent families—the Baileys, Tiptons, and Millers—made Lost Cove their home for nearly 95 years. Other families included the Bryants, Coopers, Howells, and Presnells. When families in the cove began moving away, lands were sold to families within the community but also to people outside of the community. There were various factors that contributed to the downfall of the settlement: the disapproval of a community road, discontinued passenger trains, the depleting of timber, population decrease, and education.

For many years, the residents of Lost Cove hoped that the government would build a new road into their settlement. As early as the 1930s, Lost Cove residents tried to build a road into the community. Accounts from a 1991 affidavit issued in Unicoi County by Velmer Bailey, Isaac Tipton, and Chester Bailey describe how the men, along with others, provided free labor to build a roadway that "runs from Highway 19 through White Oak Flats to what is known as Lost Cove."[2] The men provided free labor on the public road to the citizens and residents of Yancey County. The affidavit is a clear statement that the road was important to Lost Cove residents and that their efforts demonstrated determination and resiliency within a thriving community.

A new road meant children could go to high school and complete their education and that the families could sell goods, including the pulpwood they produced from timber, to local markets. The families could travel to neighboring towns like Poplar and Erwin to purchase essential goods that they could not grow or make themselves. The road could help families have jobs in neighboring towns while still keeping their homes and land. Prominent teacher Sinclair Conley believed that the average income of the families was around $300 a year. With the road, families could make more than $400-500 per year with crop output included. Mr. Conley stated in the *Asheville Citizen-Times* that "a rough road would cost not more than $10,000 to $15,000. There is a good route available."[3]

He proposed that the road should be built from the east, around the side of Flat Top Mountain. The community only needed to cut a three and one-half mile

Seven. The End of a Community

road that winds around the backside of the community near Bob and John Miller's houses. The road would appear on the side of Poplar. Mr. Conley submitted the road proposal to Governor Scott of North Carolina. Governor Scott replied to Mr. Conley and expressed interest in the project. Scott petitioned Highway Commissioner Dale Thrash to review the plans Conley submitted. Scott directed Thrash to advise and assist Mr. Conley in any way possible. While no actions were taken in 1952, Mr. Thrash did visit the cove the following year to check the route that Mr. Conley proposed.

In the *Asheville Citizen-Times* on March 14, 1953, an article titled "Building of Lost Cove Road Is Up to People of Yancey" describes Mr. Thrash's visit with Mr. Conley and Bob Bailey. The trio hiked along the four-mile route that Conley proposed. Mr. Thrash estimated it would cost the county $80,000 to build the road plus $50,000 for a bridge over the Toe River that would connect the cove to Poplar. The families could then travel to the Poplar store and send their children to high school. Since there were only 21 people residing in the cove, Thrash did not think the state could justify or approve the project. Thrash sympathized with the families who wanted to stay. He knew generations of families lived in the cove. He thought it best if the families relocated so they can have modern amenities. The families reiterated to Thrash that they didn't need an expensive road, only one that machinery and labor could build.[4]

Conley made every effort to keep the petition alive. As the *Asheville Citizen-Times* reported on May 8, 1953:

> New agreements for rights-of-way have been obtained and turned over to the State Highway and Public Works Commission offices in Burnsville. Conley said a request has been made to the SH&PWC that part of the road be built this year and part next year.[5]

The families and Conley were anxious to hear good news from the Yancey County commissioners and highway department. Dale Thrash told Conley that the road project for the community would be up to the Yancey County citizens. If citizens wanted some of the highway funds to be used for the Lost Cove road, then the project would begin. Yet earlier that week, Dale Thrash's term as highway commissioner expired. After Mr. Thrash's term, state highway authorities made the trip to survey the territory sometime during the summer months. The community's hope for a road was depleted when authorities decided that there were not enough people in Lost Cove to warrant a road. Highway authorities also maintained that if Yancey County did build a road, there would not be enough money for the county to maintain county and mountain highways. Lost Cove petitioned the county twice to build a road, once in 1952 and then again in the spring of 1953.

While the families did not like the decision, they remained determined to stay in their community. Mr. Bailey notes that "it was too expensive to build a road for the amount of families left in the cove."[6] Mr. Davis recalls that when he began preaching at Lost Cove, there were around 11 to 13 families living in the cove and the last year of his preaching only three or four families remained.[7] Mr. Bailey adds that "there were only three or four families left during the later years from 1952 to 1957."[8]

In November 1953 the community got hit with another problem. The families received word that the Clinchfield Railroad was ready to discontinue passenger services in Kentucky, Virginia, Tennessee, and South Carolina. An *Asheville Citizen-Times* article titled "Hearing Set on Clinchfield Passenger Service Request" announces that a hearing will be held on December 9, 1953, at 10 a.m. between the State Utilities Commissioners and Clinchfield Railroad. The railroad would seek permission from other state agencies to discontinue services. The counties affected in North Carolina included McDowell, Rutherford, Mitchell, and parts of Yancey. All of these counties are mountainous areas.[9]

There is no evidence that residents of Yancey County had any input into the closing of the passenger train services. The Clinchfield Railroad was the only transportation for many citizens in the mountain regions of Yancey and Mitchell counties. Without service, many families were forced to move elsewhere. Lost Cove relied upon the Clinchfield for necessary supplies, removal of cut timber, and shipment of pulpwood. The trains allowed many families to travel for shopping and supplies, and allowed family and friends to visit those in Lost Cove. The Clinchfield Railroad, like the Tweetsie Railroad, decided that short-haul passenger services were no longer profitable. Passenger services from Elk Horn, Kentucky, to Spartanburg, South Carolina, would come to a halt if the Clinchfield decided to cease services. By late June 30, 1953, the railroad was claiming they had lost $119,276 due to a decrease in passenger services.[10]

Modern life snuffed out the rural isolated towns throughout western North Carolina and northeastern Tennessee. By May 1955, the Clinchfield ceased passenger services for the 277-mile route from Kentucky to South Carolina. Lost Cove families had to succumb to the outside world's modern ways. The outside world became dependent upon the individual automobile while train transportation depended upon coal outputs. Lost Cove families held out for several more years before the last family left.

Faye Miller, a former teacher in Lost Cove, remembers that the discontinued passenger trains forced her to give up her teaching job during the 1950s. She adds that she had to walk three to four miles up the railroad tracks to reach the school.[11] The new highways and new automobiles offered transportation that the railroad could not provide. Economic resources like timber began dwindling in Lost Cove. Residents began moving out by early 1950s.

Around the 1950s, Clifford Miller remembers, "the supply of timber finally gave out and brought on hard times."[12] The fertile lands produced the last of the oak, pine, poplar, and ash trees. Lost Cove's landscape craved new trees but none were to be found. Though families had triumphed over hard times in the past, now times were different. The ability to earn income in Lost Cove began to fade once timber was depleted. Lost Cove's earlier self-reliance had given way to dependence, and people wanted a new life in neighboring towns, new jobs, and new schools.

Additionally, since school systems were consolidating their smaller schools due to the economy, the board of education pressured Yancey County officials to make arrangements for boarding Lost Cove High School students in nearby Bee Log, North Carolina. Students walked out of Lost Cove on Sunday and returned on Friday afternoon.[13] The families became victims of a new world that depended on transportation and income. Isaiah Bailey recalls how he had to walk everyday around the winding Poplar trail to get to school. Isaiah Bailey and Priscilla Bailey Knode left Lost Cove to further their education. Other reasons for families leaving the cove centered on military services. Young men like J.C. Bryant, Okie Bailey, and Homer Tipton left Lost Cove for the military forces, while some say the families simply grew tired of struggling in the later years. The isolated life proved too hard to handle.

According to an article in the *Raleigh News and Observer*, "of the thirteen families who were the last to leave, one moved to a home near Burnsville, North Carolina, while the others went to Erwin and Jonesborough, Tennessee. Those employable are working at various jobs. The school children are in regular attendance at nearby schools."[14] Mr. Bryant's family moved to Erwin, while he joined the army and headed to Korea in 1950. Even in the 1950s, his family often returned to Lost Cove for apple picking and visits with the families that were left. Life in Lost Cove was not the same as it had been.[15]

Isaiah Bailey's family was the last family to leave Lost Cove. Velmer Bailey states in an article published in the *Johnson City Press Chronicle* on April 3, 1958: "We don't want to leave, but we have no choice. The others have left and we can't stay here alone."[16] Velmer Bailey; his wife, Servilla; sons Okie, Isaiah, and Hosea; and daughter, Priscilla left Lost Cove on January 1, 1958. The only sign left of the community were words written on a wooden wall behind the pulpit in the church. Mr. Velmer Bailey wrote as follows:

> School closed forever at Lost Cove, December 17, 1957. Sinclair Conley, 75 years old. Last revival conducted by Clyde Fender, November 1956. Last Sunday school, November 26, 1957. Very sad.[17]

Mr. Bailey states that they took with them what they could carry. They took two cows out of the cove as well. That day, no trains ran along the Nolichucky River. The family hiked out, down the railroad tracks to Unaka Springs. Though Velmer did not want to leave the community, Isaiah knew the family would never return.[18] Even residents like Hazel Miller believed that, if possible, they'd return, because all the families felt safe.[19]

Throughout the years Lost Cove lands were sold and re-sold. The schoolhouse, which the Board of Education in Yancey County owned, sold to several families outside of the cove. Families sold their lands to members of their extended family as well as outsiders. Families with surnames Keeley, Canoy, Street, Thomas, and Maas now own land in Lost Cove. Records indicate that Lost Cove families began selling their lands in 1937.

Frank and Jane Bryant, J.C. Bryant's parents, sold their land to Harley and Mamel Bailey on July 1, 1937. The cost was $42 for the parcel adjoining the lands of I. Mac English and Wiley Tipton. The 37 acres began on the west side of Deep Hole Branch. The branch lay near the opening of Lost Cove trail from the railroad trail. The line ran from the forked white pine to the top of the ridge to Dock Tipton's line at rock cliffs. The land sat along the wire fence before the noticeable rock at the entry of the settlement. Harley and Mamel lived in the cove for several years before they moved to Erwin. There are several instances when land was bought by families in the cove from other families then resold to people outside of the community.

In 1941 Jettie Bailey, widowed wife of William, sold her land to Chester and

Carrie Tipton Bailey. The land cost only $25 and bordered her other lands. The boundary lines began on "a buckeye near the old cold springs Will Bailey corner including ⅓ interest in spring thence with Will Bailey Line to a Pine stump."[20] Chester and Carrie lived in Lost Cove until 1955 and then moved to Unaka Springs. They lived in the house across from Unaka Springs Hotel.

Clifford and Hazel Bailey Miller acquired land from E.L. Briggs and his wife, Eloise, in June 1948. Clifford and Hazel lived in Lost Cove during their childhood. The 30 acres cost them $10 and other valuables. The land adjoined land owned by the United States Forest Service, Bob Miller, and John Miller:

> Beginning on the stake below the Schoolhouse or on the East side of the Schoolhouse, said stake being on the South side of the public road; thence South to the line of John Miller in a southerly direction to a bunch of small lynns in the Branch; thence West with Mack English's line to a chestnut oak on top of the ridge in the line of Sam Miller; thence North with said Miller's line and Howell line following the crest of the ridge to a chestnut in the Howell line on the point of the ridge; thence with the Howell line to a stake in the public road; thence a Easterly direction with the public road to the beginning, containing, 30 acres or less.[21]

Clifford was 32 years old when he bought land from E.L. Briggs. Clifford and Hazel lived in the cove in their own home for 12 years, until 1950 when they moved to Erwin.

During the 1950s, many newspapers throughout North Carolina and the United States highlighted the Lost Cove settlement and its families. Articles depicted isolation, resilient family life, and the exit of some Lost Cove families and land sales. The *Asheville Citizen-Times* even headlined an article "Deserted Lost Cove can be Bought for a Price—about $20,000" in its Sunday edition on March 16, 1958. The writer, Doris Dumond, announced that the modern world had lured many Lost Cove families away from their isolated community. She appealed to the city folk who were bored of the fast life, those who wanted to enjoy peace in the mountains and the joy of living next to the forest. While there were no Lost Cove family names mentioned in the article, she wrote:

> The owners are asking from $600 to $3,500 for their individual lots, which range from 20 to 50 acres each. Altogether the price is around $20,000 for the entire tract of 300 acres "more or less" (the land has never been properly surveyed, and is believed to be more than 300 acres).[22]

Dumond's depiction of the pristine settlement with its springs and orchard captured the attention of many buyers, some of whom bought land without ever setting foot in Lost Cove. Instead of families passing their land down through generations, some lands were bought by Ernie Briggs from Burnsville, North Carolina; Charles Stern from Washington State; and several businessmen from Greensboro, North Carolina. Within four months, several parcels of Lost Cove sold to one man.

In July 1958, D.E. Koonts (Daniel Emmett) and his wife, Nannie, bought two separate land tracts from several Miller families. D.E. Koonts was owner of Daniel's Cleaners and Dryers in High Point as well as Koonts Cleaning Company in Greensboro. On July 18, 1958, two Miller couples—Swin and Martha and Ulis and Faye—sold their lands to Koonts.

Swin and Martha sold two tracts of land for $10. The land adjoined the lands of

Seven. The End of a Community

Jettie Bailey, I. Mac English, and others and was known as the Arch Bennett place. The lines led up the ridge to Wiley Tipton's place to where Rex Hedrick's line joined. The land contained 57 acres. The second tract adjoined the land of Dock Tipton and others. It ran southwest to a mahogany tree located on Wiley Tipton's line, then headed northeast to a hemlock pine near the road. This tract was 16 acres. Koonts' land also contained a right-of-way of 20 feet that led from the railroad tracks to the cemetery that sat on a knoll near Wiley Tipton's property line.[23] For only $10 Koonts secured 63 acres of land from Swin and Martha Miller. Koonts also bought land from Ulis and Faye Miller that day.

Ulis Miller sold his land to Koonts for $10. The land began at the mouth of Deep Hole Branch. As mentioned before, the 37 acres ran to the back line of I.R. Love's acreage. This land contained the same right-of-way as Swin and Martha Miller's land. The distance was about one-half mile and also lay near the cemetery. The land, first owned by Frank Bryant, was sold three times before Mr. Koonts purchased the tracts. The acreage remained with families in Lost Cove until Mr. Koonts.

Koonts did not remain the owner of these lands for too long. Within three weeks he sold the land to another businessman from Greensboro, Charles Keeley. Keeley was a prominent businessman of the Southern Rubber Company. D.E. Koonts sold his land to Keeley for $10 on July 30, 1958. The land included all three tracts that Koonts bought from the Miller families. Now, Charles Keeley owned the most acreage of land by an outsider in Lost Cove. Keeley, like Koonts, heard of Lost Cove land due to numerous articles in the newspapers. The territory, known for hunting throughout the western Carolinas, was prime territory for deer and bear. Like Koonts, Keeley wanted a piece of Lost Cove so he, along with others from the Greensboro area, could hunt in the mountains. Within two years, other families within the cove started to sell their lands to Keeley.

Clifford and Hazel Miller sold their land on December 16, 1960, for $600. The deed shows that Keeley's land joined the land of John Miller and the United States government. The 30-acre land deed also provides information on mineral rights:

> The Grantors hereby retain and reserve to themselves all the minerals of every description on, under or about the above described property, with the right to work same in any manner desired with the right of ingress, egress and the right to build roads to any mines or mineral deposits on side property, the right to the use of any water on said lands for mining purposes, the right to the use of timer for mining purposes; and the right to build power lines to any mines or mineral deposits on said property, such rights having been reserved by E.L. Briggs, and wife, Eloise Briggs, in deed conveying property to Grantors, deed dated the 26th of June 1948....[24]

The land first owned by E.L. Briggs clearly states that mineral rights belong to the grantor, even after he sold the land to Clifford Miller. Eventually Clifford Miller did retain mineral rights to his new land by selling it in 1960 to C.A. Keeley. While power did not exist in the cove, Keeley could build power lines for use to any mines and mineral deposits found on the property. This is the first descriptive information found that indicates mines and mineral deposits in Lost Cove territory. The only other details were from Albert Tipton and the "dead man's gold." Albert Tipton indicates that he, along with his brothers, discovered gold rocks when they attended the moonshine still while their father remained in the Buncombe County jail back in the 1920s.

One of the most important pieces of property within the cove was the schoolhouse, which doubled as the Mountain View Free Will Baptist Church. The sale of the schoolhouse began on August 13, 1958. The Yancey County Board of Education appointed Hubert D. Justice, secretary of the Board of Education, to sell and advertise for public sale. When the Board of Education advertised the sale on September 27, 1958, E.L. Briggs became the highest bidder at $75. Justice reported the bid, yet the bid became null when a higher bid was filed in the office of the superior court clerk in Yancey County that same day. The clerk directed Mr. Justice to advertise the sale of the property once again. Justice advertised the re-sale of the schoolhouse at the courthouse in Burnsville. E.L. Briggs once again became the highest bidder at $125 on October 25, 1958. Again, someone else bid a higher price for the schoolhouse that day in the clerk's office.

Finally, on November 22, 1958, at 11:15 a.m., the schoolhouse sold at the courthouse door to Mack B. Ray and his wife, Dorothy. They paid $500 for the schoolhouse property. No one outspent the Rays, not even E.L. Briggs, who first bid for the property. The sale went through on December 4, 1958, and was confirmed by the Board of Education; the chairman of the board, W.H. Peterson; and Mr. Justice, the secretary of the board.[25] E.L. Briggs' hope of owning the school was shattered by the Rays' higher bid. No documents show who may have outbid the couple the first two times the school went up for sale. The Board of Education wanted more money for the school and that is why the sale never went to E.L. Briggs and his wife. Mack and Dorothy Ray owned the land for nearly 10 years before they sold it to Keeley.

Another known outside family is the Sterns, who were from Pond Oreille County, Washington State and were Seventh Day Adventists. Charles Stern; his wife, Elizabeth; and their two children, Becky and Ben, purchased land in the cove in 1958. There is no information on how Charles Stern heard about Lost Cove. Like others, Stern probably read newspaper articles across the nation on Lost Cove and its exodus. In a 1959 article titled "Lost Cove Found by New Settlers," *Erwin Record* writer Harvey Miller wrote about Mr. Briggs selling his Lost Cove land and reported that "a family or group of Seventh Day Adventist[s]" had moved into the cove.[26] The Sterns owned nearly 50 acres of land for 10 years. The Sterns stayed in the cove for less than two or three years. No one knows which house the Sterns lived in or the names of other Seventh Day Adventists who may have moved into the cove also. Deeds are the best informative documents that were found on their owned lands.

While the Sterns were from Washington State, most of the lands were sold to people who had a connection to Koonts and Keeley and were from Guilford County, North Carolina. The third person to own land was Ruth T. Walker. Ruth Jessie Thacker Walker was the wife of William Sidney Walker. Walker was a buyer for tobacco and a farmer. They resided in Reidsville, North Carolina. Ruth acquired John Miller's land on July 10, 1961. The land adjoined holdings of C.A. Keeley, Ulis Miller, and the United States government. Her lands began

> on an Oak that stands on the North side of a small branch not far below the schoolhouse; then East or nearly so, to a Sourwood and Spruce Pine near the bank of a branch; thence South 40

Seven. The End of a Community

East about 84 poles, following the United States Government line to the Southeast corner; thence North or nearly so along the Unites States property, to a Lynn, a conditional corner made by and between Sam Tipton and Mose Tipton, his brother; thence a straight or direct line to the beginning, containing twenty acres more or less.[27]

There are no records indicating how Ruth heard about Lost Cove lands. The only legitimate evidence suggests that she and her husband were friends to Koonts and Keeley. Ruth owned the 20 acres for nine years. In July 1970 she sold the land to B.L. Thomas of Rockingham County for $10. Byron Thomas owned land in the cove until the late 2010s. There is one more person who lives in Guilford County who owns land to this day in Lost Cove, and his name is Norman Canoy.

On August 8, 2017, Norman Canoy sat down with me for an interview. Mr. Canoy lives outside of Greeneville, South Carolina, with his wife, Katherine Long Canoy. Canoy has two daughters, Norma Newton and Karen Alexander. Nicknamed Rooster and Old Norm, Mr. Canoy is a strikingly tall and honorable man. He is 83 years old and his intelligence and factual accounts provide important information to Lost Cove's later years. Canoy's story begins from the time the last family left Lost Cove in 1957.

Mr. Canoy and Mr. Keeley were friends, and Canoy worked for Keeley in Greensboro, North Carolina, during the 1950s. Mr. Charles Keeley of Greensboro, North Carolina, learned about Lost Cove through a friend from Morganton, North Carolina, and read article upon article on families leaving the cove when news broke throughout the United States and in local newspapers in Greensboro. Canoy states that "Keeley read articles out of the *Oakland Tribune* and other local newspapers about the settlement and an article even appeared in *Life* magazine right before 1957."[28] Canoy states that Mr. Keeley was fascinated with the cove. When he heard tales of people hiking into the cove and stripping and stealing the items the families left behind, Keeley sent a real estate agent down from Greensboro to talk with some of the families who were possibly interested in selling their land.[29] After Keeley purchased land, the pair took a trip into the cove.

Canoy first went into the settlement from the old sled trail on the Poplar side. The land is rugged and hard to walk. They toured the land for several hours. They checked Keeley's land lines and deeds. The men didn't stay in the cove too long that day, due to the sun setting. In 1960 the pair returned, but this time they walked the railroad tracks from Unaka Springs. Canoy states that all of the houses were still there except for one that had begun to fall down. After their visit, Canoy decided to buy some land. Both men loved to hunt, and Lost Cove is prime territory for deer. Canoy bought his first property in 1967. On October 19, Canoy purchased land from Ethel Ryles of Muscogee County, Georgia. Ethel Ryles was the daughter of John M. Howell and Olivia Bailey.

Norman Canoy's land purchase cost him a mere $10 for 50 acres of land. The deed book says the land formerly known as the John M. Howell land adjoins the lands of Velmer Bailey, H. Cooper, the United States government and others:

Beginning on a Spruce Pine and Maple in a branch known as the Fall Branch; then East to a Chestnut Oak; then up the ridge to a stake; then up the same ridge to a Chestnut; then West to a Buckeye; then down the branch to the beginning, containing 20 acres, more or less.

Second Tract: Adjoins the same lands as first tract; "beginning at the road at the H. Cooper corner, crossing an old field to a point of the ridge running with the H. Cooper lin; thence up a ridge to a stake at the road that leads across Flat Mountain; thence up the same ridge to a Chestnut Tree in the I. Mac English line; thence with I. Mac English line to a Buckeye near the Drip Rock on Fall Branch; thence down Fall Branch with its meanders to the Jettie Bailey line; thence with the Jettie Bailey line to a road and gate; thence with the upper side of the said road to the beginnings, containing 30 acres more or less."[30]

Mr. Canoy's land contains Velmer Bailey's apple orchard as well. The orchard, even in the late 1990s, produced some of the best, biggest apples ever seen. Within one year, Canoy purchased more land from the last known original family in the cove.

On June 6, 1968, Ulis Miller and his wife, Faye J. Miller, deeded to Norman W. Canoy and his heirs a certain tract of land adjoining the lands of John Howell, Velmer Bailey, and the U.S. Forest Service lands. Ulis Miller previously purchased this same track of land from Charles Stern and his wife, Elizabeth, on April 18, 1968, for $6000. The land that Canoy bought included two tracts of land. These tracts included nearly 50 acres of land and also joined Sam Cooper's land. This deed connects to the first deed on record in Lost Cove, which dates to 1898 when J.R. Young and his wife, Ellen, purchased land in the cove. Norman Canoy now owns 95 acres of land.

In 1968, Canoy sold a small piece of land back to Ulis and Faye Miller for $10. The deed book describes the land in question as follows:

Beginning at the road at the H. Cooper corner, and running thence in an Southerly direction, a straight line a distance of about 90 feet, to a stake in the said Cooper line; thence running in an easterly direction on the southerly side of an old road a distance of about 660 feet, more or less, to a stake in the old Jettie Bailey line; thence running in a Northerly direction with the said old Jettie Bailey line, a distance of about 120 feet, more or less, to a stake; thence running in a westerly direction with the northerly line of the old road, a distance of about 520 feet, more or less, to the point of beginning. And being a part of the same land conveyed to Norman Canoy, Inc., by deed from Ethel Ryles dated October 19, 1967.[31]

Ulis Miller still owns this property in Lost Cove. His daughter, Teresa Bowman, now has the deed to show his property lines.

During the 1960s, Keeley and Canoy hired Grant B. Ward to serve as caretaker in Lost Cove. Mr. Ward was from Green Mountain, North Carolina. He was born on March 9, 1934. Keeley and Canoy hired Mr. Ward due to the amount of people hiking into the cove to pillage through the houses. When the families left the settlement, they believed they would return to their homes, but modern life kept them away. Grant Ward took care of the property until the late 1970s. The one-armed, gun-toting man scared many hikers away during those years. Grant Ward is said to have been an expert on Lost Cove, but all the families in the cove already left before he entered. Mr. Keeley's first purchase of land did not occur until 1958 and Canoy did not buy land in the settlement until 1967. Canoy and Keeley hunted several times in the cove while Mr. Ward cared for their property. Norman Canoy has a huge deer displayed in his home from a hunt in the cove.

From the 1970s to the early 1990s, land in the cove changed hands again among Keeley, Chester Bailey, Virginia Bryant, and Marie Tipton. The Yancey County deed books provide important information regarding Lost Cove land lines. Since the land switched hands quite often in the settlements inception, referring to old deeds and

Seven. The End of a Community

new deeds can be puzzling due to the buying and selling of land within families. The original families passed down their properties to some family members, yet many, like Keeley, sold their land to friends.

On February 27, 1975, Charles Keeley and his wife, Helene, sold some of his land to Byron L. Thomas and Norman Canoy. The land included the schoolhouse. The land both men inherited also contained 30 acres. The school land, first sold to Mack Ray and his wife, then to Keeley, now landed in the hands of Thomas and Canoy. Two tracts from the original document are included along with an excerpt that read: "And being the same lands or schoolhouse site as described in a deed dated December 4, 1958, from the Board of Education of Yancey County to Mack B. Ray and wife, Dorothy D. Ray, recorded in Deed Book 122, at page 131."[32] The land included one and one-half acres and was near the line of W.E. Uptegrove's property. It is interesting to find this small bit of information within this particular deed. William E. Uptegrove was a wealthy businessman from New York City and his property sat close to the school.

It is unknown when and how W.E. Uptegrove attained property in Lost Cove. Outsiders often heard of the cove from other businessmen. Did Uptegrove have contact at some point with I. Mac English, who owned the sawmill in the early years of the settlement? There are many newspaper accounts that speak of Uptegrove's visits to the mountains of North Carolina and Tennessee. His business, W.E. Uptegrove and Brothers, manufactured veneers, cigar boxes, and fine woodwork in New York. Uptegrove did own a plant in Johnson City during the late 1890s. He bought the old furniture and factory at an auction sale in 1897 from the clerk and master.[33] His newly bought plant was called the American Cigar Box Lumber Company and was located on North Roan Street.

Uptegrove often traveled to Johnson City for business purposes. There are no deeds to determine how many acres Uptegrove owned in Lost Cove, how he inquired the land, or when he sold the land. One article in *The Comet* of Johnson City says Uptegrove and company, along with J.M. Buck Lumber Company of the city, acquired lands in the Flag Pond area of Unicoi County to buy timber and wanted to build a railroad line through the heart of the territory. The line was to connect with the OR&C (Ohio River and Charleston Railroad) at Red Banks along the Nolichucky River and run to Flag Pond.[34] Did he instead buy timber from English at the English sawmill near Lost Cove? Uptegrove's plant in Johnson City needed wood to make cigar boxes.

Evidence is needed to determine how involved his business may have been with the Mac English sawmill and if he purchased pine for his cigar boxes and furniture. If Uptegrove did purchase wood from English sawmill, then it would make sense to own land in the cove. Uptegrove died around June 27, 1935, in Newark, New Jersey. While Uptegrove and Mac English may have been the first outsiders to own land in the early years of the settlement, Charles Keeley, Byron Thomas, and Norman Canoy were the three outsiders who owned land after the original families left. Keeley and Thomas eventually sold their lands, while Canoy retains his even to this day.

Charles Keeley owned his Lost Cove lands for 21 years before he passed away on April 28, 1977, at the age of 81. Two years after his death, Helen inherited the four tracts of land her husband left to her. While Helen kept the land, some original families sold their lands to family members generation after generation.

On December 5, 1979, Chester Bailey and wife, Carrie, of Erwin, deeded their land to Hazel Miller and Virginia Bryant. The Baileys sold their land, which adjoined that of Jettie Bailey and others, for $10.[35] The land contained four acres. The original land deed described in this deed is recorded in the Yancey County Deed Book 86, page 440. Hazel and Virginia were Chester and Carrie Bailey's daughters. Hazel Miller was the wife of Clifford Miller. In 1990 the land that Chester Bailey once owned fell into the hands of his granddaughter, Joan C. Maas. Virginia sold her part of the land to her daughter for $10. Hazel Miller, Virginia's sister, owned her part of the land until 2000. On September 7, 2000, Hazel signed her land over to Joan. The document provides no details regarding the cost of the land. The grantee paid a valuable amount to Hazel, her aunt. The four acres of land is still owned by the original family, the Baileys, passed down through generations. Hazel, Virginia's sister, lives in Erwin to this day. On August 23, 2017, Virginia "June" died in Michigan. Joan still owns land in Lost Cove. The Tiptons, one of the original families, will own land for the longest time period, while the Baileys and Millers will be the last of the original families to keep their land.

On May 14, 1991, Marie Tipton, wife of Kenneth and daughter-in-law to Wiley, sold some of her land to Daniel Scott Street and Philip Todd Street from Shallotte, North Carolina. Marie Tipton's land consisted of 42 acres, yet she only sold one acre to the Street men. The deed book describes the land in question as follows:

> Beginning at the United States Forest Services aluminum pipe and runs with the Forest service line to a birch, thence with the Kenneth Tipton line to a poplar, thence to an oak, thence to a Cucumber, thence to a Maple in the US Forest Service line..., containing one acre more or less.[36]

Though the Street brothers owned a small piece of her land, it would be 22 years before Marie Tipton sold the last of her 41 acres to the United States Forest Service. On August 30, 2003, Marie sold her land for $50,604.00. The forest service land tract no. P-328, part of the Pisgah National Forest, was witnessed and signed in Yancey County. Her lands would no longer be sold to outsiders or passed down to her daughter. Marie Tipton died in 2004, within one year of selling her land. She was not the only one to sell her land in the 2000s.

On December 18, 2012, Charles S. Keeley III, co-executor of his father Charles S. Keeley II's estate, along with his wife and Tyler Ross Keeley, deeded their grandfather Charles Keeley's land to the Southern Appalachian Highlands Conservancy. The conservancy is a non-profit organization that works to conserve the habitat and lands of the Appalachian Mountains throughout North Carolina and Tennessee. The organization creates partnerships with private landowners and public agencies by managing and owning the lands deeded to them.

The land that Charles Keeley purchased from D.E. Koonts included the lands that once belonged to E.L. Briggs and Ulis Miller. Keeley owned more than 100 acres of land in 1958. He deeded 31 acres, which included the schoolhouse property, to Byron Thomas and Norman Canoy in 1975. Charles Keeley's land deeded to the conservancy includes a

95.12 acre parcel as shown on a survey for Southern Appalachian Highland Conservancy by Kee Mapping & Surveying dated December 10, 2012 and recorded in Plat Book 4 at page 17, Yancey County Registry. Save and except a right-of-way 20 feet wide leading from the Clinchfield Railroad Company right of way to the cemetery, and also excepting the cemetery containing about 1 ½ acres as shown on said survey.[37]

The Keeley family's deed allowed the conservancy to own, manage, and maintain the property that he once owned. In an interview with Norman Canoy in 2017, he addresses a controversy with the Southern Appalachian Highland Conservancy. Mr. Canoy owns nearly 95 acres of land in the cove yet now one tract is in question. Canoy has always received bills for his land taxes from Yancey County Register of Deeds. Sometime in 2017, he quit receiving a bill to pay his taxes on 45 acres of land he owns. Somehow the conservancy acquired Canoy's land without permission. Did Canoy's land get lumped into the sale with Keeley's land via a surveying mistake? The land had to be surveyed by someone. If Canoy's land did fall into the conservancy's hands without permission, then he should be able to retain his land. The registry of deeds, surveyors, and lawyers are looking into the problem. Canoy will be the only outsider to keep his land by the summer of 2018.

On May 30, 2018, Juanita C. Thomas, executor of Byron Lewis Thomas, deeds her husband's land to T. Russell Fox and his wife, Brandy D. Fox, of Burnsville, North Carolina. The pair bought the land, which consisted of the property that Thomas and Canoy bought from Charles Keeley in 1975, for $10. The land contains two tracts: one is one and one-half acres and the other 20. The couple now own part of Canoy's land with him. Mr. Fox could be related to Trina Presnell Fox, who once lived in Mac English's house in Lost Cove, after he left the settlement. This last deed is the only deed left associated with Lost Cove.

Today, some families still own land in Lost Cove. Mr. Ulis Miller owns one of the three houses still standing. Mr. Miller owns two tracts within Lost Cove. One tract is four acres and the second tract is three and one-half acres. Mr. Bailey's uncle's daughter owns five acres of land in Lost Cove. June Bryant inherited her father's land and owned the land until she deeded it to her daughter, Joan Maas. According to Mr. Bailey, the government (National Forest Service) kept buying up the land from the descendants. Not too long ago, Mrs. Tipton's 62 acres was bought by the government. Only five people that he knows own land in Lost Cove.[38]

For decades the Baileys, Tiptons, and Millers were the prominent families in Lost Cove. Families such as the Bennetts, Bryants, Coopers, and Howells were either married to women from the prominent families or bought land in the community from the families. The Arrowoods and Presnells came into the community to work the sawmill during the 1930s and 1940s. Their short life in the cove is a time that they all will remember and cherish.

Until the middle 1990s, there were at least eight houses still standing in the settlement and no overgrowth or fallen trees. The Unaka Mountains rise beyond the northeast. Flat Top Mountain lies above the settlement, overlooking the beautiful landscape. The rolling fields and colorful trees come to life. Maples, oaks, pines, and locust line the truck path down to the railroad tracks. The orchards still provide apples and the American chestnut, which once thrived throughout the Appalachians, remains. Yes ... the chestnut still lives in Lost Cove.

Though no trespassing signs line the pathway into Lost Cove, many hikers, including former residents, still walk the rugged trail around the mountain to visit the cemetery and to catch a glimpse of the community. Along the trail one can see Swin Miller's 1938 Chevy hunkered down near a tree with bullet wounds scattered across the body. The rusted truck hauled timbers and families up and down the road to the railroad. The springs still run in Lost Cove, though they flow softer than they once did. The cemetery sits alone, although no weeds hang on to the stones. In May of 2007, fires swept through Lost Cove, burning much forest. All of the houses are gone except for two: Bob Miller's house, which sits below the schoolhouse, and Chester Bailey's house, which sits near the bottom of the Forest Service Trail from Flat Top Mountain. There are many old chimneys that rise above the overgrowth and weeds that can still be seen.

Life once ran deep through this community. The fertile grounds provided good farming for the families, while the timber ensured good income. Moonshine helped families have extra help before and during the Depression. Family members were born and others died during the years. The pristine cemetery holds more than 30 graves, with babies and teenagers, seniors and the middle-aged. The railroad no longer carried passengers as coal became a necessity throughout the country. The much-needed road into the community became a funding issue with the Yancey County road superintendent and citizens. Youth wanted to seek and further their high school education, while young men left for World War II and the Vietnam and Korean wars. Families could no longer stay outside of the modern world. Life changed in the cove. Families left the settlement but always thought they would return. The former residents of Lost Cove still remember their lives, their love of land, and their triumphs in the settlement.

In 2019, I stood on the railroad tracks, taking a deep breath before the climb into Lost Cove. The hike from Unaka Springs, Tennessee, into the settlement is long yet memorable. Once you step onto the railroad tracks near the historic Unaka Springs Hotel, time slows down. I've hiked into Lost Cove more than 20 times since being a child. Stories of train derailments, runaway trains, and death echo throughout the history books and oral histories. The terrain along the gorge is peaceful yet haunting. The railroad tracks cradle the mountainside, leaving little room between you and the CSX trains. There are some cracks and crannies where hikers can escape the trains or river, but you never want to get caught on the tracks around the rock walls, unless you know how to climb. The raging Nolichucky is swift and deep. The picturesque river is known for deaths, taking lives without hesitation. The river slithers like a snake below the tracks, raging and surging into the unknown.

Two and one-half miles on railroad tracks can take a toll on your shins. Crossties bear years of hardships and rusted rivets lay scattered along the rocks. Once you step off the tracks, a new world of perception emerges. The lush forest overshadows the rutted out truck trail that once carried timber down the rutted out road to the railroad tracks. The steep hike up the rain-swollen trail takes you on a journey in time. Gurgling springs create small pools of water for lichens and salamanders. Massive

Seven. The End of a Community

poplars, oaks, and pines line the beaten road. Sunlight shimmers through the thick forest growth, creating beams of light that bounce off the plush moss on the boulders.

The overgrown trail makes it hard to distinguish family homesteads, barn foundations, and outside buildings like chicken coops and corncribs. One can still see the schoolhouse steps and take a walk beside the Reverend Bob Miller's house, but the land is slowly folding the house over into the ground. The conservancy still manages the 95 acres they maintain in the cove. Volunteers and staff hike into the cove taking their members with them to view the lands. Hikers, hunters, and occasional river raft guides and rafters enter now, catching a glimpse of the once lively community.

Appendix
Sketches of Lost Cove Interviewees

Mrs. Geneva Tipton McNabb (b. 1918)—89 years old when interviewed—resided in Erwin, Tennessee. After leaving Lost Cove, Mrs. McNabb's family moved to Erwin. She married Harry McNabb in 1942. She worked for the Southern Pottery Company, Industrial Garments, Hoover, and NN, Inc. before retiring. Mrs. McNabb had three children: James Wiley, Eldora, and Tammy Camille. Geneva was a wonderful woman who painted replicas of the old pottery patterns on dried out gourds to sell during the fall festivals. She lived next to her sister Edna. Geneva Tipton McNabb passed away on January 11, 2011. Her son, James Wiley, died on December 21, 2011. Her daughters, Eldora "Pug" and Camille, live in Erwin.

Mr. J.C. Bryant (b. 1932)—75 in 2007—resided in Erwin, Tennessee. After leaving Lost Cove at the age of 18, J.C. joined the army and fought in the Korean War. He married Dixie Lee Tipton in 1954. He and Dixie Lee had four children: Kathy Ann, Marcella, Randy, and Jeff. J.C. provided the best information for me during this process. I will long remember his smart wits and loveable character. J.C. passed away on June 20, 2020, in Erwin.

Geneva Tipton McNabb (2007). Photograph by the author.

Mr. Homer Tipton (b. 1932)—75 when interviewed—resided in Marion, Indiana. He served in the Korean War with the Seventh Infantry Division. He married Ore Lee Watts in Erwin, Tennessee, in 1960. The couple moved to Muncie, Indiana, after his service. They had six children: Homer Jr., William, Angela, Roy Lee, Amy, and Michael. Homer is J.C. Bryant's brother-in-law. His father, King David, was born in Lost Cove. Homer passed away on February 14, 2014, in Grant County, Indiana.

Mr. Isaiah Bailey (b. 1940) was 67 when we spoke and residing in Erwin, Tennessee. After leaving Lost Cove at the age of 18, Mr. Bailey, his parents, brothers, and sister moved to the Lamar

Homer Tipton and J.C. Bryant (2007). Photograph by the author.

community in Washington County, Tennessee. He married Nellie Lynn Bailey in 1942. They have one child, Angela Bailey. Mr. Bailey retired from NFS (Nuclear Fuel Services) in 2006. His family resides in Erwin, Tennessee.

Mr. Verno Davis (b. 1915) was 92 in 2007 and resided in Erwin, Tennessee, along Spivey Mountain. After leaving his preaching job in Lost Cove, Mr. Davis preached in various churches in North Carolina and Tennessee. He married Gay-Nell Hensley in 1922. They had seven children: Verdie, Evelyn, Anita, Sandra, Gwendolyn, Gerald Lynn (who died at childbirth) and a lone surviving son, the Reverend R.J. Davis. Mr. Davis was a warm, humble man who helped tremendously on church customs and sermons. Mr. Verno Davis passed away on February 9, 2013.

Norman Canoy (b. 1935), 85, resides outside of Clemson, South Carolina. He

Isaiah Bailey (2007). Photograph by the author.

Verno Davis, wife Gaynell (left), and daughter Gwendolyn (2007). Photograph by the author.

was born on May 14, 1935, in Asheboro, North Carolina. Norman is the son of Wilson and Reba May Farlow Canoy. He is married to Katherine Long Canoy. Norman has two daughters: Karen Alexander and Norma Newton. Norman is an avid Clemson Tiger fan and always attends the football games.

Ms. Betty Bryant Peterson (b. 1934), 86, resides in Erwin, Tennessee. She was born on Christmas Day. She is the daughter of Jim and Naomi Bryant of White Oak Flats, North Carolina. After leaving her homestead in White Oak Flats, Betty moved to Nashville. She worked for the Maxwell House Hotel as a server. She met Gerald Peterson, a paratrooper from Portland, Oregon. He was stationed at Fort Knox. They married in 1953 in Roswell, Georgia. The couple adopted a four-day-old girl in 1962. Their daughter, Brenda, lives in Lexington, Kentucky. Betty is a grandmother and loves when her daughter and grandchildren visit her home.

Teresa Miller Bowman (b. 1953) lives in Erwin, Tennessee. She is the daughter of Ulis and Faye Johnson Miller. Teresa married Doug Bowman on August 31, 1974. Doug is the son of J.R. and Judy Bowman of Unicoi County. Teresa retired from the Unicoi County School System. She and Doug have two daughters, Julia and Lindsay. The couple resides in Erwin, Tennessee.

Joseph Michael Bailey (b. 1952) is the son of Edwin Yates Bailey and Jenny Lee Witcher. He was born in Philadelphia, Pennsylvania. His father, Edwin, was born in Lost Cove. Joseph has two brothers, Terry Allen and James Edwin. He is married to Janet Lee Vines. Joe retired from teaching after 36 years. Joe has three stepchildren: Amy, Kim, and Seth. The couple resides in Hampton, Tennessee, and Joe works as a part-time security guard for Fish Springs Marina.

Camille McNabb Flett (b. 1958) resides in Erwin, Tennessee. Her sister, Eldora "Pug," resides with Camille and her husband, Roddy Flett. Her brother, James Wiley, died in 2011 at the age of 63. Camille and Roddy have been married for four years. Roddy is the son of Arnot and Williamina Inkster Flett of Orkney Island, Scotland.

James L. Johnson (b. 1954) was born on March 24, 1954, in Point Pleasant, New Jersey. He is the son of Kenneth and Dolly Jane Miller Johnson. Jim is married to Joy Lynn Heumer, and the

Norman Canoy with daughters Karen Alexander (left) and Norma Newton (2017). Photograph by the author.

couple has two children: Jessica and Joshua. Every year Jim returns to Unaka Spring in Erwin to live during the summer months. He lives in Chester Bailey's old house. Jim owns the old Unaka Springs Hotel. His cousin Richard Bailey, Polly's son, owns the old church that sits above the Unaka Springs Hotel. Richard, son of Polly and Harley Bailey, lives in Fredericksburg, Virginia.

Lost Cove Speaks
Christy A. Smith

Hidden in the mountain's bosom,
    Past the devil's washing bowls and state line,
        A trail winds up the ridge.
            Railroad tracks bend and disappear beneath your feet.
           A community's yarn spins.
        One hundred years weathered the ground's path. Old logging trails slide through
           the slanted trees. A community's silence speaks:
              I was plumb tarred when they left. They warped
        my body and drove me into the ground. I've seen many
    a gully washer and almost tumbled into the crick.
Been dragged and worn to death only stones lay in my path.
I was sad that there coal beds came when passenger trains was thriving.
    People couldn't go to town without money and timber was becoming scarce.
    My ole craggy trail rutted out and the trucks couldn't reach bottom.
        I did all I could for this here peoples but the railroad quit takin' my
            passengers. Even now I feel tarred but hikers keep coming and I
                like feeling their shoes on my skin.
            *L*ook at me, I was alone for many years wasting in the ravines. My ole
            rusty body couldn't be saved, so
            I just laid here rested. I've been beaten and bruised
        traveling up that there ole trail for years, now I lay wasting,
      hidden in this cranny. Heck, the only time I get eyed is when
    hikers come through, even they just stand on that there trail and look
down at me and just start rocking. I've held so much timber my back
hurts, but I kept trudging along, helping my folks. They always kept me
  pretty, but now I just sit rusted and decayed. I'm sad
        because nobody comes here anymore. It's been a coon's age
          since I've had thanks and all. Since I am old and run
            down, I can't be saved. Yep, I thank they got to be
              somebody telling my story.
                I've held your story longer than
              most, since I was the one that helped the
            people and kept them safe from bears and bobcats.
        Jest look at me now, I's been rotting for years and never
      complained to my peoples. I used to keep them bodies
    warm at night and gave them good ground to sleep on. I had four
or five families living in my house, cooking, sleeping, and eating on
my floors. I've been peeled back by falling wallpaper all my born days, but I
  never complained. My windows are all broken, my stove doesn't work
    anymore and my ole corroded box springs stay home to rats. I'm used to

Lost Cove Speaks

having smoke rise up in my face. Heck it would take all day for them to
    just air me out.
        I remember folk setting on my sturdy porch jest
            swinging and telling stories. They'd laugh and sing all the
      time, always waiting for the next story or supper time. I've had plenty
of folks wear my body thin, but I don't care. They have been the heart of this
here community and so have I , but now I'm sad and tarred that they ne'er coming
back. They said one day they would bring me back to life, but I just sit here waiting for
    that there time to come.
*W*ell, I've been waiting since that there first day
    when they started digging into me. They planted
        and reaped my body thin, while I was thirsting for water and food.
        But they sure did nurse my body with water from that there spring,
      when I was dry. I helped that family flourish with crops, herbs and
        corn. I brought in money they had to keep going back and
          forth to town, but that stopped when the trains quit coming. I sure
        do wish they would have stayed up here in these mountains.
          I did my best, but there wasn't enough care to keep them here.
        *B*ut I kept them here for all this time.
      I'm the only one that there seems to be no bellyache from.
      I've been the soul of this here community. I've wept
    each time they dug and loosened my soil. I've had
    headstones poke my head and coffins lying so tired against my skin.
Even I don't know how I've lasted all my born days. There are so
many folks living in me: grandmas, mothers, grandpas, fathers, children, and soldiers.
  I remember that there time when that little girl died from tuberculosis.
    They sang and wept so loud that rain washed down my cheeks.
      My body was tired but I remained at peace with fresh flowers and leaves
        growing round me. I stand lonely though, up here by myself tucked
          away in the underbrush. Not nearly a hiker comes to see me.
           I just fade like the etching on them headstones.
              *D*on't be so hard on yourself. They bent and bended me
         so hard, my belly was about to fall off
           into the river, once. They have been keeping me grounded for years. I've
      been the backbone to this here community. I helped and
    carried them to town. They always rode me with pride. Every time
they stepped onto my tracks they would smile and stare at the cliff
rocks and the raging Nolichucky. I miss stopping along the river's gorge.
  Heck, I had to brake ½ mile up track to stop. They never set heavy metal on me
    or lost their path. I never was so drained until coal came. Wasn't too long
      and I had to say goodbye myself. That there day was the hardest born
        day of my life. Now all I see are hikers and they walk
          on me every day catching a glimpse of Lost Cove.

Chapter Notes

Preface

1. Aldo Leopold, *A Sound County Almanac, and Sketches Here and There* (New York: Oxford University Press, 1989), 223.

Introduction

1. Everett M. Kivette, "Epitaph for Lost Cove: Few Outsiders Ever Saw the Fabled Community, and Fewer Ever Will," *The State Magazine* 27 (March 1971): 1.
2. Pat Alderman, *All Aboard* (Erwin, TN: Y's Men's Club, 1968), 14.
3. John Preston Arthur, *Western North Carolina: A History from 1730 to 1913* (Johnson City, TN: Overmountain Press, 1996), 179.
4. Samuel Byrd, interview by Christy A. Smith, Burnsville, NC, January 23, 2009.

Chapter One

1. Alderman, *All Aboard*, 14.
2. Ibid.
3. Frank Elliott, "The Ghost Town of the Nolichucky: Walking into Lost Cove North Carolina," Blue Ridge Country 10 (May/June 1997): 42.
4. Ibid., 42.
5. J.L. Lonon, *Tall Tales of the Rails on the Carolina, Clinchfield, and Ohio* (Johnson City, TN: Overmountain Press, 1989), 27.
6. Ibid.
7. Ibid., 24.
8. Bailey, Sr., vol. 1, 139.
9. Ibid., 131.
10. Ibid.
11. The National Archives. (2010), Compiled Service Records of Volunteer Union Soldiers Who Served in Organizations from the State of North Carolina. Retrieved from https://www.fold3.com/image/264727095.
12. Ibid.
13. National Archives, Pension Rolls, # 388.
14. Alderman, *In the Shadow*, 62.
15. Robert H. Fowler, "Lost Cove Is Completely Shut In by 4,000-Foot Mountains," *Greensboro Daily News*, August 8, 1951.
16. Isaiah Bailey, interview by Christy A. Smith, Erwin, TN, October 4, 2007.
17. Alderman, *All Aboard*, 14.
18. Gordon McKinney, "The Civil War in Appalachia," in *The Appalachians: America's First and Last Frontier*, ed. Mari-Lynn Evans, Robert Santelli, and Holly George-Warren (New York: Random House, 2004), 33.
19. Ibid., 35.
20. Ibid., 34. McKinney describes western North Carolina's loyalty during the Civil War era.
21. Ina Van Noppen and John Van Noppen, *Western North Carolina Since the Civil War* (Boone, NC: Appalachian Consortium Press, 1973), 6.
22. Phillip S. Paludan, *Victims: A True Story of the Civil War* (Knoxville: The University of Tennessee Press, 1981), 69–70.
23. Don Haines, "Gone, But Not Forgotten: For Those Who Lived There, the Community of Lost Cove Retains a Special Place in Their Hearts," *Our State Magazine*, October 2004, 152.
24. Ibid.
25. Bryant interview, March 9, 2007.
26. O. Blackmun, "War Comes to the Hills," in *Western North Carolina: Its Mountains and Its People to 1880* (Boone, NC: Appalachian State University, 1977), 343–355.
27. Ibid., 346.
28. Ron V. Killian, *A History of the North Carolina Third Mounted Infantry Volunteers: March 1864 to August 1865* (Berwyn Heights, MD: Heritage Books, Inc., 2008), 1.
29. Ibid., 28.
30. Ibid., 5.
31. Ibid.
32. Ibid., 6–7.
33. Ibid., 11.
34. Geneva Tipton McNabb, interview by Christy A. Smith, Erwin, TN, September 20, 2007.
35. Compiled Service Records of Volunteer Union Soldiers of North Carolina, NARA, Catalog ID #300398. Retrieved from www.fold3.com.
36. Ibid., 13.
37. Ibid., 17.
38. Ibid., 22.
39. The National Archives, Pension Rolls, #388.
40. McNabb interview, September 20, 2007.
41. Ibid.

42. "Lost Cove Moonshiners," *Asheville Daily Gazette*, February 22, 1898.
43. Arthur, 1. Notes by Captain Gudger are deposited by him with his report with the secretary of state at Raleigh. See Pub. Doc. 1887, and *Dugger v. McKesson*, 100 N.C., p.1.
44. Lloyd Bailey, Sr., ed., *The Heritage of the Toe River Valley: Avery, Mitchell, and Yancey Counties, North Carolina, Vol. 2* (Marceline, MO: Walsworth Publishing Co., 1997). 94.
45. J.L. Lonon, *Tall Tales of the Rails on the Carolina, Clinchfield, and Ohio* (Johnson City, TN: Overmountain Press, 1989), 24.
46. Patricia Duane Beaver, "Family, Land, and Community," in *Appalachia: Social Context Past and Present*, ed. Bruce Ergood and Bruce E. Kuhre (Dubuque, IA: Kendall and Hunt Publishing Co., 1991), 299.

Chapter Two

1. Durwood Dunn, *Cades Cove: The Life and Death of a Southern Appalachian Community 1818–1937* (Knoxville: The University of Tennessee Press, 1988), 186.
2. Elliot, 42.
3. Bryant interview, March 9, 2007.
4. *Ibid*.
5. *Ibid*.
6. *Ibid*.
7. Pat Alderman, *In the Shadow of the Big Bald: About the Appalachians and Their People* (Mars Hill, NC: Bald Mountain Development Corporation, 1972), 64.
8. Haines, 42.
9. Bryant interview, March 9, 2007.
10. *Ibid*.
11. *Ibid*.
12. Homer Tipton, interview by Christy A. Smith, Erwin, TN, September 6, 2007.
13. *Ibid*.
14. McNabb interview, September 26, 2007.
15. *Ibid*.
16. *Ibid*.
17. Bryant interview, March 9, 2007.
18. McNabb interview, September 26, 2007.
19. *Ibid*.
20. *Ibid*.
21. Bryant interview, March 9, 2007.
22. *Ibid*.
23. *Ibid*.
24. Isaiah Bailey interview, October 4, 2007.
25. *Ibid*.
26. Bryant interview, March 9, 2007.
27. McNabb interview, September 26, 2007.
28. Bryant interview, March 9, 2007.
29. "Last Family Leaves Isolated Cove Section, Never to Return," *Johnson City Press Chronicle*, April 2, 1958, 83–85.
30. McNabb interview, September 26, 2007.
31. Frank Elliott, "The Ghost Town of the Nolichucky: Walking into Lost Cove," *Blue Ridge Country*, May/June 1997, 42–43.
32. McNabb interview, September 26, 2007.
33. Haines, 155.
34. *Ibid*.
35. Guthrie interview, August 9, 2019.
36. Haines, 155.
37. John B. Alderman, Historical Materials, 1970–78, Archives of Appalachia, East Tennessee State University, Series II, Box 5:5.
38. Bailey interview, September 27, 2007.

Chapter Three

1. William Way, Jr., *The Clinchfield Railroad: The Story of a Trade Route Across the Blue Ridge Mountains* (Chapel Hill: The University of North Carolina Press, 1931), 98.
2. Mary Hattan Bogart, *Conquering the Appalachians: Building the Western Maryland and Carolina, Clinchfield & Ohio Railroads Through the Appalachian Mountains* (Dexter, MI: Thomson-Shore, Inc., 2000), 42.
3. William Way, Jr., *The Clinchfield Railroad: The Story of a Trade Route Across the Blue Ridge Mountains* (Chapel Hill: The University of North Carolina Press, 1931), 156.
4. South and Western Railway Files, Construction of Train Track Revision, Archives of Appalachia at East Tennessee State University.
5. Bryant interview, March 9, 2007.
6. Bogart, 67.
7. Bryant interview, March 9, 2007.
8. *Ibid*.
9. Way, 271. Way provides a list of general laws on the railway held by the Carolina, Clinchfield, and Ohio.
10. James A. Goforth, *Building the Clinchfield: A Construction History of America's Most Unusual Railroad* (Erwin, TN: GEM Publishers, 1989), 34.
11. *Ibid*., 34.
12. Ronald L. Lewis, "Appalachian Myths and the Legacy of Coal," in *The Appalachians: America's First and Last Frontier*, ed. Mari-Lynn Evans, Robert Santelli, and Holly George-Warren (New York: Random House, 2004), 76. The article focuses on how the railroads played an important role in coal production and transportation.
13. Carolina, Clinchfield, and Ohio Railway vertical files. Archives of Appalachia: East Tennessee State University.
14. Way, 261. Way addresses stations for which no time is shown for the trains to stop.
15. McNabb interview, September 26, 2007.
16. Bryant interview, March 9, 2007.
17. *Ibid*.
18. *Ibid*.
19. McNabb interview, September 26, 2007.
20. Isaiah Bailey interview, October 4, 2007.
21. McNabb interview, September 26, 2007.
22. Camille McNabb Flett interview, July 2, 2020.
23. Jim Johnson interview, August 5, 2020.
24. Wilbur R. Miller, *Revenuers & Moonshiners: Enforcing Federal Liquor Law in the Mountain South,*

1865–1900 (Chapel Hill: The University of North Carolina Press, 1991), 152.

25. Bailey, vol. 2. 113.

26. Carolina, Clinchfield, and Ohio Railroad files, 1899–1983, Industrial Agent Correspondence, 1909–1925, Archives of Appalachia, East Tennessee State University, Series III, Box 28-x 87.

27. Ibid.

28. Alderman, *In the Shadow of the Big Bald: About the Appalachians and Their People*, 62.

29. Ibid.

30. Ibid.

31. McNabb interview, September 26, 2007.

32. Isaiah Bailey interview, October 4, 2007.

33. *American Lumberman*, September 22, 1923,.80.

34. "Britton is Delegate of Masonic Society," *The Winston Salem Journal*, June 22, 1919, 12.

35. McNabb interview, September 26, 2007.

36. Bryant interview, March 9, 2007.

37. Alderman, 62.

38. Carolina, Clinchfield, and Ohio File, Archives of Appalachia, East Tennessee State University, Industrial Agent Correspondence, 1909–1925, Series III, Box 62-x 977. Sidetrack agreement at Lost Cove, North Carolina. June 28, 1916.

39. Ibid.

40. Bryant interview, March 9, 2007.

41. Haines, 155.

42. Forest History Society, "Champion Pulp and Paper Mill in Canton, NC Timeline," accessed March 22, 2020, https://foresthistory.org/digital-collections/champion-pulp-and-paper-mill-in-canton-nc-timeline/.

43. Bryant interview, March 9, 2007.

44. "Forest Fires in Tennessee Creep to Town Borders," *Asheville Citizen-Times*, September 10, 1925, 1.

45. Homer Tipton interview, September 6, 2007.

46. "Flames under control," *The Bristol Herald Courier*, September 13, 1925, 1.

47. "Latest Menace on Devil's Creek, State Line Marker," *The Knoxville Journal*, September 13, 1925, 1.

48. Clinchfield Railroad Company Correspondence, March 29, 1926.

49. Clinchfield Railroad Company Correspondence, May 26, 1927.

50. Clinchfield Railroad Company Correspondence, March 17, 1928.

51. Clinchfield Railroad Company Correspondence, February 6, 1929.

52. Clinchfield Railroad Company Correspondence, April 12, 1929.

53. Clinchfield Railroad Company Correspondence, February 3, 1931.

54. Clinchfield Railroad Company Correspondence, July 9, 1931.

55. Clinchfield Railroad Company Correspondence, January 3, 1933.

56. J. M English Son's Company Correspondence to Clinchfield Railroad, August 9, 1938.

57. Death Certificate, Tennessee Deaths 1914–1966. *Isaac MacCall English*. Retrieved from www.familyresearch.org

58. Ibid., Annie Minerva English.

59. Bryant interview, September 27, 2007.

60. Ibid.

61. Lonon, 25.

62. Ibid.

63. Bailey, vol. 1, 187.

Chapter Four

1. Tom Robertson, "Moonshine on the Mountain," in *The Appalachians: America's First and Last Frontier*, ed. Mari-Lynn Evans, Robert Santelli, and Holly George-Warren (New York: Random House, 2004), 84.

2. Shapiro, 104.

3. Wilbur R. Miller, *The Revenuers and Moonshiners: Enforcing Federal Liquor Law in the Mountain South, 1870–1990* (Chapel Hill: The University of North Carolina Press, 1991), 99–100.

4. Camille McNabb Flett interview, July 2, 2020.

5. Loyal Durand, Jr., "Mountain Moonshining in East Tennessee," *Geographical Review* 46 (April 1956): 168–181.

6. McKinney, 85.

7. Robertson, 84.

8. Wilbur Miller, "The Revenue: Federal Law Enforcement in the Mountain South, 1870–1900," *The Journal of Southern History* 55, no. 2 (May 1989): 195–216.

9. Shapiro, 30.

10. Arthur, 272. Arthur discusses the history of moonshine, its definition, and how it is made.

11. Miller, 31.

12. Miller, 36.

13. Jess Carr, *The Second Oldest Profession: An Informal History of Moonshining in America* (Radford, VA: Commonwealth Press, Inc., 1978), 33.

14. Lloyd Bailey, Sr., ed. *News from Yancey: Articles from Area Newspapers (1840–1900)* (Burnsville: Yancey Graphics, 1983), 69.

15. *The Falcon*, Elizabeth City, NC, June 10, 1887.

16. Arthur, 334.

17. Miller, 181.

18. Ibid.

19. Thomas Michie,. *The Encyclopedic Digest of North Carolina Reports: Being a Complete Encyclopedia and Digest of All the North Carolina Case Law Up to and Including Volume 167, North Carolina Reports, and Volumes 1 to 83, Southeastern Reporter* (Charlottesville, VA: The Michie Company, Law Publishers, 1916).

20. *The Southwestern Reporter Volume 182: Comprising All the Current Decisions of the Supreme and Appellate Courts of Arkansas, Kentucky, Missouri, Tennessee and Texas* (St. Paul: West Publishing Company, 1916).

21. "Spectacular Raid of Three Stills near the State Line," *Johnson City Press Chronicle*, June 12, 1924, 9.

22. Ibid.

23. "Many Convictions on Whiskey Charges," *Asheville Citizen-Times*, November 7, 1924, 7.
24. *Ibid.*
25. Alfred Tipton, "The True Story," 1972.
26. "Large Still Is Taken by Yancey County Officers," *Asheville Citizen-Times*, August 7, 1931, 15.
27. Kellner, 230.
28. Anonymous.
29. *Ibid.*
30. Bryant interview, March 9, 2007.
31. Bryant interview, March 9, 2007.
32. Durand, 170.
33. *Ibid.*
34. McNabb interview, September 26, 2007.
35. Alfred Tipton, "A True Story," 1972.
36. Bryant interview, September 6, 2007.
37. Richard Bailey interview, August 5, 2020.
38. Esther Kellner, *Moonshine: Its History and Folklore* (Indianapolis: The Bobbs-Merrill Company, 1971), 37.
39. *Ibid.*, 37–38.
40. Bryant interview, September 6, 2007.
41. Tipton interview, September 6, 2007.
42. Bryant Interview, September 27, 2007.
43. Robertson, 86.

Chapter Five

1. Howard Dorgan, *Giving Glory to God in Appalachia: Worship Practices of Six Baptist Subdenominations* (Knoxville: The University of Tennessee Press, 1987), 38.
2. Deborah Vansau McCauley, *Appalachian Mountain Religion: A History* (Chicago: University of Illinois Press, 1995), 2.
3. Bill Leonard, ed. *Christianity in Appalachia: Profiles in Regional Pluralism* (Knoxville: The University of Tennessee Press, 1999), 122.
4. Leonard, 123.
5. Bailey, vol.2, 113.
6. *Ibid.*
7. *Ibid.*
8. *Ibid.*
9. *Ibid.*
10. McCauley, 129.
11. Howard Dorgan, *Giving Glory to God in Appalachia: Worshipping Practices of Six Baptist Subdenominations* (Knoxville: The University of Tennessee Press: 1987), 114.
12. *Ibid.*, 39.
13. Bryant interview, September 6, 2007.
14. Bryant interview, September 6, 2007.
15. Bryant interview, September 6, 2007.
16. Davis interview, September 18, 2007.
17. McNabb interview, September 26, 2007.
18. *Ibid.*
19. Deborah V. McCauley, "Grace and the Heart of Appalachian Mountain Religion," in *Appalachian Social Context Past and Present*, eds. Bruce Ergood and Bruce E. Kuhre (Dubuque, IA: Kendall & Hunt Publishing Co., 2003), 358.
20. Verno Davis, interview by Christy A. Smith, Erwin, TN, September 28, 2007.

21. *Ibid.*
22. Bryant interview, September 6, 2007.
23. Davis interview, September 18, 2007.
24. Isaiah Bailey interview, October 4, 2007.
25. Bailey, vol.2, 113.
26. Davis interview.
27. Bailey, vol. 2, 113.
28. Allen Jackson, "Fasting and Prayer," posted July 25, 2015, http://faithbaptistgb.org/fasting-and-prayer/.
29. Bailey, Velmer (February 1,1996). Fasts of Velmer Bailey. [Describes Velmer Bailey Fasting Entries from 1952–1961]. Holy Bible entries.
30. *Ibid.*
31. *Ibid.*
32. Jim Johnson interview, August 5, 2020.
33. "To Play Santa Claus," *Asheville Citizen-Times*, December 7, 1952, 15, https://www.newspapers.com/image/195363776/?terms=lost%2Bcove%2Bchildren%2Bvisit%2Basheville.
34. "Photographer Tells of Wait.," *Statesville Daily Record*, December 18, 1952, 16, https://www.newspapers.com/image/10587133/?terms=photographer%2Btells%2Bof%2Bwait.
35. *Ibid.*
36. "Children from Lost Cove Have Big Time Seeing the Sights of the City" *Asheville Citizen-Times*, December 20, 1952, 14, https://www.newspapers.com/image/195390571/?terms=lost%2Bcove%2Bchildren.
37. "11 Youngsters from Lost Cove Coming to City," *Asheville Citizen-Times*, December 18, 1952, 15, https://www.newspapers.com/image/195387113/?terms=11%2Byoungsters.
38. "Children from Lost Cove Have Big Time Seeing the Sights of the City," *Asheville Citizen-Times*, December 20, 1952, 14, https://www.newspapers.com/image/195390571/?terms=lost%2Bcove%2Bchildren.
39. "Santa Finally Arrives at Lost Cove," *Asheville Citizen-Times*, December 21, 1952, 44, https://www.newspapers.com/image/195392910/?terms=lost%2Bcove%2Bchildren.
40. "Operation Santa of Five Airmen Slowed to Walk," *The Palm Beach Post*, December 21, 1953, 7, https://www.newspapers.com/image/131562801/?terms=santa%2Band%2Bhelpers%2Bclimb%2Bmountain.
41. "Santa Moving Infantry Style," *The Galveston Daily News*, December 21, 1953, 2, https://www.newspapers.com/image/23300408/?terms=santa%2Bmoving%2Binfantry%2Bstyle.
42. "Air Force Crew Delivers Presents to Lost Cove," *Kingsport News*, December 21, 1953, 8, https://www.newspapers.com/image/68744687/?terms=air%2Bforce%2Bcrew%2Bdelivers%2Bpresent%2Bto%2Blost%2Bcove.
43. *Ibid.*
44. Betty Peterson interview, October 26, 2020.
45. James K. Crissman, *Death and Dying in Central Appalachia: Changing Attitudes and Practices* (Chicago: University of Illinois Press, 1994), 106.
46. *Ibid.*, 107.

47. Isaiah Bailey interview, October 4, 2007.
48. CDC. "Achievements in Public Health, 1900–1999: Control of Infectious Diseases," *Morbidity and Mortality Weekly Report* 48(29) (July 30, 1999): 621–629.
49. Lost Cove Cemetery Memorials. (n.d.). Find a Grave. Retrieved March 1, 2020, from www.findagrave.com.
50. *Ibid.*, Tipton.
51. Death certificate for Bonnie Miller, 3, June, 1938, File No. 004219366, North Carolina State Board of Health.
52. Kris Hawkins Rosalina interview, August 2020.
53. Death certificate for Coolidge Miller, 15, February, 1943, File No. 004220247, North Carolina State Board of Health.
54. Lloyd Bailey, Sr., ed. *The Heritage of the Toe River Valley: Avery, Mitchell, and Yancey Counties, North Carolina, Vol.4* (Marceline, MO: Walsworth Publishing Co., 1997), 320.
55. Roy Guthrie interview, August 9, 2019.
56. "Civilian Conservation Corps," History.com, May 11, 2010, https://www.history.com/topics/great-depression/civilian-conservation-corps.
57. Death Certificate for Russell Tipton, 2 April, 1936, File No. 1876–1880 1936. Film# 004218679. North Carolina State Board of Health.
58. Crissman, 69.
59. *Ibid.*, 70.
60. *Ibid.*, 60.
61. Bryant interview, September 6, 2007.
62. Tipton interview, September 6, 2007.
63. Crissman, 116.
64. *Ibid.*
65. *Ibid.*, 44.
66. *Ibid.*, 49.
67. Bryant interview, September 6, 2007.
68. *Ibid.*
69. McNabb interview, September 26, 2007.
70. Alderman, *In the Shadow of the Big Bald: About the Appalachians and Their People*, 62.
71. McNabb interview, September 26, 2007.
72. *Ibid.*
73. Betty Bryant Peterson interview, October 26, 2020.
74. Haines, 154.
75. Teresa Miller Bowman interview, May 25, 2020.
76. "Lost Cove: It's Out of This World Except for Road," *Asheville Citizen-Times*, October 5, 1952, 13.
77. Lloyd Bailey, Sr., vol.1, 185.
78. Robert H. Fowler, "Lost Cove Is Completely Shut In by 4,000-Foot Mountains," *Greensboro Daily News*, August 8, 1951, 2.
79. Isaiah Bailey interview, October 4, 2007.
80. Lloyd Bailey, vol. 1, 185.
81. Haines, 154.
82. Robert H. Fowler, "Lost Cove Is Completely Shut In by 4,000-Foot Mountains," *Greensboro Daily News*, August 8, 1951, 2.
83. *Ibid.*, 2.
84. George McCoy, "Lost Cove: It's Out of This World," *Asheville Citizen-Times*, October 5, 1952.
85. Robert H. Fowler, "Lost Cove Is Completely Shut In by 4,000-Foot Mountains," *Greensboro Daily News*, August 8, 1951.
86. Haines, 154.
87. Isaiah Bailey interview, October 4, 2007.
88. McNabb interview, September 26, 2007.
89. "A Town Where Time Stands Still," *Oakland Tribune Parade*, March 8, 1953, 116, https://www.newspapers.com/image/276841299/.
90. Bailey, Chad Fred, interview by Christy A. Smith on March 23, 2020.
91. Isaiah Bailey interview, October 4, 2007.
92. *Ibid.*
93. Lloyd Bailey, *Images of Yancey County: Pictorial History of a Western North Carolina City* (Burnsville, NC: Yancey History Association, 1993), 66.
94. McCoy, 36.
95. *Ibid.*, 67.

Chapter Six

1. Dunn, 179.
2. Patricia Duane Beaver, "Family, Land, and Community," in *Appalachia: Social Context Past and Present*, ed. Bruce Ergood and Bruce E. Kuhre (Dubuque, IA: Kendall and Hunt Publishing Co., 1991), 299.
3. Eller, 38.
4. Yancey County NC Census—1860 Agricultural Census.
5. http://files.usgwarchives.org.
6. North Carolina Deaths, 1931–1944, Image #115. Retrieved from www.familysearch.org.
7. United States Census—1900. Retrieved from www.familysearch.org.
8. United States Census—1940. Retrieved from www.familysearch.org.
9. "Gravestone of Yellow Jacket John Bailey and wife Lovada Ray Bailey," 2002. Monument inscription, Yellow Jacket John Bailey Cemetery, Relief, North Carolina.
10. Chad Bailey informant, 2015.
11. *Ibid.*
12. https://southernappalachian.wordpress.com/2013/01/22/lost-cove-ghost-town-in-the-national-forest/, Gale Ratliff.
13. Tennessee, County Marriages, 1790–1950, Image #447. Retrieved from www.familysearch.org.
14. Joseph Bailey interview, February 4, 2020.
15. Tennessee County Marriages, 1790–1950, Image #342. Retrieved from www.familysearch.org.
16. Obituaries: John Orville Bailey, *Johnson City Press*, November 28, 1992, p.2.
17. North Carolina Deaths, 1906–1930, Image #1570. Retrieved from www.familysearch.org.
18. Tennessee County Marriages, 1790–1950, Image #623. Retrieved from www.familysearch.org.
19. United States Census, 1940. Retrieved from www.familysearch.org.
20. United States Census, 1860, North Carolina, Yancey, Image #128. Retrieved from www.familysearch.org.
21. North Carolina County Marriages, 1762–

1979, Image #544. Retrieved from www.familysearch.org.
22. United States Census, 1940. Retrieved from www.familysearch.org.
23. North Carolina Deaths, 1906-1930, Image #2397. Retrieved from www.familysearch.org.
24. North Carolina County Marriages, 1762-1979, Image #892. Retrieved from www.familysearch.org.
25. Tennessee Death 1914-1966, Image #1528. Retrieved from www.familysearch.org.
26. Camille McNabb Flett interview, July 2, 2020.
27. Tipton, Paul (2010, December 19). *Albert Tipton*. Retrieved from www.findagrave.com.
28. North Carolina Marriage Register, 1881-1912, Image #261. Retrieved from www.familysearch.org.
29. Tennessee County Marriages, 1790-1950, Image #794. Retrieved on www.familysearch.org.
30. North Carolina Deaths, 1906-1930, Image #690. Retrieved on www.familysearch.org.
31. North Carolina Death Records, Wiley Tipton, #004219384 Image #2139. Retrieved on www.familysearch.org.
32. Woodby, Madge, tombstone. www.findagrave.com.
33. Tennessee State Marriage Index, 1780-2002. Isaac Tipton and Juanita Ambrose. Retrieved from www.familysearch.org.
34. Tennessee County Marriages, 1790-1950, Image #268. Retrieved from www.familysearch.org.
35. Tennessee County Marriages, 1790-1950, Image #188. Retrieved from www.familysearch.org.
36. Tennessee County Marriages, 1790-1950, Image #76. Retrieved from www.familysearch.org.
37. United States Census, 1910, Image #10. Retrieved from www.familysearch.org.
38. North Carolina Marriages, 1762-1979, Image #42. Retrieved from www.familysearch.org.
39. United States Census, 1920, North Carolina, Yancey Ramsey Township, Image #26. Retrieved from www.familysearch.org.
40. Tennessee County Marriages, 1790-1950, Image#719. Retrieved from www.familysearch.org.
41. United State Census, 1910, North Carolina Yancey, Ramsey Township, Image #5. Retrieved from www.familysearch.org.
42. Tennessee Deaths, 1914-1966, Image #2046. Retrieved from www.familysearch.org.
43. Tennessee Deaths, 1914-1966, Image #639. Retrieved from www.familysearch.org.
44. Tennessee County Marriages, 1790-1950, Unicoi County, Image #214. Retrieved from www.familysearch.org.
45. Tennessee County Marriages, 1790-1950, Unicoi County, Image #74. Retrieved from www.familysearch.org.
46. United States Census, 1940, Tennessee, Unicoi County, Image #12. Retrieved from www.familysearch.org.
47. Tennessee County Marriages, 1790-1950, Unicoi County, Image #69. Retrieved from www.familysearch.org.
48. United States Census, 1940, Tennessee, Unicoi County, Image #6. Retrieved from www.familysearch.org.
49. Tennessee County Marriages, 1790-1950, Unicoi County, Image #540. Retrieved from www.familysearch.org.
50. United States Census, 1940, Tennessee, Unicoi County, Image # 6. Retrieved from www.familysearch.org.
51. United State Census, 1930, Virginia, Buchanan County, Image #17. Retrieved from www.familysearch.org.
52. United States Census, 1940, Tennessee, Unicoi County. Image #17. Retrieved from www.familysearch.org.
53. *Veterans Affairs BIRLS Death File* (/title/848/veterans-affairs-birls-death-file :accessed May 4, 2020), database and images, https://www.fold3.com/title/848/veterans-affairs-birls-death-file.
54. Memories of District C, Civilian Conservation Corps, 1934, p.47.
55. United States Census 1940, Hawaii Territory, Honolulu. Image #342. Retrieved from www.familysearch.org.
56. World War II Enlistment Records, #3404 4203. Retrieved from www.fold3.com/record/87680913-wiley-tipton.
57. Tennessee County Marriages, 1790-195, Unicoi, Image #667. Retrieved from www.familysearch.org.
58. Tennessee County Marriages, 1790-1950, Sullivan, Image #132. Retrieved from www.familysearch.org.
59. United States Census, 1940, California, Sausalito, Image #8. Retrieved from www.familysearch.org.
60. Tennessee County Marriages, 1790-1950, Unicoi, Image #187. Retrieved from www.familysearch.org.
61. United States Census, 1910, North Carolina, Yancey County, Ramsey Township, Image # 6. Retrieved from www.familysearch.org.
62. United States Census, 1930, Tennessee, Unicoi County, Image #11. Retrieved from www.familysearch.org.
63. Tipton, David, MC. Compiled Service Records of Volunteer Union Soldiers, Image #260641055. Retrieved from www.fold3.com/image/260641055.
64. United States Census, 1880, North Carolina, Mitchell, Harrell, Image #3. Retrieved from www.familysearch.org.
65. United States Census, 1870, North Carolina, Mitchell, Harrell, Image #6. Retrieved from www.familysearch.org.
66. Tipton, Sidney. Compiled Service Records of Volunteer Union Soldiers, Image #260831255. Retrieved from www.fold3.com/images/260831255.
67. North Carolina Marriage Register, Yancey County, Image #544. Retrieved from www.familysearch.org.
68. United States Census, 1870, North Carolina,

Notes—Chapter Six

Yancey County, Jacks Creek, Image #24. Retrieved from www.familysearch.org.

69. North Carolina Marriages, Registry of Marriages, Yancey County, Image #281. Retrieved from www.familysearch.org.

70. Tennessee Deaths, 1914–1966, Image #1803. Retrieved from www.familysearch.org.

71. United States Census 1900, North Carolina, Mitchell County, Image #19. Retrieved from www.familysearch.org.

72. North Carolina Deaths, 1906–1930, Image #927. Retrieved from www.familysearch.org.

73. United States Census 1900, North Carolina, Mitchell, Harrell Township, Image #3–4. Retrieved from www.familysearch.org.

74. United States Census 1910, Tennessee, Carter, Civil District 3, Image #33. Retrieved from www.familysearch.org.

75. United States Census 1900, North Carolina, Yancey County, Ramsey Township, Image #14. Retrieved from www.familysearch.org.

76. North Carolina Marriages, 1762–1979, Yancey, Image #371. Retrieved from www.familysearch.org.

77. North Carolina Deaths, 1906–1930, Image #2261. Retrieved from www.familysearch.org.

78. Tennessee Death Certificates, 1914–1966, Image #1376. Retrieved from www.familysearch.org.

79. Tennessee County Marriages, 1790–1950, Unicoi, Image #534. Retrieved from www.familysearch.org.

80. Rosalina, Kris Hawkins, interview by Christy A. Smith, July 7, 2020.

81. National Selective Service Registration Card, D.S.S. Form 1 #1497, Image #683832931. Retrieved from www.fold3.com.

82. Tennessee Death Certificates, 1914–1966, Unicoi, Image #1804. Retrieved from www.familysearch.org.

83. Tennessee County Marriages, 1790–1950, Unicoi, Image #509. Retrieved from www.familysearch.org.

84. Tennessee Death Certificates, 1914–1966, Image #2023. Retrieved from www.familysearch.org.

85. Tennessee County Marriages, 1790–1950, Washington County, Image #108. Retrieved from www.familysearch.org.

86. Betty Bryant Peterson interview, October 26, 2020.

87. Obituaries Esta Ada Arrowood, *Antigo Times*, May 3, 2016. Retrieved from https://antigotimes.com/2016/05/esta-ada-arrowood-99/.

88. Unicoi County Army Enlistment Card, July 1, 1941. Retrieved from www.fold3.com/image/683834808.

89. North Carolina Obituaries, Yancey County, Image #1853. Retrieved from www.familysearch.org.

90. "Obituaries, Calvin Coolidge Miller," *Johnson City Press*, February 16, 1943, 2.

91. North Carolina Marriage Register, Mitchell County, Red Hill Township, Image #178. Retrieved from www.familysearch.org.

92. United States 1920 Census Records, Yancey County, Ramsey Township, North Carolina, Image #29. Retrieved from www.familysearch.org.

93. Teresa Miller Bowman interview, August 16, 2020.

94. United States 1930 Census Records, Yancey County, Ramsey Township, North Carolina, Image #26. Retrieved from www.familysearch.org.

95. Jim Johnson interview, August 5, 2020.

96. *Ibid.*

97. *Ibid.*

98. Tennessee County Marriages, 1790–1950, Unicoi County, Image #185. Retrieved from www.familysearch.org.

99. "Obituaries, Phil Miller," *Johnson City Press*, July 11, 2008, 2.

100. North Carolina Death Certificates, Bonnie Miller, Image #1209. Retrieved from www.familysearch.org.

101. Jim Johnson interview, August, 5, 2020.

102. United States Draft Registration Card, Kenneth Johnson, #10105, Belmar, New Jersey. Retrieved from www.fold3.com.

103. United States Draft Registration Card, Ulis Miller, #11542, Unicoi County, Tennessee. Retrieved from www.fold3.com.

104. Teresa Bailey Bowman interview, August 2020.

105. North Carolina Marriage Certificates, Yancey County, Ramsey Township, Image #769. Retrieved from www.familysearch.org.

106. United States Census Records, Yancey County, North Carolina. Retrieved from www.familysearch.org.

107. United States Census 1940, Mitchell County, North Carolina, Image #11. Retrieved from www.familysearch.org.

108. United States Census 1940, Washington County, Tennessee, Image #22. Retrieved from www.familysearch.org.

109. Roy Guthrie interview, August 9, 2019.

110. "Obituaries, Harvey T. Bryant, Sr.," Image #957. Retrieved from www.familysearch.org.

111. "Obituaries, Dula Hensley," *Johnson City Press*, May 10, 1997, 2.

112. United States Census, 1940, Yancey County, Ramsey Township, North Carolina, Image #13. Retrieved from www.familysearch.org.

113. North Carolina Death Certificates, Yancey County, Ramsey Township, North Carolina, Image #522. Retrieved from www.familysearch.org.

114. Tennessee Death Certificates, 1914–1966, Image #2512. Retrieved from www.familysearch.org.

115. North Carolina Death Certificates, Yancey County, Ramsey Township, North Carolina, Image #912. Retrieved from www.familysearch.org.

116. Lloyd Bailey, Sr., ed. *The Heritage of the Toe River Valley: Avery, Mitchell, and Yancey Counties, North Carolina, Vol.1* (Marceline, MO: Walsworth Publishing Co., 1994), 187.

117. *Ibid.*

118. United States Census 1880, Yancey County, Ramsey Township, North Carolina, Image #16. Retrieved from www.familysearch.org.

119. United States Census, 1910, North Carolina, Yancey, Ramsey Township, Image #5. Retrieved from www.familysearch.org.

120. Register of Marriages, Yancey County, North Carolina, Image #257. Retrieved from www.familysearch.org.

121. North Carolina Deaths, 1931–1994, Marion, McDowell County, Image #1796. Retrieved from www.familysearch.org.

122. United States Census 1930, Yancey County, Ramsey Township, North Carolina. Retrieved from www.familysearch.org.

Chapter Seven

1. George W. McCoy, "Lost Cove: It's Out of This World," in *The Heritage of the Toe River Valley: Avery, Mitchell, and Yancey Counties, North Carolina, vol.1,* ed. Lloyd Bailey, Sr. (Marceline, MO: Walsworth Publishing Co., 1994), 35.

2. Unicoi County Affidavit in Yancey County, North Carolina Deed Book: CRP 244: 62.

3. "Lost Cove: It's Out of This World Except for Road," *Asheville Citizen-Times*, October 5, 1952, 13.

4. "Building of Lost Cove Road Is Up to People of Yancey," *Asheville Citizen-Times*, March 14, 1953, 9.

5. "New Efforts Made to Get Road for Lost Cove Section," *Asheville Citizen-Times*, May 8, 1958, 19.

6. Bailey interview, October 2007.

7. Davis interview.

8. Bailey interview, October 2007.

9. "Hearing Set on the Clinchfield Passenger Service Request," *Asheville Citizen-Times*, November 13, 1953, 11.

10. "First it was the Tweetsie," *Asheville Citizen-Times*, September 15, 1953, 4.

11. Haines, 155.

12. *Ibid.*

13. Bailey's *Images of Yancey County*, 67.

14. "The Lost Land of the Lost Cove," *Raleigh News and Observer*, January 1, 1961.

15. Bailey interview.

16. "Last Family Leaves Isolated Cove Section, Never to Return," *Johnson City Press Chronicle*, April 3, 1958, 83.

17. Haines, 153.

18. Isaiah Bailey interview, October 4, 2007.

19. Haines, 155.

20. Yancey County, North Carolina, Deed Book 86: 440.

21. Yancey County, North Carolina, Deed Book 117:124.

22. "Deserted Lost Cove can be bought for a Price—about $20,000," *Asheville Citizen-Times*, March 16, 1958, 15.

23. Yancey County, North Carolina, Deed Book 120: 363.

24. Yancey County, North Carolina, Deed Book 117:124.

25. Yancey County, North Carolina, Deed Book 122:131.

26. " Lost Cove Found by New Settlers," *The Erwin Record*, April 8, 1959, 1.

27. Yancey County, North Carolina, Deed Book 121:258.

28. Canoy, Norman, interview by Christy A. Smith, August 12, 2017.

29. *Ibid.*

30. Yancey County, North Carolina, Deed Book 140:19.

31. Yancey County, North Carolina, Deed Book 140:499.

32. Yancey County, North Carolina, Deed Book 159: 27.

33. "Sold at Last, the Old Furniture Factory Goes Into New Hands," *The Comet, Johnson City, Tennessee,* November 25, 1897, 3.

34. "Will Build a Railroad," *The Comet,* Johnson City, Tennessee, March 2, 1899, 3.

35. Yancey County, North Carolina, Deed Book 180:67.

36. Yancey County, North Carolina, Deed Book 229:422.

37. Yancey County, North Carolina, Deed Book 680:245.

38. Isaiah Bailey interview, October 4, 2007.

Bibliography

"Air Force Crew Delivers Presents to Lost Cove." *Kingsport News*, December 21, 1953. Retrieved from www.newspapers.com.
Alderman, John B. Historical Materials, 1970–78, Archives of Appalachia, East Tennessee State University, Series II, Box 5:5.
Alderman, Pat. *All Aboard*. Erwin, TN: Y's Men's Club, 1968.
Alderman, Pat. *In the Shadow of the Big Bald: About the Appalachians and Their People*. Mars Hill, NC: Bald Mountain Development Corporation, 1972.
Alderman, Pat. *The Wonders of the Unakas in Unicoi County*. Erwin, TN: Pat Alderman, 1964.
American Lumberman. September 22, 1923.
Arthur, John Preston. *Western North Carolina: A History from 1730 to 1913*. Johnson City, TN: Overmountain Press, 1996.
Bailey, Chad Fred. Interview by Christy A. Smith. March 23, 2020.
Bailey, Isaiah. Interview by Christy A. Smith. Erwin, TN, October 4, 2007.
Bailey, Joseph. Interview by Christy A. Smith. February 4, 2020.
Bailey, Lloyd. *Images of Yancey County: Pictorial History of a Western North Carolina City*. Burnsville, NC: Yancey History Association, 1993.
Bailey, Lloyd, Sr., ed. *News from Yancey: Articles from Area Newspapers 1840–1900*. Burnsville, NC: Yancey Graphics, 1983.
Bailey, Lloyd, Sr., ed. *The Heritage of the Toe River Valley: Avery, Mitchell, and Yancey Counties, North Carolina, Vol. 1*. Marceline, MO: Walsworth Publishing Co., 1994.
Bailey, Lloyd, Sr., ed. *The Heritage of the Toe River Valley: Avery, Mitchell, and Yancey Counties, North Carolina, Vol. 2*. Marceline, MO: Walsworth Publishing Co., 1997.
Beaver, Patricia Duane. "Family, Land, and Community." In *Appalachia: Social Context Past and Present*, edited by Bruce Ergood and Bruce E. Kuhre. Dubuque, IA: Kendall and Hunt Publishing Co., 1991.
Blackmun, O. "War Comes to the Hills." In *Western North Carolina: Its Mountains and Its People to 1880*, 343–355. Boone, NC: Appalachian State University, 1977. Retrieved February 21, 2020, from www.jstor.org/stable/j.ctt1xp3mp5.26.
Bogart, Mary Hattan. *Conquering the Appalachians: Building the Western Maryland and Carolina, Clinchfield & Ohio Railroads Through the Appalachian Mountains*. Dexter, MI: Thomson-Shore, Inc., 2000.
Bowman, Teresa Miller. Interview by Christy A. Smith. September 10, 2020.
"Britton Is Delegate of Masonic Society." *The Winston-Salem Journal*, June 22, 1919.
Bryant, J.C. Interview by Christy A. Smith. Erwin, TN, March 9, 2007.
Bryant, J.C. Interview by Christy A. Smith. Erwin, TN, September 6, 2007.
Bryant, J.C. Interview by Christy A. Smith. Erwin, TN, September 27, 2007.
"Building of Lost Cove Road Is Up to People of Yancey." *Asheville Citizen-Times*, March 14, 1953.
Byrd, Samuel. Interview by Christy A. Smith. Burnsville, NC, January 23, 2009.
Canoy, Norman. Interview by Christy A. Smith. August 12, 2017.
Carolina, Clinchfield, and Ohio Railroad Records (1909–1954). Archives of Appalachia, East Tennessee State University, Industrial Agent Correspondence, Series III, Box 62, X-977.
Carolina, Clinchfield, and Ohio Railroad Records (1899–1983). Archives of Appalachia, East Tennessee State University, Industrial Agent Correspondence, Series III: Box 28, X-87.
Carr, Jess. *The Second Oldest Profession: An Informal History of Moonshining in America*. Radford, VA: Commonwealth Press, Inc., 1978.
CDC. "Achievements in Public Health, 1900–1999: Control of infectious diseases." *Morbidity and Mortality Weekly Report* 48(29) (July 30, 1999): 621–629.
"Children from Lost Cove have Big Time Seeing the Sights of the City." *Asheville Citizen-Times*, December 20, 1952. Retrieved from www.newspapers.com.

Bibliography

Clinchfield Railroad Company Correspondence. March 29, 1926.
Clinchfield Railroad Company Correspondence. May 26, 1927.
Clinchfield Railroad Company Correspondence. March 17, 1928.
Clinchfield Railroad Company Correspondence. February 6, 1929.
Clinchfield Railroad Company Correspondence. April 12, 1929.
Clinchfield Railroad Company Correspondence. February 3, 1931.
Clinchfield Railroad Company Correspondence. July 9, 1931.
Clinchfield Railroad Company Correspondence. January 3, 1933.
Compiled Service Records of Volunteer Union Soldiers of North Carolina, NARA, Catalog ID #300398. Retrieved from www.fold3.com.
Crissman, James K. *Death and Dying in Central Appalachia: Changing Attitudes and Practices*. Chicago: University of Illinois Press, 1994.
Davis, Verno. Interview by Christy A. Smith. Erwin, TN, September 18, 2007.
Death certificate for Bonnie Miller. June 3, 1938. File No. 004219366. North Carolina State Board of Health.
Death certificate for Coolidge Miller. February 15, 1943. File No. 004220247. North Carolina State Board of Health.
Death certificate for Russell Tipton. April 2, 1936. File No. 1876–1880 1936. Film #004218679. North Carolina State Board of Health.
Death Certificate. Tennessee Deaths 1914–1966. Isaac MacCall English. Retrieved from www.familyresearch.org.
"Deserted Lost Cove can be bought for a Price—about $20,000." *Asheville Citizen-Times*, March 16, 1958.
Dorgan, Howard. *Giving Glory to God in Appalachia: Worship Practices of Six Baptist Subdenominations*. Knoxville: The University of Tennessee Press, 1987.
Dunn, Durwood. *Cades Cove: The Life and Death of a Southern Appalachian Community 1818–1937*. Knoxville: The University of Tennessee Press, 1988.
Durand, Loyal, Jr. "Mountain Moonshining in East Tennessee." *Geographical Review* 46 (April 1956): 168–181.
"11 Youngsters from Lost Cove Coming to City." *Asheville Citizen-Times*, December 18, 1925. Retrieved from www.newspapers.com.
Elliott, Frank. "The Ghost Town of the Nolichucky: Walking Into Lost Cove, North Carolina." *Blue Ridge Country* 10 (May/June 1997): 41–43.
Evans, Mari-Lynn, Robert Santelli and Holly George-Warren, eds. *The Appalachians: America's First and Last Frontier*. New York: Random House, 2004.
The Falcon. Elizabeth City, NC, June 10, 1887.
"First It Was the Tweetsie." *Asheville Citizen-Times*, September 15, 1953.
"Flames Under Control." *The Bristol Herald Courier*, September 13, 1925.
Flett, Camille McNabb. Interview by Christy A. Smith. July 2, 2020.
"Forest Fires in Tennessee Creep to Town Borders." *Asheville Citizen-Times*, September 10, 1925.
Forest History Society. "Champion Pulp and Paper Mill in Canton, NC Timeline." Accessed March 22, 2020. https://foresthistory.org/digital-collections/champion-pulp-and-paper-mill-in-canton-nc-timeline/.
Fowler, Robert H. "Lost Cove Is Completely Shut In by 4,000-Foot Mountains." *Greensboro Daily News*, August 8, 1951.
Goforth, James A. *Building the Clinchfield: A Construction History of America's Most Unusual Railroad*. Erwin, TN: GEM Publishers, 1989.
Guthrie, Roy Lee. Interview by Christy A. Smith. August 9, 2019.
Guthrie, Roy Lee. Photograph collection (1906–1951), Archives of Appalachia, East Tennessee State University, Series I, Box I, #229.
Haines, Don. "Gone, But Not Forgotten: For those who lived there, the community of Lost Cove retains a special place in their hearts." *Our State Magazine*, October 2004.
"Hearing Set on the Clinchfield Passenger Service Request." *Asheville Citizen-Times*, November 13, 1953.
History.com. "Civilian Conservation Corps." Originally published May 11, 2010. Accessed March 6, 2020. https://www.history.com/topics/great-depression/civilian-conservation-corps.
Jackson, Allen. "Fasting and Prayer." Posted July 25, 2015. http://faithbaptistgb.org/fasting-and-prayer/.
James A. Goforth Photo Collection (1906–1951). Archives of Appalachia, East Tennessee State University, Series I, Box I, photo #229.
James T. Dowdy Photograph Collection (1890–1950). Archives of Appalachia, East Tennessee State University, Johnson City, TN. Accession 107, photo #827.
J.M. English Son's Company Correspondence to Clinchfield Railroad, August 9, 1938.
John Biggs Alderman Papers (1918–1983). Archives of Appalachia, East Tennessee State University, Historical Materials, 1970–1978, Series II, Box 5:5.
Johnson, Jim. Interview by Christy A. Smith. August 5, 2020.
Kellner, Esther. *Moonshine: Its History and Folklore*. Indianapolis: The Bobbs-Merrill Company, 1971.
Killian, Ron V. *A History of the North Carolina Third Mounted Infantry Volunteers: March 1864 to August 1865*. Berwyn Heights, MD: Heritage Books, Inc., 2008.

Kivette, Everett M. "Epitaph of Lost Cove: Few Outsiders Ever Saw the Fabled Community, and Fewer Ever Will." *The State Magazine* 27 (March 1971): 1–4.
"Large Still Is Taken by Yancey County Officers." *Asheville Citizen-Times*, August 7, 1931.
"Last Family Leaves Isolated Cove Section, Never to Return." *Johnson City Press Chronicle*, April 2, 1958.
"Latest Menace on Devil's Creek, State Line Marker." *The Knoxville Journal*, September 13, 1925.
Leonard, Bill, ed. *Christianity in Appalachia: Profiles in Regional Pluralism*. Knoxville: The University of Tennessee Press, 1999.
Leopold, Aldo. *A Sand County Almanac, and Sketches Here and There*. New York: Oxford University Press, 1989.
Lewis, Ronald L. "Appalachian Myths and the Legacy of Coal." In *The Appalachians: America's First and Last Frontier*, edited by Mari-Lynn Evans, Robert Santelli, and Holly George-Warren, 75–83. New York: Random House, 2004.
Lonon, J.L. *Tall Tales of the Rails on the Carolina, Clinchfield, and Ohio*. Johnson City, TN: Overmountain Press, 1989.
Lost Cove Cemetery Memorials. (n.d). Find a Grave. Retrieved March 1, 2020 from www.findagrave.com.
"Lost Cove Found by New Settlers." *The Erwin Record*, April 8, 1959.
"Lost Cove Moonshiners." *Asheville Daily Gazette*, February 22, 1898.
"The Lost Land of the Lost Cove." *Raleigh News and Observer*, January 1, 1961.
"Many Convictions on Whiskey Charges." *Asheville Citizen-Times*, November 7, 1924.
McCauley, Deborah Vansau. *Appalachian Mountain Religion: A History*. Chicago: University of Illinois Press, 1995.
McCauley, Deborah Vansau. "Grace and the Heart of Appalachian Mountain Religion." In *Appalachian Social Context: Past and Present*, edited by Bruce Ergood and Bruce E. Kuhre, 355–362. Dubuque, IA: Kendall and Hunt Publishing Co., 2003.
McCoy, George. "Lost Cove: It's Out of This World." *Asheville Citizen-Times*, October 5, 1952.
McCoy, George W. "Lost Cove: It's Out of This World." In *News from Yancey: Articles from Area Newspapers 1840–1900*, edited by Lloyd Bailey, Sr. Burnsville, NC: Yancey Graphics, 1983.
McKinney, Gordon. "The Civil War in Appalachia." In *The Appalachians: America's First and Last Frontier*, edited by Mari-Lynn Evans, Robert Santelli, and Holly George-Warren, 33–37. New York: Random House, 2004.
McNabb, Geneva Tipton. Interview by Christy A. Smith. Erwin, TN, September 21, 2007.
Memories of District C, Civilian Conservation Corps, 1934, p.47.
Michie, Thomas, ed. *The Encyclopedic Digest of North Carolina Reports: Being a Complete Encyclopedia and Digest of All the North Carolina Case Law Up to and Including Volume 167, North Carolina Reports, and Volumes 1 to 83, Southeastern Reporter*. Charlottesville, VA: The Michie Company, Law Publishers, 1916.
Miller, Wilbur R. "The Revenue: Federal Law Enforcement in the Mountain South, 1870–1900." *The Journal of Southern History* 55, no. 2 (May 1989): 195–216.
Miller, Wilbur R. *Revenuers & Moonshiners: Enforcing Federal Liquor Law in the Mountain South, 1865–1900*. Chapel Hill: The University of North Carolina Press, 1991.
"Moonshine," Google Online; available from http://www.freerepublic.com; Internet; accessed 20 October 2007.
The National Archives. (2010). Compiled Service Records of Volunteer Union Soldiers Who Served in Organizations from the State of North Carolina. Retrieved from https://www.fold3.com/image/264727095.
National Selective Service Registration Card, D.S.S. Form 1 #1497, Image #683832931. Retrieved from www.fold3.com.
"New Efforts Made to Get Road for Lost Cove Section." *Asheville Citizen-Times*, May 8, 1958.
North Carolina Death Certificates, Bonnie Miller, Image #1209. Retrieved from www.familysearch.org.
North Carolina Death Certificates, Yancey County, Ramsey Township, North Carolina, Image #522. Retrieved from www.familysearch.org.
North Carolina Death Certificates, Yancey County, Ramsey Township, North Carolina, Image #912. Retrieved from www.familysearch.org.
North Carolina Death Records, Wiley Tipton, #004219384 Image #2139. Retrieved from www.familysearch.org.
North Carolina Deaths, 1906–1930, Image #690. Retrieved from www.familysearch.org.
North Carolina Deaths, 1906–1930, Image #927. Retrieved from www.familysearch.org.
North Carolina Deaths, 1906–1930, Image #1570. Retrieved from www.familysearch.org.
North Carolina Deaths, 1906–1930, Image #2261. Retrieved from www.familysearch.org.
North Carolina Deaths, 1906–1930, Image #2397. Retrieved from www.familysearch.org.
North Carolina Deaths, 1931–1944, Image #115. Retrieved from www.familysearch.org.
North Carolina Marriages, Registry of Marriages, Yancey County, Image #281. Retrieved from www.familysearch.org.
North Carolina Marriages, 1762–1979, Yancey, Image #371. Retrieved from www.familysearch.org.

North Carolina County Marriages, Yancey, 1762–1979, Image #544. Retrieved from www.familysearch.org.
North Carolina County Marriages, Yancey, 1762–1979, Image #892. Retrieved from www.familysearch.org.
North Carolina County Marriages, Yancey, 1762–1979, Image#42. Retrieved from www.familysearch.org.
North Carolina Marriage Certificates, Yancey County, Ramsey Township, Image #769. Retrieved from www.familysearch.org.
North Carolina Marriage Register, Mitchell County, Red Hill Township, Image #178. Retrieved from www.familysearch.org.
North Carolina Marriage Register, Yancey County, Image #544. Retrieved from www.familysearch.org.
North Carolina Obituaries, Yancey County, Image #1853. Retrieved from www.familysearch.org.
"Obituaries, Calvin Coolidge Miller." *Johnson City Press*, February 16, 1943.
"Obituaries, Dula Hensley." *Johnson City Press*, May 10, 1997.
"Obituaries, Esta Ada Arrowood." *Antigo Times*, May 3, 2016. Retrieved from https://antigotimes.com/2016/05/esta-ada-arrowood-99/.
"Obituaries, Harvey T. Bryant, Sr.," Image #957. Retrieved from www.familysearch.org.
"Obituaries, John Orville Bailey." *Johnson City Press*, November 28, 1992.
"Obituaries, Phil Miller." *Johnson City Press*, July 11, 2008.
"Operation Santa of Five Airmen Slowed to Walk." *The Palm Beach Post*, December 21, 1953. Retrieved from www.newspapers.com.
Paludan, Phillip S. *Victims: A True Story of the Civil War*. Knoxville: The University of Tennessee Press, 1981.
Peterson, Betty. Interview by Christy A. Smith. October 26, 2020.
"Photographer Tells of Wait." *Statesville Daily Record*, December 18, 1952. Retrieved from www.newspapers.com.
Robertson, Tom. "Moonshine on the Mountain." In *The Appalachians: America's First and Last Frontier*, edited by Mari-Lynn Evans, Robert Santelli, and Holly George-Warren, 84–87. New York: Random House, 2004.
Rosalina, Kris Hawkins. Interview by Christy A. Smith. July 7, 2020.
"Santa Finally Arrives at Lost Cove." *Asheville Citizen-Times*, December 21, 1952. Retrieved from www.newspapers.com.
"Santa Moving Infantry Style." *The Galveston Daily News*, December 21, 1953. Retrieved from www.newspapers.com.
Seventh Generation, "Bailey genealogy," Geocities online. Home page online. Available from www.geocities.com/Heartland/Plains/4277/d57.htm; Internet; accessed November 1, 2007.
Shapiro, Henry D. *Appalachia on Our Mind: The Southern Mountains and Mountaineers in the American Consciousness, 1870–1920*. Chapel Hill: University of North Carolina Press, 1978.
"Sold at Last, the Old Furniture Factory Goes Into New Hands." *The Comet*, Johnson City, Tennessee, November 25, 1897.
South and Western Railway Files, Construction of Train Track Revision, Archives of Appalachia at East Tennessee State University.
The Southwestern Reporter Volume, 182: Comprising all the current decisions of the Supreme and Appellate Courts of Arkansas, Kentucky, Missouri, Tennessee and Texas. St. Paul: West Publishing Company, 1916.
"Spectacular Raid of Three Stills near the State Line." *Johnson City Press Chronicle*, June 12, 1924.
Tennessee County Marriages, 1790–1950, Sullivan, Image #132. Retrieved from www.familysearch.org.
Tennessee County Marriages, 1790–1950, Unicoi, Image #69. Retrieved from www.familysearch.org.
Tennessee County Marriages, 1790–1950, Unicoi County, Image #74. Retrieved from www.familysearch.org.
Tennessee County Marriages, 1790–1950, Image #76. Retrieved from www.familysearch.org.
Tennessee County Marriages, 1790–1950, Unicoi, Image #171. Retrieved from www.familysearch.org.
Tennessee County Marriages, 1790–1950, Unicoi County, Image #185. Retrieved from www.familysearch.org.
Tennessee County Marriages, 1790–1950, Unicoi, Image #187. Retrieved from www.familysearch.org.
Tennessee County Marriages, 1790–1950, Image #188. Retrieved from www.familysearch.org.
Tennessee County Marriages, 1790–1950, Unicoi County, Image #214. Retrieved from www.familysearch.org.
Tennessee County Marriages, 1790–1950, Image #268. Retrieved from www.familysearch.org.
Tennessee County Marriages, 1790–1950, Image #342. Retrieved from www.familysearch.org.
Tennessee County Marriages, 1790–1950, Image #447. Retrieved from www.familysearch.org.
Tennessee County Marriages, 1790–1950, Unicoi, Image #509. Retrieved from www.familysearch.org.
Tennessee County Marriages, 1790–1950, Unicoi, Image #534. Retrieved from www.familysearch.org.
Tennessee County Marriages, 1790–1950, Unicoi County, Image #540. Retrieved from www.familysearch.org.
Tennessee County Marriages, 1790–1950, Image #623. Retrieved from www.familysearch.org.
Tennessee County Marriages, 1790–195, Unicoi, Image #667. Retrieved from www.familysearch.org.
Tennessee County Marriages, 1790–1950, Image #719. Retrieved from www.familysearch.org.
Tennessee County Marriages, 1790–1950, Image #794. Retrieved from www.familysearch.org.
Tennessee County Marriages, 1790–1950, Washington County, Image #108. Retrieved from www.familysearch.org.
Tennessee Death Certificates, 1914–1966, Image #639. Retrieved from www.familysearch.org.
Tennessee Death Certificates, 1914–1966, Image #1376. Retrieved from www.familysearch.org.

Bibliography

Tennessee Death Certificates, 1914–1966, Image #1528. Retrieved from www.familysearch.org.
Tennessee Death Certificates, 1914–1966, Image #1803. Retrieved from www.familysearch.org.
Tennessee Death Certificates, 1914–1966, Unicoi, Image #1804. Retrieved from www.familysearch.org.
Tennessee Death Certificates, 1914–1966, Image #2023. Retrieved from www.familysearch.org.
Tennessee Death Certificates, 1914–1966, Image #2046. Retrieved from www.familysearch.org.
Tennessee Death Certificates, 1914–1966, Image #2512. Retrieved from www.familysearch.org.
Tennessee State Marriage Index, 1780–2002. Isaac Tipton and Juanita Ambrose. Retrieved from www.familysearch.org.
Tipton, David, MC. Compiled Service Records of Volunteer Union Soldiers, Image #260641055. Retrieved from www.fold3.com/image/260641055.
Tipton, Homer. Interview by Christy A. Smith. Erwin, TN, September 6, 2007.
Tipton, Sidney. Compiled Service Records of Volunteer Union Soldiers, Image #260831255. Retrieved from www.fold3.com/images/260831255.
"To Play Santa Claus." *Asheville Citizen-Times*, December 7, 1952. Retrieved from www.newspapers.com.
"A Town Where Time Stands Still." *Oakland Tribune Parade*, March 8, 1953. Retrieved from https://www.newspapers.com/image/276841299/.
Unicoi County Affidavit in Yancey County, North Carolina Deed Book: CRP 244: 62.
Unicoi County Army Enlistment Card, July 1, 1941. Retrieved from www.fold3.com/image/683834808.
United States Census, 1860, North Carolina, Yancey, Image #128. Retrieved from www.familysearch.org.
United States Census, 1870, North Carolina, Mitchell, Harrell, Image #6. Retrieved from www.familysearch.org.
United States Census, 1870, North Carolina, Yancey County, Jacks Creek, Image #24. Retrieved from www.familysearch.org.
United States Census, 1880, North Carolina, Mitchell County, Harrell, Image #3. Retrieved from www.familysearch.org.
United States Census 1880, Yancey County, Ramsey Township, North Carolina, Image #16. Retrieved from www.familysearch.org.
United States Census, 1900. Retrieved from www.familysearch.org.
United States Census 1900, North Carolina, Mitchell, Harrell Township, Image #3–4. Retrieved from www.familysearch.org.
United States Census 1900, North Carolina, Mitchell County, Image #19. Retrieved from www.familysearch.org.
United States Census 1900, North Carolina, Yancey County, Ramsey Township, Image #14. Retrieved from www.familysearch.org.
United State Census, 1910, North Carolina Yancey, Ramsey Township, Image #5. Retrieved from www.familysearch.org.
United States Census, 1910, North Carolina, Yancey County, Ramsey Township, Image #6. Retrieved from www.familysearch.org.
United States Census, 1910, North Carolina, Yancey County, Ramsey Township, Image #10. Retrieved from www.familysearch.org.
United States Census 1910, Tennessee, Carter, Civil District 3, Image #33. Retrieved from www.familysearch.org.
United States Census, 1920, North Carolina, Yancey Ramsey Township, Image #26. Retrieved from www.familysearch.org.
United States 1920 Census Records, Yancey County, Ramsey Township, North Carolina, Image #29. Retrieved from www.familysearch.org.
United States Census, 1930, Tennessee, Unicoi County, Image #11. Retrieved from www.familysearch.org.
United State Census, 1930, Virginia, Buchanan County, Image #17. Retrieved from www.familysearch.org.
United States 1930 Census Records, Yancey County, Ramsey Township, North Carolina, Image #26. Retrieved from www.familysearch.org.
United States Census—1940. Retrieved from www.familysearch.org.
United States Census 1940, Hawaii Territory, Honolulu. Image #342. Retrieved from www.familysearch.org.
United States Census, 1940, California, Sausalito, Image #8. Retrieved from www.familysearch.org.
United States Census 1940, Mitchell County, North Carolina, Image #11. Retrieved from www.familysearch.org.
United States Census, 1940, Yancey County, Ramsey Township, North Carolina, Image #13. Retrieved from www.familysearch.org.
United States Census, 1940, Tennessee, Unicoi County, Image #6. Retrieved from www.familysearch.org.
United States Census, 1940, Tennessee, Unicoi County, Image #12. Retrieved from www.familysearch.org.
United States Census, 1940, Tennessee, Unicoi County, Image #17. Retrieved from www.familysearch.org.
United States Census 1940, Washington County, Tennessee, Image #22. Retrieved from www.familysearch.org.
United States Draft Registration Card, Kenneth Johnson, #10105, Belmar, New Jersey. Retrieved from www.fold3.com.

Bibliography

United States Draft Registration Card, Ulis Miller, #11542, Unicoi County, Tennessee. Retrieved from www.fold3.com.

Van Noppen, Ina, and John J. Van Noppen. *Western North Carolina Since the Civil War*. Boone, NC: Appalachian Consortium, 1973.

Veterans Affairs BIRLS Death File (/title/848/veterans-affairs-birls-death-file: accessed May 4, 2020), database and images, https://www.fold3.com/title/848/veterans-affairs-birls-death-file.

Way, Willam, Jr. *The Clinchfield Railroad: The Story of a Trade Route Across the Blue Ridge Mountains*. Chapel Hill: University of North Carolina Press, 1931.

"Will Build a Railroad." *The Comet, Johnson City, Tennessee*, March 2, 1899.

Woodby, Madge. Tombstone. www.findagrave.com.

World War II Enlistment Records, #34044203. Retrieved from www.fold3.com/record/87680913-wiley-tipton.

Yancey County, North Carolina, Deed Book 86: 440.

Yancey County, North Carolina, Deed Book 117:124.

Yancey County, North Carolina, Deed Book 120: 363.

Yancey County, North Carolina, Deed Book 121:258.

Yancey County, North Carolina, Deed Book 122:131.

Yancey County, North Carolina, Deed Book 140:19.

Yancey County, North Carolina, Deed Book 140:499.

Yancey County, North Carolina, Deed Book 159: 27.

Yancey County, North Carolina, Deed Book 180:67.

Yancey County, North Carolina, Deed Book 229:422.

Yancey County, North Carolina, Deed Book 680:245.

Yancey County NC Census—1860 Agricultural Census.

Index

Numbers in ***bold italics*** indicate pages with illustrations

African American Preacher 74–75
Aiken, A.E. 21, 59
Alderman, Pat 5, 10, 13, 24, 49
Arrowood, Esta Miller 125–127
Arrowood, Percy 126–127
apple orchard(s) 25, 31, 39, 100, 104, 154; *see also* orchard(s)
Arthur, John Preston: *Western North Carolina: A History from 1730 to 1913* 9, 21, 58, 60
Asheville Citizen Times 39, 51, 62, 75, 77, 89–90, 146–148, 150

Bailey, Carrie Tipton ***69***, 87, 105, 111–112, 129, 131, 150, 156
Bailey, Chad Fred 4, 104–105; photographs by 24–27, 31–32, 34–37, 56, 68, 72, 76, 78, 87, 92, 95–97, 106–108, 135
Bailey, Chester 10, 23, ***48***, 67, 82, 84, 87, 102, 105, 112, 129, 131, 146, 149–150, 154, 156, 158, 164
Bailey, Harley 68–69, 105, 113, ***120-121***
Bailey, Hosea ***25-27***, 33–***35***, ***56***, 77–***78***, 92–93, ***94-97***, 104–105, ***108***
Bailey, Isaiah 3, 8, 15, ***26***, ***32***, ***34***, 37, 40, 47, 50, ***56***, 77, 80, 87, 89–90, 93, ***96***, 97–98, 104–105, ***106-108***, 147–149, 157, 161, ***162***
Bailey, Jettie Hedrick 68, 81–82, 102–105, 107, 112–113, 124, 142–144, 149, 151, 154, 156
Bailey, John Orville 102, 107
Bailey, John "YellowJacket" 14, 102–***103***
Bailey, Joseph 3–4, 105; photographs by 120–121
Bailey, Lloyd, Sr. 10, 14–15, 49, 55, 67–68, 72, 81, 107, 110, 141
Bailey, Lovada Ray 14, 102
Bailey, Mamel Tipton 105–106, 111, 113, ***120-121***, 149
Bailey, Polly Ann Miller 75, ***86***, 128, 130–131, ***137***, 164
Bailey, Rebecca Deyton 17, 100–102, 119
Bailey, Richard 4, 64, 128, 131, 164
Bailey, Servilla ***56***, 68, ***72***, 104, ***106-108***, 149
Bailey, Stephen Morgan 7, 13–17, 19–20, 23, 109–110, 112, 118–119, 141, 143; children 100–109
Bailey, Velmer 15, 23, 25, 33–34, 37, 39, 50, 55, 68–69, 71, 74, 77, 81–82, 84–86, 93, 97, 102, 104–105, 146, 149, 153–154; photographs of 24, 26–27, 36, 56, 68–69, 72–73, 79, 96, 106–107
Bailey, William (Will) 102–103, 143, 149–150
baptisms 66, 69–71
Beaver, Patricia: "Family, Land, and Community" 10, 99
Bennett, Archibald (Arch) 19–20, 111, 151; family 141–142

boundary dispute 13, 21, 60; *see also Dugger vs. McKeeson; McCarty vs. Carolina Lumber Company*
boundary lines 5–7, 9, 13, 21, 59–61, 150; *see also* boundary dispute
Bowman, Teresa Miller 3–4, ***86***–87, ***88-89***, 127–128, 131, 154, 163; photographs by 27–28, 30, 67, 69, 91–94, 134, 136–137
Briggs, E.L. 150–152, 156
Bryant, Emma 125
Bryant, Frank 23, 46, 64, 74, 80, 126; family 132–138, 149, 151
Bryant, Harvey 112, 132, 134
Bryant, Jane Miller 80; family 132–***138***
Bryant, J.C. 3–4, 7–8, 17, 23–24, 26, 28, 30–31, 33–34, 37, 39, 42, 44, 46–47, 50–51, 55, 63–64, 70–72, 74–75, 80–85, ***90***, 123, 132, ***137-138***, 149, 161, ***162***
Bryant, Virginia June Bailey ***69***, 105, 112, 134, 154, 156
Byrd, Samuel 4, 7, 10

Caldwell Lumber Company 49
Cane Bottom 1, 23, 42–43, 47–49, 74
Canoy, Norman 3, 10, 153–157, 162, ***164***
Caro-Tenn 40, 50
Carolina, Clinchfield, and Ohio Railroad (CC&O) 1, 3, 10, 22, 41–44, 46, ***47***, 49–50, 52, 132
Carr, Jess: *The Second Oldest Profession: An Informal History of Moonshining in America* 10, 59
church services 9, 69
Civilian Conservation Corps (CCC) 82, 113, 116, 127–128
communion 70, 84
Conley, Sinclair ***30***, 77, 85, 89–90, 92–94, 98, 104, 132, 146–147, 149
Cooper, Jeff 39–40, 130, 139
Cooper, Samuel 61–62, 117–118, 125 141, 154
Cooper, William Harrison 141, 153–154
CSX Railroad 1, 5, 7, 158

Davis, Verno Harris 3, 71–72, 147, 162, ***163***
Devil's Creek 10, 49–54, 127
Dick, Judge R.P. 60
Dorgan, Howard: *Giving Glory to God in Appalachia: Worship Practices of Six Baptist Sub-denominations* 10, 66, 70
Dugger vs. McKeeson 61
Dumond, Doris 8, 150

Elliott, Frank: "The Ghost Town of the Nolichucky: Walking into Lost Cove North Carolina" 13

Index

English, I. Mac 23, 33, 35, 41, 49–55, 145, 149, 151, 154–155, 157

fasting 66, 69, 72, 74
fire 51–53
Flat Top Mountain 5–7, 29–30, 146, 157
Flett, Camille McNabb 3–4, 48, 58, 110, 116–117, 161, 163; photographs by 121–123
foot washing 69–71
Fox, Trina Presnell 10, 25, 55, 145, 157
funeral services 70, 81–82, 84, 127, 139

Garland, Martha 132, 144
Goforth, James 44–**45**
Gudger, James M. 9, 21, 61
Guthrie, Roy Lee 3, 39–40, 81–82, 133, *139*, 164
Guthrie, Trula Mae Bryant 39, 82, 132–134, 143

Haines, Don: "Gone, But Not Forgotten" 17, 25, 39–40, 51, 86, 90
Hedrick, Mack 102, 124; family 142–144
Hedrick, Rickles Rex 143
The Heritage of the Toe River Valley 10, 14, 49
Hermit of Lost Cove 59–60, 110; *see also* Tipton, John D.
Howell, John 85, 132; family 144–145, 150, 153
Howell, Lizzie 39–40, 133, 143
Hyams, Jeff 60

Jacks Creek Freewill Baptist Association 66, 68, 71
J.M. English & Son's Company 54
Johnson, Dolly Jane Miller 48, 75, *86*, 128, 130,-131, *137*, *140*, 163
Johnson, Hank Sherman "Old Pop" 1–2; moonshine 57, 64
Johnson, Jim 4, *48*, 75, 129, 163–164; photographs by 135, 140
Johnson, Robert (Bob) Franklin 1–2, 64

Keeley, Charles 149, 151–157
Kirk, George W. 15, 18–20
Knode, Priscilla Bailey 8, *27*, 77, **93–96**, 104–**108**, 148–149

Lonon, J.L: *Tall Tales of the Rails* 13–14, 22, 55
Lost Cove cemetery 80, 82, *83*, 105, 110–111, 114, 125, 127, 133, 139, 143
Lost Cove School 66–**67**, *87*, 90, 92, 98
Lost Cove Station 23, 43–44, 46–47, 90

McCarty vs. Carolina Lumber Company 61
McCauley, Deborah: *Appalachian Mountain Religion: A History* 66, 69; "Grace and the Heart of Appalachian Mountain Religion" 71
McKinney, Gordon: "The Civil War in Appalachia" 10, 16, 58
McNabb, Geneva Tipton 3, 10, 17, 19–20, 24, 31, 33, 39, 48, 58–59, 62, 81, 85, 110, 114–117, 121, 123–124, 161
Miller, Arch 23, 80, *134*; family 124–141
Miller, Bonnie 68, 81, *84*, *86*, 128, 130, *135*
Miller, Clifford 23, *30*, 39–40, 50–51, 55, 69, 81, *86*, 105, 112, 128–129, *135*, 148, 150–151, 156
Miller, Elsie 77, *93*, 127
Miller, Faye Johnson 85–86, *88*, 89, 92, 131, *136*, 148, 150–151, 154, 163
Miller, Hazel Bailey 10, *28*, 39, 81, *86*, 105, 112, 129, 131, 149–151, 156
Miller, Hulda Webb 112, 128–131, **134–135**

Miller, John 7, 14, 23, *25*, *30*, *36*, 39, 64, 68, 77, 81, 84, *120*, 125; family 128–131, 147, 150–152
Miller, Lucinda (Sindy) Hedrick 23, 80, 82; family 124–141; Hedrick family 142–144
Miller, Martha 23, 27, *29*, *69*–70, 144, 150–151; *see also* Garland, Martha
Miller, Phil *86*, 128–130, *137*
Miller, the Rev. Robert (Bob) 23, *37*, 68, 70, 72, 81; family 125–128, 132, 150, 158–159
Miller, Swin 8, 23, *30*, 38, 40, 55, *56*, 63, *69*, *75*, *77*, 80, 90, 131–132, 144, 158
Miller, Ulis 17, *27*, 86, 90, *137*, 151–152, 154, 156–157
Miller, Vester 77, 139–140
Miller, Wilbur R: *Revenuers and Moonshiners: Enforcing Federal Liquor Law in the Mountain South, 1865-1900* 49, 58–60
moonshine 2, 7, 9–10, 57–65
Mountain View Free Will Baptist Church 66–*67*, 68–69, 72–*73*, *76*, 104, 125, 152

National Archives 15–16
Neal, J.R. 9, 21
Nolichucky Gorge 1–2, 6–8, 23, 41–42, 49–50; *see also* Nolichucky River
Nolichucky River 3, 9, 13–14, 22–23, 41–42, 47, 59, 109, 125, 129, 149
North Carolina Third Mounted Infantry 15, 17–20, 109, 118, 141

Peterson, Betty Bryant 3, 7, 80, 85, 126, 163
Peterson, Briscoe *31*, 40
Phetteplace, L.H. 50–51
Poplar, North Carolina 5–8, 15, 23–24, 29, *31*, 38–44, *47*, 50, 72, 75, 80, 89–90, 100–102, 105, 110, 113–114, 119, 123–125, 132, 143, 146–148, 153
post office 8, 40
Presnell, Robert K. 54–55, 145–146, 157
pulpwood 7, 50–51, 55, 146, 148

revenuers 49, 57, 59–63
revivals 69–72, 80, 104, 127, 131

Santa Claus 75–80
shanty houses 1, 42, 52–53
sidetrack 1, 8, 42, 50–52, 55
sled trail 7, 153
South and Western Railway 41–42, *43*, *46*
Southern Appalachian Highland Conservancy 156–157
"Spectacular Raid of Three Stills Made Near the State Line" 61–62
Sterling Lumber Company 53
Stern, Charles 55, 150, 152, 154
surveyors 61, 157; *see also* Neal, J.R.

Third NC Mounted Infantry 15, 17–20, 109, 118, 141–142
Thomas, Byron 153, 155–157
Tipton, Albert 62, 114, 116, 151
Tipton, Augusta Bailey 82, 104, 107–108, 123–124
Tipton, Caroline Peterson 20, 80, 85; children 109–124
Tipton, Dock Landon 4, 21, 58–59, 61–62, 81, 110, 114–118, *121–122*, 149, 151
Tipton, Elva Bailey 102, 105
Tipton, Everett *69*, 80, *89*, 111, 113
Tipton, George 81, 108, 123–124
Tipton, Hester Price 23, 81–82, 85, 105, 111, *120*
Tipton, Homer 3, 29, 51, 149, 161, *162*

Index

Tipton, John D. 17, 19–21, 40, 59–60, 80, 82, 84–85, 90, 138, 141–143; children 109–124
Tipton, Kenneth *86*, 111, 113, 156
Tipton, King David (Dave) *122*–123, 161
Tipton, Marie Tinker 113, 154, 156
Tipton, Samuel Harrison 120–124
Tipton, Usley Hensley 91, 114, *121–122*
Tipton, Wiley 21, 40, 50, 80, 82, *84*, 85, 111, *120*, 140, 151
Tipton, the Rev. Wiley 20, 110, 120, 124
Toe River 1, 5, 9, 13, 15, 18, 21–22
Toe River Association of Free Will Baptist 66

Unaka Springs 2, 7, 41, 43–44, 49, 51, 61, 64, 71, 87, 89, 130, 149, 153, 158; *see also* Unaka Springs Hotel
Unaka Springs Cemetery 111

Unaka Springs Free Will Baptist Church 105, 129, 131
Unaka Springs Hotel 3, 52, 131, 150, 164
Uptegrove, W.E. 155

Van Noppen, Ina: *Western North Carolina Since the Civil War* 10, 16
Van Noppen, John: *Western North Carolina Since the Civil War* 10, 16

White Oak Flats 5, 7, 85, 102, 104, 126, 128, 130–132, 146, 163
William, Way: *The Clinchfield Railroad* 41–42

Young, Carl 85–*86*, 130